# TEACHING GRAPHIC NOVELS

## PRACTICAL STRATEGIES FOR THE SECONDARY ELA CLASSROOM

# KATIE MONNIN

*Teaching Graphic Novels*
*Practical Strategies for the Secondary ELA Classroom*

By Katie Monnin

Cover illustration: Hope Larson
Cover and book design: Mickey Cuthbertson

Library of Congress Cataloging-in-Publication Data

Monnin, Katie.

Teaching graphic novels : practical strategies for the secondary ELA classroom / Katie Monnin.

p. cm.

Includes bibliographical references and index.

ISBN-13: 978-1-934338-40-7 (pbk.)

ISBN-10: 1-934338-40-0 (pbk.)

1. Language arts. 2. English language--Study and teaching (Secondary) 3. Graphic novels--History and criticism. 4. Literacy. I. Title.

LB1631.M588 2010

428.0071'2--dc22

2009040723

*Chiggers* by Hope Larson is published by Atheneum Books for Young Readers, an imprint of Simon & Schuster Children's Publishing Division; *Adventures in Cartooning* by James Sturm, Andrew Arnold, and Alexis Frederick-Frost, *Alan's War* by Emmanuel Guibert, *American Born Chinese* by Gene Luan Yang, *Bourbon Island: 1730* by Appollo and Lewis Trondheim, and *Laika* by Nick Abadzis are published by First Second Books; *Gettysburg: The Graphic Novel* by C.M. Butzer is published by HarperCollins; *Maus* by Art Spiegelman is published by Pantheon; *Spiral-Bound* by Aaron Renier is published by Top Shelf; and *The 9/11 Report: A Graphic Adaptation* by Sid Jacobson and Ernie Colón is published by Hill and Wang.

Maupin House publishes professional resources for K-12 educators. Contact us for tailored, in-school training or to schedule an author for a workshop or conference. Visit www.maupinhouse.com for free lesson plan downloads.

Maupin House Publishing, Inc.
2416 NW 71 Place
Gainesville, FL 32653
www.maupinhouse.com
800-524-0634
352-373-5588
352-373-5546 (fax)
info@maupinhouse.com

10 9 8 7 6 5 4 3 2 1

This book is dedicated to my very best friends and most enthusiastic supporters:

## SAM & MAX

# CONTENTS

ACKNOWLEDGMENTS ........................................................ IX

FOREWORD BY FRANÇOISE MOULY ........................................ XI

INTRODUCTION-WHY TEACH GRAPHIC NOVELS IN ENGLISH LANGUAGE ARTS? AND WHY NOW? ...... XV

CHAPTER 1-READING THE GRAPHIC NOVEL: GRAPHIC NOVEL VOCABULARY ..........................1

Featured resource texts: Scott McCloud's *Making Comics*; Jessica Abel and Matt Madden's *Drawing Words & Writing Pictures*; and James Sturm, Andrew Arnold, and Alexis Frederick-Frost's *Adventures in Cartooning*

*Chiggers* by Hope Larson
*Laika* by Nick Abadzis
*American Born Chinese* by Gene Luan Yang
*Alan's War* by Emmanuel Guibert

**Appendix A:** *Basic graphic novel vocabulary found in Chapter 1*

CHAPTER 2-TEACHING READING COMPREHENSION WITH GRAPHIC NOVELS ..........................15

*Chiggers* by Hope Larson
*Bourbon Island: 1730* by Appollo and Lewis Trondheim

**Lesson Idea 2.A: Teaching Reading Comprehension in Middle School ELA** ..................................... 18
**Lesson Idea 2.B: Teaching Reading Comprehension in High School ELA** ......................................... 27

**Appendix B:** *Three story-mapping handouts for teaching reading comprehension with graphic novels in middle school ELA*

**Appendix C:** *Three story-mapping handouts for teaching reading comprehension with graphic novels in high school ELA*

## CHAPTER 3-TEACHING GRAPHIC NOVEL FICTION ...................................... 39

*American Born Chinese* by Gene Luan Yang

**Lesson Idea 3.A:** Teaching Graphic Novel Fiction in Middle School ELA..........................44

**Lesson Idea 3.B:** Teaching Graphic Novel Fiction in High School ELA..........................56

**Appendix D:** *The Literate Eye reading strategy*

**Appendix E:** *The Literate Eye reading strategy for middle school ELA students*

**Appendix F:** *Reference list of graphic novel adaptations of traditional print-text fiction*

**Appendix G:** *A blank version of the Literate Eye reading strategy for high school ELA students*

**Appendix H:** *Supplement to the Literate Eye reading strategy for high school ELA students*

## CHAPTER 4-TEACHING GRAPHIC NOVEL NONFICTION ................................. 67

*Gettysburg: The Graphic Novel* by C.M. Butzer

*Laika* by Nick Abadzis

*The 9/11 Report: A Graphic Adaptation* by Sid Jacobson and Ernie Colón

*Alan's War* by Emmanuel Guibert

**Lesson Idea 4.A:** Teaching Informational Nonfiction Graphic Novels in Middle School ELA ....... 72

**Lesson Idea 4.B:** Teaching Creative Nonfiction Graphic Novels in Middle School ELA..................78

**Lesson Idea 4.C:** Teaching Informational Nonfiction Graphic Novels in High School ELA............88

**Lesson Idea 4.D:** Teaching Creative Nonfiction Graphic Novels in High School ELA ..................... 95

**Appendix I:** *Nonfiction Collaboration Stair-Step for Middle School Readers*

**Appendix J:** *Nonfiction Collaboration Stair-Step Supplement (middle school or high school)*

**Appendix K:** *Nonfiction Collaboration Journey for Middle School Readers*

**Appendix L:** *Nonfiction Collaboration Journey Supplement (middle school or high school)*

**Appendix M:** *Nonfiction Collaboration Stair-Step for High School Readers*

**Appendix N:** *Nonfiction Collaboration Journey for High School Readers*

**Appendix O:** *Nonfiction Graphic Novel Reference List for Middle School and High School ELA*

## CHAPTER 5-TEACHING MEDIA LITERACY WITH GRAPHIC NOVELS..................... 103

*Laika* by Nick Abadzis

*Spiral-Bound* by Aaron Renier

*Maus* by Art Spiegelman

**Lesson Idea 5.A:** Teaching Media Literacy with Graphic Novels in Middle School ELA.................114

**Lesson Idea 5.B:** Teaching Media Literacy with Graphic Novels in High School ELA.....................118

**Appendix P:** *"Graphic Novel Media and Me: Reading and Responding to Print-text Literacies and Image Literacies" middle school ELA reading strategy for teaching media literacy with graphic novels*

**Appendix Q:** *"And the Meaning Is..." middle school ELA reading strategy for teaching media literacy with graphic novels*

*Appendix R:* "Build It!" reading strategy for middle school ELA

*Appendix S:* "Graphic Novel Media and Me: Reading and Responding to Print and Image Literacies" reading strategy in high school ELA

*Appendix T:* "If I Could Please Respond to This Graphic Novel..." reading strategy and writing activity for high school level ELA

*Appendix U:* "I Write It!" writing activity for teaching middle school ELA media literacy with graphic novels

## CHAPTER 6 - SOME SUGGESTIONS FOR TEACHING GRAPHIC NOVELS TO ENGLISH LANGUAGE LEARNERS ...... 123

**Lesson Idea 6.A:** Teaching Comics with Early Language Learners.................................126

**Lesson Idea 6.B:** Teaching Emergent Language Learners with Comics.............................128

**Lesson Idea 6.C:** Teaching Emergent Language Learners with Early Reader Graphic Novels ..... 130

**Lesson Idea 6.D:** Teaching Soon-to-be-fluent Language Learners with Early Reader Graphic Novels or Graphic Novels ...........................................................132

*Appendix V:* Four stages of language learning, objectives that support the use of graphic novels and comics at each stage, and recommended graphic novels and comics

*Appendix W:* KWL chart for emergent language learners

*Appendix X:* Elements of story and story map activity for teaching language-learning students about the reading-writing connection

*Appendix Y:* Reader's theatre handout

## APPENDICES .................................................................. 133

*Appendix A:* Basic graphic novel vocabulary found in Chapter 1 ....................................... 133

*Appendix B:* Three story-mapping handouts for teaching reading comprehension with graphic novels in middle school ELA .......................................................................139

*Appendix C:* Three story-mapping handouts for teaching reading comprehension with graphic novels in high school ELA ............................................................................143

*Appendix D:* The Literate Eye reading strategy...................................................... 149

*Appendix E:* The Literate Eye reading strategy for middle school ELA students .....................150

*Appendix F:* Reference list of graphic novel adaptations of traditional print-text fiction ................. 152

*Appendix G:* A blank version of the Literate Eye reading strategy for high school ELA students.......154

*Appendix H:* Supplement to the Literate Eye reading strategy for high school ELA students ............ 155

*Appendix I:* Nonfiction Collaboration Stair-Step for Middle School Readers...........................160

*Appendix J:* Nonfiction Collaboration Stair-Step Supplement (middle school or high school)...........162

*Appendix K:* Nonfiction Collaboration Journey for Middle School Readers ............................163

*Appendix L:* Nonfiction Collaboration Journey Supplement (middle school or high school)...............165

*Appendix M:* Nonfiction Collaboration Stair-Step for High School Readers............................ 166

*Appendix N:* Nonfiction Collaboration Journey for High School Readers ............................. 168

*Appendix O:* Nonfiction Graphic Novel Reference List for Middle School and High School ELA ..........171

***Appendix P:*** *"Graphic Novel Media and Me: Reading and Responding to Print-text Literacies and Image Literacies" middle school ELA reading strategy for teaching media literacy with graphic novels* ..................................................................................................................... 175

***Appendix Q:*** *"And the Meaning Is..." middle school ELA reading strategy for teaching media literacy with graphic novels* ........................................................................................................188

***Appendix R:*** *"Build It!" reading strategy for middle school ELA* ................................................ 189

***Appendix S:*** *"Graphic Novel Media and Me: Reading and Responding to Print and Image Literacies" reading strategy in high school ELA* ..............................................................................192

***Appendix T:*** *"If I Could Please Respond to This Graphic Novel..." reading strategy and writing activity for high school level ELA* ..................................................................................................... 207

***Appendix U:*** *"I Write It!" writing activity for teaching middle school ELA media literacy with graphic novels* ................................................................................................................................. 212

***Appendix V:*** *Four stages of language learning, objectives that support the use of graphic novels and comics at each stage, and recommended graphic novels and comics* ..........................215

***Appendix W:*** *KWL chart for emergent language learners* ...........................................................216

***Appendix X:*** *Elements of story and story map activity for teaching language-learning students about the reading-writing connection* ................................................................................................ 217

***Appendix Y:*** *Reader's theatre handout* ...................................................................................... 220

## GRAPHIC NOVEL REFERENCE LIST FOR MIDDLE SCHOOL ELA FICTION .............. 221
## GRAPHIC NOVEL REFERENCE LIST FOR HIGH SCHOOL ELA FICTION ................. 222
## CROSS-INDEX OF MIDDLE SCHOOL GRAPHIC NOVELS AND THEMES ................... 223
## CROSS-INDEX OF HIGH SCHOOL GRAPHIC NOVELS AND THEMES ..................... 226
## REFERENCES ................................................................................ 229
## SOME HELPFUL GRAPHIC NOVEL WEBSITES ............................................. 232
## INDEX ........................................................................................ 233

# ACKNOWLEDGMENTS

*T*he writing of this book has been an absolutely amazing experience, and there are a number of people who deserve my heartfelt appreciation.

First and foremost, my editor at Maupin House, Emily Raij. Emily is not only the best editor on the planet, but also my friend. In the years to come, I hope to continue to know Emily as both a friend and a colleague.

A name that will probably appear in the acknowledgments of everything I ever write is Dr. Nancy Padak, Distinguished Professor of Education at Kent State University. Nancy Padak has always believed in me, even when I showed some of my own signs of doubt. She is my forever-mentor. Thank you, Nancy.

Dr. Belinda Zimmerman, Assistant Professor of Literacy at Kent State University, also deserves a shout-out. Belinda, remember the fork in the road? We choose wisely, my friend. I admire you each and every day and am thankful for your friendship. No matter how much times passes, we are forever-friends.

Dr. Wanda Hedrick also deserves recognition, for I believe she is ultimately responsible for bringing me to the state of Florida (a place I LOVE to live!) and especially to the University of North Florida. Because of you, Wanda, I am able to wake up each day and go to an awesome job at an awesome university and, then, when the day is done, take my dogs to the beach.

I also want to thank Françoise Mouly for her support of this book. Françoise has been a graceful, brilliant mentor to me, and I look forward to working with her in the years to come.

When I wrote my dissertation a few years ago, my guiding mentor was someone I didn't even know, Dr. James "Bucky" Carter, and his book *Building Literacy Connections with Graphic Novels* (2007). Today, I have the honor of calling Bucky a friend and a colleague. Thank you, Bucky, for all of your support and advice.

Since I was little, I have dreamed of writing a book. This being my first book, I was sometimes pretty nervous. And one of my greatest fears kept resurfacing over and over again, especially in my dreams: "The cover must be cool, Katie!" Hope Larson's cover could not please me more. I am thrilled to know her and to have had her graciously draw the cover for this book. Hope, it is perfect! When you agreed to do the cover, I couldn't stop smiling. And for good reason . . . .

To the graphic novel community at large, thank you! When I emailed you guys, you responded. When I called, you returned my calls. I am honored to have especially worked with the following graphic novelists in the making of this book: C.M. Butzer, Nick Abadzis, Hope Larson, Gene L. Yang, Appollo, Lewis Trondheim, Brian Fies, and Sara Varon.

The following behind-the-scenes graphic novel and comics representatives also made this book possible and deserve a hearty thanks: Gina Gagliano of First Second Books; John Hogan of *Graphic Novel Reporter* (graphicnovelreporter.com); Caitlin Plovnick, John Shableski, and Janna Morishima, all at Diamond Books; and Bob Levy and Jim Davis at the Professor Garfield Foundation.

Finally, I want to thank Henry Vachon. Henry, you gave birth to all of the ideas in this book. So, perhaps an understatement, but, thank you, Henry! I cannot wait to see what an awesome young man you will surely become!

Katie Monnin

# FOREWORD

## — Françoise Mouly —

Françoise Mouly is the art editor of *The New Yorker* and editorial director of TOON Books, the first high-quality comics designed for early readers. Her most recent book is *The TOON Treasury of Classic Children's Comics*, of which she is a co-editor with her husband, Pulitzer Prize-winning cartoonist Art Spiegelman.

As many teachers, librarians, and parents will attest, children LOVE comics! Comic books were first published around 1938, branching away from newspaper comics, and were the first pop culture fad to engulf kids—before rock-and-roll, rap music, or "Grand Theft Auto." By the late 40s, most children (and certainly most boys) read, collected, and exchanged comic books. The intensity of the kids' embrace and the lurid excesses of some crime and horror comics scared many adults. In 1954, a highly regarded psychologist, Dr. Fredric Wertham, made headlines when he denounced the comics medium itself in his incendiary book, *Seduction of the Innocent*. Senate hearings were held to investigate the connection that Wertham claimed existed between comics and juvenile delinquency, and many communities organized public comic book burnings. By the 60s, comic books were virtually left for dead, leaving a barren field populated mostly by superhero comics appealing only to a narrow group of hardcore fans.

Four decades and a couple of generations later, Dr. Katie Monnin, assistant professor of literacy, proposes to use comics, or, as the contemporary euphemism has it, graphic novels, in the classroom. Many educators are indeed intrigued by the recent explosion of graphic novels, manga, and other works created in the medium of comics, but teachers have to be prepared to justify using a medium that still has a tinge of the illicit, especially when so few of their students are ready for "real books." Some may still consider comics a dumbed-down version of literature, while others, who might be willing to experiment, are confounded by the profusion of new publishing in the field: comics, graphic novels, manga—many of which are not at all appropriate for children. Some wonder how they will answer when challenged: kids might like comics, but not everything kids like is good for them, and won't comics rot students' brains?

Fortunately, Dr. Monnin wholeheartedly tackles all the issues that will confront any educator ready to embark upon the innovative approach of bringing graphic novels in the classroom. Dr. Monnin gives us a clearly articulated presentation of how one can exploit students' almost visceral attraction towards comics and turn the medium into a rich tool for fostering the students' interests and literacy skills throughout their schooling. Visual literacy is seldom addressed in our educational system, and there's a dearth of vocabulary or critical apparatus for talking about comics, especially in the context of the classroom. English language arts practitioners, who readily make sense of the most complex works of literature, can be less than comfortable in front of a painting or a comic book.

Conversely, a dispiritingly common view holds that the whole point of becoming literate for the child progressing from kindergarten to first and second grade is for that student to learn to leave the pictures behind. Those educators who think of pictures only as "crutches" for struggling readers risk remaining blind to the rich grammar and syntax of visual communication.

Thirty years ago, my husband, cartoonist Art Spiegelman, and I launched *RAW* magazine to demonstrate that "Comics: they are not just for kids anymore!" The tipping point for acceptance has now certainly been reached, when comics and graphic novels are regularly reviewed with other books, receive awards and literary prizes, are taught in universities, and are the subject of museum shows. Sadly, in the bid to rehabilitate the medium, the children's love for comics got side-stepped and swept under the rug. Ten years ago, I started a new division, *RAW Junior*, to publish quality comics for young readers, for which the motto could almost be: "Comics: they are not just for adults anymore!"

The recent embrace of comics and graphic novels by innovative librarians and educators is a hopeful sign of a changing wave, a turn toward a new literacy that can embrace and build on visual communication. As a matter of fact, last year, the NCTE Executive Committee emphasized the need to redefine literacy: "Because technology has increased the intensity and complexity of literate environments, the twenty-first century demands that a literate person possess a wide range of abilities and competencies, many literacies." In a world where students are bombarded by thousands of pictures every day, why not embrace comics (or graphic novels), a printed medium that allows students to probe and dissect, read and re-read a treasure trove of visual information, the re-reading itself a process that will help them build a whole range of visual literacy skills?

Visual communication deals with symbols, otherwise known as cartoons. Cartoons in turn are simple, but they are not simplistic. Our brain is wired to extract meaningful patterns out of complex pictures, to make cartoons out of realistically detailed pictures. Babies recognize a "have a nice day" face before they recognize their mother's face. Those cartoons in turn become the building blocks of the way we think. As Jim Davis, the creator of *Garfield the Cat*, a comic strip syndicated in 2,570 journals and newspapers and probably the most well-known comic strip in the world, points out, when one hears the word *table*, one does not picture the letters T-A-B-L-E; one sees a cartoon, an idea-picture of a table in the mind's eye. That idea-cartoon represents all the tables one has sat at, tables on which to eat, to write, to draw, or even a table one once climbed onto to dance. Cartoons are distillations of many complex ideas, boiled down to their common essence. A *New Yorker* cover by Saul Steinberg is a simple cartoon—he often drew with a child's colored pencils—but it contains deeply layered worlds of meaning. Reading a cartoon and a comic strip is analyzing a set of universal symbols and bringing into play all of a readers' skills: inference, deduction, projection, interpretation.

Comics have always had a unique ability to draw young readers into a story through the drawings; as the series of pictures is interpreted, the meaning is extracted and children fall in love with the active act of reading. As Dr. Monnin shows, comics are not movies on paper; they have their own language and are far more complex than simply a series of illustrations for a text. In truth, instead of being "dumbed down" by comics, the systematic use of symbols in the comics medium demands that the reader use his or her imaginative and interpretative powers. As Dr. Barbara Tversky, professor of psychology at Stanford University and an advisor to TOON Books explains: "Comics use a broad range of sophisticated devices for communication. They make use of a multi-modal language that blends words, pictures, facial expressions, panel-to-panel progression, color, sound effects, and more to engage readers in a compelling narrative." Many of the issues that emerging readers have traditionally struggled with are instantly clarified by comics' simple and inviting format.

When teachers embrace graphic novels, comics, and cartoons, a wonderful thing happens: children are way ahead of them. Kids are eager to talk about images, their understanding is often extremely sophisticated, and they can well articulate their appreciation. Students' love of pictures is intuitive—teachers usually don't have to show them how to find Waldo; rather the contrary. I, for one, am endlessly amazed by children's ease with visual complexity—they are among the most attentive and demanding readers I have ever worked for. If we can, as Dr. Monnin suggests here, take advantage of the many possibilities inherent in the comics medium, if we open up to a literacy that students are eager for, to a form of printed communication that is intuitively clear to children and will motivate them, then we can all, working together, become more broadly literate in the twenty-first century.

# WHY TEACH GRAPHIC NOVELS IN ELA? AND WHY NOW?

After I finished speaking about graphic novels at the 2008 National Council of Teachers of English (NCTE) annual conference, a middle school teacher said the following:

"I get it. I do. Graphic novels get kids motivated to read. During SSR [sustained silent reading] most kids have one. But the reality is that I have to teach my curriculum. I have to teach 'real' literature."

On another occasion, a graduate student in an advanced literacy course said:

"I can totally see the story in the pictures, Katie. I'm with you. My kids love 'em. They have 'em. But how can I say that the graphic novel is literature and goes with what I have to teach?"

Whether a statement or a question, the point is the same: Despite the ELA teacher's enthusiasm for and interest in the graphic novel, and that of their students, the applicability of the graphic novel to ELA teaching and learning is currently in question.

## THE PURPOSE OF THIS BOOK

The exciting and passionate intention of *Teaching Graphic Novels* is to respond to this concern, and, in doing so, offer ELA teachers classroom-based and curriculum-aligned lesson ideas for teaching the graphic novel in their secondary ELA classrooms—both in terms of reading and writing.

Thus, the guiding question for *Teaching Graphic Novels* is: How can secondary ELA educators teach their stated curriculum with graphic novels?

To answer this question, this book will begin with a discussion about what it means to be literate during the greatest communication revolution of all time (Kress, 2003). During our current communication revolution, the worlds of print-text literacy and image literacy share the stage (Buckingham, 2003; Kress, 2003; The New London Group, 1996). They are co-stars. They are partners.

To help us better visualize our modern literacy climate, let's imagine a stage with two actors upon it. Both stand mid-stage, dressed the same, ready to take on their roles. The one actor—let's call him "Print-text"—will be voicing his lines in words. He has always been the star, the veteran entertainer. The other actor—"Image-text"—is the new guy, and he will be acting out his message visually. They will both be given equal amounts of space and time on the stage. And they will each tell the story. Both will communicate meaning, yet they will do so in their own unique formats, sometimes standing alone, sometimes standing together.

Because of this new, shared literacy stage, today's ELA teachers have the good fortune to be living and teaching during what seems like the most exciting time in the history of ELA teaching and learning. We are the teachers who will redefine what counts as valuable literature, and literacy, for generations to come. What we do with the relationship between print-text literacies and image literacies has never before been attempted. This opportunity is more than exciting and more than seismic to the future of ELA.

## HOW THIS BOOK IS ORGANIZED

This book is organized into two major sections. The first section, which starts with the Introduction, begins by offering a brief, historical explanation about the significance of teaching modern ELA students to read and write with both print-text literacies and image literacies. Chapter 1 then continues this conversation by explaining graphic novel terminology.

The second section, beginning with Chapter 2, then turns its attention to aligning graphic novels to the ELA curriculum. Specifically, Chapters 2-6 address how to align graphic novels to the following major areas of ELA teaching and learning: reading comprehension, fiction, nonfiction, media literacy, and English language learning.

Each chapter uses the graphic novel vocabulary discussed in Chapter 1. This book also suggests exemplary middle-school- and high-school-level graphic novels for your ELA classrooms. But these are merely suggestions. You are encouraged to expand upon these suggestions. If you would like to share your favorite graphic novel selections, lesson ideas, reading strategies or general thoughts, I invite you to do so on the *Teaching Graphic Novels* blog: http://teachinggraphicnovels. blogspot.com.

I look forward to continued conversations with all of you as we pursue teaching graphic novels together in the following chapters.

## WHAT'S A GRAPHIC NOVEL ANYWAY?

Before we look at how to teach graphic novels in ELA, it might be helpful to have some history on the graphic novel itself and why it should now count as a valuable format of literature in ELA teaching and learning.

In the late 1960s and early 1970s, some visionary comic artists (including Jim Steranko and Will Eisner) wanted to respond to society's assumption that comics were juvenile in nature and intended merely for adolescent reading pleasure. These assumptions, they felt, were false and were guided by strong misunderstandings about the supposed linkage between comics and juvenile delinquency. Responding to these misunderstandings, then, comic artists were determined to prove that image literacies could not only appeal to a much larger audience—youth and adult readers alike—but also operate on a serious, literary level (a level worthy of esteemed attention).

In 1978, Eisner wrote and illustrated *A Contract with God*. He called his text a "graphic novel," and popularized the term. Prior to 1978, Steranko had published *Red Tide*.

In terms of ELA teaching and learning, these publications were seismic. They had proven that the graphic novel format could fit alongside the ELA curriculum, deeply exploring issues of characterization, plot, setting, theme, symbols, and so on. And although the comics industry was interested in telling these deeper, more literary-level stories that could be read like traditional literature in ELA classrooms, the early graphic novels merely made a small splash in what was later to become a much bigger pond.

In the late 1980s, this much bigger pond found itself experiencing a wave of excitement with the publication of Art Spiegelman's graphic novel *Maus I* (1986), and then, in the early 1990s, the Pulitzer Prize-winning *Maus II* (1991). And even though other significant graphic novels had been published both before *Maus* and after *Maus*, *Maus I* and *Maus II* specifically captured the general public's reading interests (including that of the ELA community). Readers from outside the comics and the graphic novel worlds were reading graphic novels. The graphic novel had made it to the main stage.

"Ok, Katie," you may want to say at this point, "I remember that. I read *Maus I* and *Maus II*. But that was the late 1980s and early 1990s. I see all kinds of graphic novels now. At bookstores. At the library. Everywhere! I never saw them everywhere like this before now. Why now?"

Although there are many reasons for the rise in graphic novel popularity today[1] (the introduction of manga in the U.S., a regeneration of traditional comics, the growing graphic novel readership from around the world, and, perhaps, even the number of movies based on graphic novels), I would like to discuss one specific moment in time as a turning point in my own teaching of ELA.

And although my explanation is personal in nature, it is linked to a moment in time we all share.

The day I realized the significance of teaching students to read and write with both print-text literacies and image literacies was September 11, 2001. I was in my second week of teaching, twenty-four years old, and with thirty seventh-grade ELA students.

The following is an account of about ten seconds of time on that day.

---

1    IT IS COMMONLY KNOWN AMONG GRAPHIC NOVEL READERS, CREATORS, AND SCHOLARS THAT GRAPHIC NOVELS HAVE BEEN POPULAR OUTSIDE OF THE U.S. SINCE THE MID-1980S.

*The principal enters the room and whispers something into my ear.*

*I stop teaching, move toward the TV, and barely manage to say, "Miss L. has asked me to turn on the television for something important," as the second plane hits the World Trade Center.*

On September 11, 2001, the power of images to convey meaning took on a whole new level of significance in classrooms around the world.

And even though it is a bit far-fetched to think that day specifically led to a general social interest in graphic novels, it was on that day that I, personally, realized that most of my students did not know how to understand what they were seeing.

Perhaps it's not related at all, and perhaps it's only a result of my passionate interest in the graphic novel, but I cannot help but note—and point out—that graphic novel sales skyrocketed post 9/11.

At a minimum, it is worthwhile to note that from 2002 onward there has been an increase in the public's desire to read with both print-text literacies and image literacies, such as those found in graphic novels.

### Chart 1: The rise in graphic novel sales from 2001–2006

| TOTAL $ SALES OF GRAPHIC NOVELS | |
|---|---|
| **2001** | $75 million |
| **2002** | $130 million |
| **2003** | $195 million |
| **2004** | $245 million |
| **2005** | $295 million |
| **2006** | $330 million |

GRABOIS, A. (2007). GRAPHIC NOVELS. RETRIEVED AUGUST 20. 2007, FROM HTTP://WWW.BENEATHTHECOVER.COM/2007/08/20/GRAPHIC-NOVELS/

# A BRIEF HISTORY OF TEACHING LITERATURE IN ELA: FROM A FIVE-FOOT BOOKSHELF TO A GRAPHIC NOVEL

Over time, ELA teaching and learning has seen a persistent and growing rise in the use of print-text literacies alongside image literacies. Today, that history can be seen to point to the significance of the graphic novel as one of the best vehicles for teaching reading and writing. The following is a concise, brief history of how image literacies have become more and more significant in ELA teaching and learning during the last century.

The rise of image literacies in ELA actually, and ironically, begins in the 1890s, with a man named Charles W. Eliot and his determined focus on print-text literacies. Eliot, president of Harvard University in the 1890s, was the chair of the Committee of Ten, a group composed of education stakeholders who were selected to decide upon a standard ELA curriculum for high school students. In the end, the Committee of Ten decided that students should be required to read what is now seen as "traditional" or "canonical" literature. Eliot even bragged that this literature could all be found on a five-foot-long bookshelf in his office. On the bookshelf: print-text literature written by mostly white, male, British authors. The message was clear: ELA teachers must only teach these print-text literacies by these authors.

In 1911, the National Council of Teachers of English (NCTE) took issue with the committee's recommendations. NCTE suggested and advocated to ELA teachers that they not feel enslaved by the committee's canonical, print-text literacy recommendations but, instead, consider the interests of their students.

In the 1920s and 1930s, basing their beliefs in the work of I.A. Richards (1929) and Louise Rosenblatt (1938), literacy scholars further argued that reader response theory—the idea that, when the reader and the text come together, they create a unique, aesthetic meaning—also serve as an avenue for text selection. Once again, ELA teachers were encouraged to reconsider the Committee of Ten's recommendations. And, in this case, reader response theory suggested that ELA educators be influenced by students as individual readers who could each interpret literature in their own unique ways.

In 1952, two decades after the surge in reader response theory, Dora V. Smith coined the name of our content area with the publication of *The English Language Arts*. Expanding the ELA teacher's view of teaching to move beyond reading and writing instruction, Smith suggested that speaking and listening also be valued as acts of literacy in ELA classrooms—an early step in how ELA teachers not only selected literature, but also defined literacy.

ELA teachers began to have two major concerns when selecting literature:
1. How am I defining literacy in my ELA classroom?
2. As a result, what and whose literature am I defining as valuable?

In 1963, *The Newsom Report* pushed these two questions further. According to the report, half of Britain's adolescent population felt marginalized by the ELA curriculum. And, as a result, the report recommended that ELA teachers expand their definition of what counted as literacy by including more image-dominant literacies—popular culture literacies, like those found in comic books, film, television, and so on. If ELA teachers could reach out to students with more image-dominant, popular culture literacies, the report posited, ELA students would most likely become more successful literacy learners.

On top of redefining what counted as literacy in their ELA classrooms, teachers of the 1960s also focused on breaking down traditional, divisive literary boundaries: between races, cultures, genders, age groups, and so on. Essentially, ELA teachers found themselves teaching students not only to value their own reader responses, but also to value the reader responses of a diverse array of people. Critical-reading lenses like African-American Theory, Queer Theory, Reader Response Theory, Marxist Theory, Feminist Theory, and many more took on a stronger presence in the ELA classroom.

Eliot's five-foot bookshelf was becoming just one example of who, and what type of literacy, could and should be valued in classrooms.

In the early 1980s, Howard Gardner's *Frames of Mind* (1983) presented another significant stepping stone for ELA teachers. Besides placing value on a student's or a group's reading lens, teachers realized they should also pay attention to their students' individual learning styles, or intelligences. Originally, Gardner listed eight different intelligences.

Two of these intelligences were especially significant to ELA, and ELA teachers began to ask: "Are the students in my classroom more verbal-linguistic learners (more inclined to succeed with print-text literacies), or are the students in my classroom more visual-spatial learners (more inclined to succeed with visual literacies of image and space)?" The answers to these questions should, Gardner argued, influence the teacher's pedagogical approach; the answers should, in other words, help ELA teachers determine whose literature, and what types of literacy, to value in their classrooms.

Around the same time Gardner discussed different types of intelligences, Len Masterman (1985) suggested that students be taught media literacy, which emphasized both print-text literacies and image literacies. And media literacy education scholars of the 1980s and the 1990s agreed (Clark, 1983; Fehlman, 1992; Hart & Benson, 1996; Hobbs, 1997, 2007; Hoffman, 1998; The New London Group, 1996).

In 2003, well-known literacy scholar Gunther Kress took a look back at the growing significance of teaching to a variety of literacies. But, in looking back, Kress also looked forward. He posited that, due to the growing significance of teaching to a variety of literacies, we are teaching (and our students are learning!) during the greatest communication revolution of all time.

*Teaching Graphic Novels* presents one idea for teaching both print-text literacies and image literacies in modern ELA classrooms. Valuing the graphic novel as one modern literacy format worthy of more attention in our schools, *Teaching Graphic Novels* steps into this particular historical moment and offers ELA teachers and teacher-educators classroom-based and standards-aligned lesson ideas for teaching graphic novels in modern ELA classrooms.

## READING THE GRAPHIC NOVEL: GRAPHIC NOVEL VOCABULARY

"A FRIEND IS SOMEONE WHO GIVES YOU A BOOK YOU HAVE NOT READ."
- Abraham Lincoln -

In 1999 I was in graduate school at the University of Dayton in Dayton, Ohio. And I was about to meet a very significant, new friend.

"You should totally read this."

"I am not reading a picture book."

"It's a graphic novel. Seriously, you should."

"No."

But my new friend insisted that I take the graphic novel home and give it a try. When I got home that night, I promptly tucked *Maus I* (1986) behind some of my favorite "real" novels by Austen, Dickens, Fitzgerald, Morrison, and Hemingway.

A few days later, while cleaning, I accidentally knocked over all of my so-called favorite, "real" novels. As they spilled off the shelf and onto the floor, the last book to fall was *Maus* (1986). It hit me on the head.

Being somewhat superstitious, I decided to read it.

By the time I finished reading, I wondered why I had never read a graphic novel before.

I started to ask questions about the graphic novel: How do the words and the images work together to tell a literary-level story and, according to the NCTE/IRA standards for teaching ELA, how can graphic novels be aligned to the ELA curriculum?

I spent my time in doctoral school in pursuit of possible answers to these questions.

Please note that for your teaching convenience, each of the following figures in Chapter 1 can be found in **Appendix A** and are intended for your classroom use.

## READING THE GRAPHIC NOVEL GUTTER AND PANEL

The most helpful and significant resource for my early work with graphic novels was Scott McCloud's *Understanding Comics* (1993). Using a comic book format and style, McCloud educates his reader about reading with both print-text literacies and image literacies. And although he uses the word "comics" in his title, his advice can be applied to any act of reading that involves both print-text and image literacies (many of the media literacies covered in the ELA curriculum[2]). The ELA community specifically acknowledged McCloud's work (McCloud, 1993; McCloud, 2000; McCloud, 2006) a few years ago when NCTE asked him to be a keynote speaker at their annual conference. Thus, despite the fact that McCloud comes from the worlds of comics and graphic novels, his work has transcended boundaries and has found a unique home in ELA teaching and learning.

According to McCloud, the most foundational graphic novel vocabulary term is *gutter*. The gutter is the space between the panels, the moment in time when the reader moves from one panel to the next panel and comes to some sort of understanding between the two. In other words, readers make inferences between panels. McCloud writes that, "Here, in the limbo of the gutter, human imagination takes two separate images and transforms them into a single idea" (66).

But before we can go any further with the idea of the gutter, let's make sure we also understand the graphic novel *panel*. In another extremely teacher-friendly resource text for learning about graphic novels, *Drawing Words & Writing Pictures* (2008), graphic novelists Jessica Abel and Matt Madden advise teachers to think about each panel as its own composition. Each panel, they write, "functions as a single effective and attractive unit in terms of tone, texture, balance, line, shape, and other visual elements" (156). A graphic novel panel is the visual or implied boundary, and the contents within it, that tell a piece of the story. If we bring Abel and Madden's definition of a panel together with McCloud's definition of the gutter, graphic novel readers will find that: **While each panel contains its own element of the story to be told, the gutters that fall in between the panels are the "glue-like" moments that bind the panels—and the story—together.**

On the next page is an example of a sequence of panels and gutters from the copyright and dedication pages of Hope Larson's graphic novel *Chiggers* (2008) (see Figure 1.1).

---

2  Teaching Graphic Novels and the ELA media literacy curriculum is specifically addressed in Chapter 5.

# Figure 1.1: Examples of reading the gutter from Larson's graphic novel *Chiggers*

Reprinted with the permission of Atheneum Books for Young Readers, an imprint of Simon & Schuster Children's Publishing Division from *CHIGGERS* by Hope Larson. Copyright © 2008 Hope Larson.

In the first panel, the reader finds a shirt labeled with the character's name, Abby. Next, the reader travels through the gutter to the second panel, and, in this second panel, finds a packed suitcase. As the reader moves from the first panel, through the gutter, and to the second panel, she brings her understanding of the first panel together with her understanding of the second panel. Transforming her understanding of both panels into one idea, through the linkage of the gutter, the reader can infer that Abby is packing to go somewhere. In moving from the second panel, through another gutter, and to the third panel, the reader then sees Abby's room. In the third panel, Abby is putting her t-shirt into the suitcase. Again, linking the two panels with the gutter that falls between them, the reader might infer that Abby is in her room, and is, in fact, packing to go somewhere. Finally, when moving from the third panel, through another gutter, and to the fourth panel, the reader sees Abby zipping up her suitcase and conversing with her mother. We hear her respond to her mother's "Hurry it up, Abby!" with "I'm coming!" Thus, in this final gutter-reading experience, the reader can infer that Abby is not only packing, but is also in a rush.

Figure 1.2 offers student-friendly definitions for the graphic novel panel and gutter.

### Figure 1.2: Basic definitions for the graphic novel panel and gutter

**PANEL:** A visual or implied boundary, and the contents within it, that tell a piece of the story.

**GUTTER:** The space between the panels. In this space, the reader moves from one panel to the next and comes to a conclusion about what is happening.

## DIFFERENT TYPES OF GRAPHIC NOVEL PANELS AND GUTTERS

Once students understand the basic definitions for the graphic novel panel and gutter, I suggest that ELA teachers build upon this knowledge by discussing the different types of panels and gutters.

There are two types of graphic novel panels: *content panels* and *story panels*. Content panels can be broken into the following categories: word panels, image panels, or word and image panels. Figure 1.3 defines content panel and explains the three categories of graphic novel content panels.

### Figure 1.3: Three types of content panels

| THREE TYPES OF CONTENT PANELS |
| --- |
| Content panels rely on formatting or style to convey their message to the reader, whether that message be expressed with words, images, or with images and words together. |
| **1. WORD PANEL:** The contents within this type of panel ONLY use words to tell a piece of the story. |
| **2. IMAGE PANEL:** The contents within this type of panel ONLY use images to tell a piece of the story. |
| **3. WORD AND IMAGE PANELS:** The contents within this type of panel use BOTH words and images to tell a piece of the story. |

Along with the three categories of graphic novel content panels, there are eleven types of graphic novel story panels (see Figure 1.4).

**Figure 1.4: Eleven different types of story panels found in graphic novels**

## ELEVEN TYPES OF STORY PANELS

Based in the elements of story familiar to ELA teachers when teaching traditional literature, story panels develop or detail the story/text.

**1. PLOT PANEL:** These panels develop the graphic novel's plot, or the main set of events that unfold in the story.

**2. CHARACTER PANEL:** These panels develop individual or multiple characters, often referred to in ELA as *characterization*.

**3. SETTING PANEL:** These panels develop setting, the place(s) where the graphic novel takes place.

**4. CONFLICT PANEL:** These panels develop the source of conflict in the graphic novel, the tension that motivates the story.

**5. RISING ACTION PANEL:** These panels develop the set of events that stem from the conflict, give rise to that conflict, and lead to the climax in the graphic novel.

**6. CLIMAX PANEL:** These panels develop the point of greatest intensity in the story.

**7. RESOLUTION PANEL:** These panels develop the final outcome that solves the primary conflict(s) in the graphic novel.

**8. SYMBOLS PANEL:** These panels usually contain images and/or words that stand for something larger than themselves.

**9. THEME PANEL:** These panels develop the main idea(s) in the graphic novel.

**10. FORESHADOWING PANEL:** These panels develop the story by hinting at or alluding to what is to come later.

**11. COMBINATION STORY PANELS:** These panels use two or more of the above types of panels.

Once students understand the different types of graphic novel panels (content panels and story panels), we can next introduce them to the different types of graphic novel gutters. There are six common types of graphic novel gutters: moment-to-moment, action-to-action, subject-to-subject, scene-to-scene, aspect-to-aspect, and non-sequitur (McCloud, 1993).

Figure 1.5 defines the graphic novel gutter and then discusses the six most common types of gutters.

## Figure 1.5: Six different types of gutters (McCloud, 1993)

Note: Examples taken from *Laika* (2007) by Nick Abadzis (First-Second Books).
*Laika* is the story of the world's first space-traveler, a dog named Laika, who was sent into orbit on Sunday, November 3, 1957 by the Soviet Space Program.

**GUTTER:** The space between the panels

**Moment-to-moment Gutter:** From one panel to the next panel, readers witness little closure and instead simply see something from one instance to the next.
**Example:** page 11 (top panels)

**Action-to-action Gutter:** Between these panels, readers see a single subject going through s pecific transitions.
**Example:** page 14 (top panels)

**Subject-to-subject Gutter:** While sticking with a single idea, these panels move the reader from one subject to the next subject, often progressing the storyline. McCloud reminds us to "note the degree of reader involvement necessary to render these transitions meaningful" (71).
**Example:** page 162 (middle panels)

**Scene-to-scene Gutter:** In reading these panels, readers often need to exercise deductive reasoning, for these panels move the reader across "significant distances of time and space" (McCloud, 1993).
**Example:** page 195 (bottom two panels)

**Aspect-to-aspect Gutter:** Because these gutters ask readers to think about the feelings or emotions being conveyed from one panel to the next panel, they are comparable to tone or mood.
**Example:** page 169 (bottom panels)

**Non-sequitur Gutter:** Sometimes it might appear that there is no logical relationship between panels. However, graphic novelists use the non-sequitur gutter to make a point: sometimes depicting symbolism, sometimes conveying confusion, and sometimes foreshadowing something to come later. There can actually be many reasons for a graphic novelist to use this type of gutter. But the point is: when the reader comes to a non-sequitur gutter, he should assume that what at first seems illogical does in fact have some sort of greater significance. What is that significance?
**Example:** page 88 (bottom panel)

Even though some gutters may be very easily identifiable as one type of gutter (like the non-sequitur example listed above), other gutters may not be so clearly indicative of only one type. The key here is to let students know that, when they are reading graphic novel gutters, they may sometimes see more than one possibility. For instance, let's look at another example from Abadzis' *Laika* on page 175.

**Figure 1.6 Two gutter possibilities**

In this example, the gutter can be read as moving from aspect-to-aspect or from moment-to-moment. If you read the gutter as moving from aspect-to-aspect, you are paying particular attention to the facial expressions and the sense of an emotional countdown. If you read the gutter as moving from moment-to-moment, you are paying particular attention to the sense of time, a sense of moving inevitably forward, toward ignition. In short, depending on how they read the gutter, students can sometimes come up with different types of gutter possibilities. Encourage students to not only see various gutter possibilities, but also explain their own aesthetic readings of those gutters.

It is next important to explain that graphic novels will call on readers to continuously be reading from panel to gutter to panel to gutter to panel, and so forth. This is the core of the graphic novel reading experience. You read a panel, you travel through the gutter, and then you read the next panel, and so on and so on, as the story builds.

## GRAPHIC NOVEL BALLOONS

Now that you and your students understand graphic novel panels and gutters, let's talk about graphic novel balloons. The following are examples of common types of graphic novel balloons.

**Figure 1.7: Different types of graphic novel balloons**

**GRAPHIC NOVEL BALLOONS:** Typically found inside of a panel, graphic novel balloons commonly create visual boundaries.

**Word Balloon:** Word balloons enclose print-text words within a visual boundary that divides the artwork from the printed-text.

**Example:** Copyright and dedication pages of Hope Larson's *Chiggers* (2008).

Reprinted with the permission of Atheneum Books for Young Readers, an imprint of Simon & Schuster Children's Publishing Division from CHIGGERS by Hope Larson. Copyright © 2008 Hope Larson.

**Story Balloon:** Story balloons focus on progressing the storyline.

**Example:** Page 23, first panel, of Gene Luen Yang's *American Born Chinese* (2006)

**Thought Balloon:** Thought balloons focus on a character's or characters' thoughts/ideas.
**Example:** Page 177, second top panel, of Gene Luen Yang's *American Born Chinese* (2006)

**Dialogue Balloon:** These balloons focus on conversation between characters (or one character simply speaking aloud to him or herself).
**Example:** Page 96, panel on bottom left, of Emmanuel Guibert's *Alan's War: The Memories of G.I. Alan Cope* (2008, First Second Books)

**Sound Effect Balloon:** These balloons use words or images to convey a sense of sound in the story.
**Example:** Page 4, second panel, of James Sturm, Andrew Arnold, and Alexis Frederick-Frost's *Adventures in Cartooning* (2009, First Second Books)

**Balloon-less Balloons:** Sometimes graphic novelists choose not to use the visual boundary that defines the balloon feature. The words or images appear alone, as if floating inside of the panel. Since there are a number of different reasons why graphic novelists choose this feature, I recommend that students first identify ballon-less balloons and, second, use story contextualization to understand why the graphic novelist might have chosen this balloon-less style. Students should be encouraged to come up with their own balloon labels for balloon-less balloons.

**Example:** Page 182, bottom panel, of Emmanuel Guibert's *Alan's War* (2008, First Second Books)

I had to find my way in the dark to get back to the village.

Possible label for this balloon-less balloon: _____

# GRAPHIC NOVEL CRITICAL-READING PARTNERSHIPS

Congratulations! If you've made it this far, you are well on your way to being excellent graphic novel readers!

With all of the graphic novel vocabulary now in mind, then, let's turn our attention to what it means to critically read graphic novels. How can graphic novel readers, in other words, be taught to critically read and interact with a graphic novel?

In *Drawing Words & Writing Pictures*, Abel and Madden ask a similar question: "What happens when you add words to an image?" (16). They suggest thinking about an apple. When you draw an apple, you have drawn an apple. Alone, this apple has the potential to have multiple meanings. But, when a creator adds "New York" to the image of the apple, readers can actively and critically reflect on the partnership between the image and the words. Most readers will probably think of "New York, the Big Apple." Abel and Madden explain: "The word and the image do not, on the surface, mean the same thing, and so the reader is required to compare the two elements and create meaning" (16).

Since readers are called upon to compare the image of the apple with the words "New York," this is called a *critical-reading partnership of comparison*. Just as easily, however, the word "orange" could have been coupled with the image of the "apple," reminding readers of the contrasting and clichéd phrase "comparing apples and oranges." In this case, graphic novel readers would call the critical-reading partnership between the apple and the orange a *critical-reading partnership of contrast*. Figure 1.8 outlines the most common types of critical-reading partnerships; it also offers space and time for ELA students to work on their own to find and label other and/or new critical-reading partnerships.

But before we look at Figure 1.8, let's think about another example offered by Abel and Madden. Think about the word "temptation." When the word "temptation" is added to the image of the apple, the critical-reading partnership becomes one of reference. Many readers might reference their knowledge of the story of Adam and Eve in the Garden of Eden, and the temptation of the apple. The images and the words, in this example, are a reference point for each other. This type of critical-reading partnership is called a *critical-reading partnership of reference.*

Sticking with the apple, Abel and Madden then introduce what I would call a *story-extension partnership*. Drawing a falling apple alongside numbered seconds and the words "past," "present," and "future," they explain that in some panels the images and the words introduce motion and the passing of time, thus leading the reader to think forward, toward the next panel and what might happen (similar to the effect created by a moment-to-moment gutter). In a *story-extension partnership*, the story progresses or moves forward.

Figure 1.8 presents common types of graphic novel critical-reading partnerships. Please note: These partnerships can exist between words, between images, and/or between images and words together.

**Figure 1.8: Common types of critical-reading partnerships found in graphic novels**

| COMMON TYPES OF CRITICAL-READING PARTNERSHIPS FOUND IN GRAPHIC NOVELS | |
| --- | --- |
| **PARTNERSHIP NAME** | **DESCRIPTION** |
| **Critical-reading Partnership of Comparison and/or Contrast:** A partnership between images, words, or images and words that asks the reader to compare and/or contrast what he or she is reading. | **Example:** Apple image + "New York" = New York, the Big Apple (compare) OR apple image + "orange" = comparing apples and oranges (contrast) |
| **Critical-reading Partnership of Reference:** A partnership between words, images, or images and words that asks the reader to activate his or her own schema or background knowledge. | **Example:** Apple image + "temptation" = Adam and Eve in the Garden of Eden |
| **Story-extension Partnership:** A partnership of words, images, or images and words that progresses the story and moves it forward. Many ELA teachers will bring the terminology for the elements of story (discussed further in chapters 3 and 4) together with the story-extension partnership. | **Example:** Falling apple image + passing of time and motion = Time is passing and the apple is falling. The story is moving forward. The reader is wondering what will happen and where the apple might land; specifically, in terms of elements of story, this partnership extends the story's plot. |

SOURCE: ABEL & MADDEN, 2008

Along with asking students to label these common types of critical-reading partnerships, I recommend that you ask students to find and label other, or new, types of critical-reading partnerships as well. At the end of Appendix A, the classroom-friendly version of Figure 1.8 offers students space and time to find and label other critical-reading partnerships.

## CHAPTER 1 HIGHLIGHTS

In this chapter, we focused on understanding graphic novel vocabulary. The following is a list of highlights from this chapter.

- The panel: A visual or implied boundary, and the contents within it that tell a piece of the story.
  o The two different types of gutters: content panels and story panels.
- The gutter: The space between the panels.
  o The six different types of gutters (Abel & Madden, 2008): moment-to-moment, action-to-action, scene-to-scene, aspect-to-aspect, subject-to-subject, and non-sequitur.
- Graphic novel balloons: Typically found inside of a panel, balloons visually section off important elements of the story.
  o And the five different types of balloons: story balloons, thought balloons, dialogue balloons, sound balloons, and balloon-less balloons.
- Graphic novel critical-reading partnerships: The ways in which readers apply meaning to words and images in a graphic novel (McCloud, 1993).
  o The three different types of graphic novel critical-reading partnerships: comparison or contrast, reference, and story-extension. Students should also feel free to find and label their own critical-reading partnerships.

# CHAPTER 2

## TEACHING READING COMPREHENSION WITH GRAPHIC NOVELS

"A NOVEL IS NOT AN ALLEGORY . . . IT IS THE SENSUAL EXPERIENCE OF ANOTHER WORLD . . . EMPATHY IS AT THE HEART OF THE NOVEL . . . YOU INHALE THE EXPERIENCE."
- Azir Nafisi, Reading Lolita in Tehran -

When we teach reading comprehension with graphic novels, three windows of opportunity allow readers to enter, inhale, and comprehend the reading experience. These three windows for teaching reading comprehension with graphic novels are: the words window, the images window, and the words and images window.

Through the words window, readers concentrate on their ability to comprehend the story through the author's use of words. Through the images window, readers concentrate on their ability to comprehend the story through images. And, finally, through the words and images window, readers concentrate on their ability to comprehend the story through the author's use of words and images together.

**Figure 2.1: Three reading comprehension windows possible with graphic novels**

WORDS WINDOW

IMAGES WINDOW

WORDS & IMAGES WINDOW

As ELA teachers who have traditionally worked with print-text literacies, we are used to thinking about reading comprehension in terms of the words window; but, as mentioned before, the graphic novel presents two more windows of reader access. Thus, with graphic novels, ELA teachers must teach reading comprehension with three different access points. We should be ready, in other words, to address all three of these windows of reader access, for when students read a graphic novel, they must be competent readers of words, images, and images and words together.

The strategies for teaching reading comprehension with graphic novels in middle school and high school ELA that follow will embrace all three of these windows.

## TEACHING READING COMPREHENSION WITH GRAPHIC NOVELS IN MIDDLE SCHOOL ELA

Since graphic novels operate on a literary level, it is easy to align them to the ELA standards, just in the same way that we align traditional, print-text literature to the standards. With that in mind, let's consider some of the highlights of teaching reading comprehension in middle school ELA.

**Figure 2.2: A few key points for teaching reading comprehension in middle school ELA**

### MIDDLE SCHOOL READING COMPREHENSION

Students will be able to access and use reading strategies to comprehend grade-appropriate text.

The main idea of the reading comprehension standard in middle school ELA is that students know how to activate and use reading strategies in order to repair or foster comprehension. A long-noted and historical discussion in ELA, the focus of the reading comprehension standard is on strategies, not on skills. As we know, reading skills and reading strategies are two different sets of knowledge. A skill is an automatic, unconscious act that allows readers to decode and comprehend with speed, efficiency, and fluency. A strategy, however, is a deliberate and conscious plan. In *Clarifying differences between reading skills and reading strategies*, Afflerbach, Pearson, and Paris (2008) explain: "Reading strategies are deliberate, goal-directed attempts to control and modify the reader's efforts to decode text, understand words, and construct meanings of text" (5). Hence, with an emphasis on teaching reading comprehension strategies for repairing or fostering a student's graphic novel reading experience, we will build upon what we already know as ELA teachers. And this, my friends, is good news.

## SOME GOOD NEWS: WHAT WE KNOW AS ELA TEACHERS APPLIED TO THE GRAPHIC NOVEL

One of the most common reading comprehension strategies used with print-text literature is the story map. The story map can also be used with graphic novels. But, in the case of the graphic novel, the story map should be expanded to include the three windows through which readers can enter, access, and ultimately comprehend a graphic novel story. In other words, there are three possible story-mapping strategies that can be used with graphic novels: a story map of the words window, a story map of the images window, and a story map of the words and images window.

# LESSON IDEA 2.A: TEACHING READING COMPREHENSION IN MIDDLE SCHOOL ELA

**The Graphic Novel:** Graphic novel of your choice; in the example that will follow, we will use Larson's *Chiggers*.

**The Standard:** Middle School ELA Reading Comprehension

**The Reading Strategy:** The story map in combination with the graphic novel's three windows of reader access

**Steps for Teaching Middle School Reading Comprehension with Graphic Novels**

1. To begin teaching with the story map reading strategy, it is a good idea to first ask students to activate their schema and free-write (on scratch paper) what they think when they hear the word "map."

2. After you have given students enough time, ask them to share their ideas with the class, and keep a list on the board of their responses.

3. Now that everyone is thinking about maps, it is time to introduce students to the story map reading strategy (see and distribute Handouts 1-3 in this chapter; a blank version is provided for your use in **Appendix B**).

4. At the top of Handout 1, you will find the three windows of reader access with graphic novels explained: words window, images window, and words and images window. Please review each of these windows with students, explaining that each of the three handouts concentrates on one way to understand the story. In other words, each handout will ask them to trace the story with a specific window of reader access in mind (Handout #1: Looking through the words window, Handout #2: Looking through the images window, and Handout #3: Looking through the images and words window).

5. At this point, it's a good idea to check in and make sure that students understand the three different windows and the concept of filling in the story maps by looking through each window.

   Note: In order to help students understand, please remember that they should have already been introduced to the basic graphic novel terminology from Chapter 1.

6. Next, you have a number of choices for how to divide up the graphic novel and have the students fill out the three handouts. The two most obvious decisions are: a. Ask students to read a chapter and then complete the three handouts (for each chapter), or b. Divide the graphic novel up into sections (perhaps as a whole text or a few chapters or pages at a time), and ask students to fill out the handouts accordingly, giving them as many copies as they will need to match the way in which you have divided up the graphic novel.

With these steps in mind, let's take a closer look at the handouts and how students could respond if they were asked to read Hope Larson's graphic novel *Chiggers*.

## Figure 2.3: Hope Larson's *Chiggers* (Simon & Schuster, 2008)

### Summary
Coming back to summer camp again, Abby finds that everything has changed. Herself. Her friendships. Her interests. And, most importantly, her priorities. *Chiggers*, a thoughtful coming-of-age story, deals with one adolescent's journey to understand what it means to grow up and come into her own as a young adult.

### Creator: Hope Larson (1982-present)
Author of two other graphic novels, *Salamander Dream* and *Gray Horses* (which earned her a 2007 Special Recognition Eisner Award), Hope Larson is a young, fresh talent who is creating a lot of buzz in the ELA community. After attending the 2008 NCTE conference in San Antonio, Texas, she wrote on her blog: "More than anything else, I came away from the conference with an awareness of JUST HOW MUCH we need more comics . . . . There need to be more middle grade comics, and they need to be better." Hope lives in Asheville, North Carolina with, as she often says, her four cats and one husband.

### Interesting Information
- Chiggers are bright, tiny red larvae, mites from the Trombiculidae family, that can get under your skin and cause intense itching.
- Before illustrating her graphic novels, Hope writes what she refers to as something of a movie-like script.
- Instead of being called a graphic novelist, Hope prefers to be called a cartoonist.
- It takes Hope about one day to create a graphic novel page.
- Hope Larson designed the cover for this book!
- *Chiggers* is Hope's first graphic novel for middle school readers.

### From Hope Larson
"Hold on to the certainty that you can do anything when you grow up. The older you get, the more you'll be told to fall in line, make 'realistic choices,' play things safe . . . . Achieving your dreams has little to do with talent and a lot to do with hard work and persistence. Being nice helps a lot, too. If you've got those three qualities, anything is possible."

Figures 2.4-2.6 offer ELA teachers the three handouts explained in Lesson Idea 2.A for teaching middle school reading comprehension with graphic novels. Please remember that Handout #1 not only explains the three windows of reader access, but also references terminology from Chapter 1—terminology that is essential to learning to read graphic novels. These handouts are located in **Appendix B**.

Name: _____

## COMPREHENDING GRAPHIC NOVELS IN MIDDLE SCHOOL ELA

There are three windows to look through when reading a graphic novel.

**1.** **The Words Window:** As you read through the words window, you will focus on all of the words in the graphic novel. For this window, it would be a good idea to recall the different types of word balloons.

**2.** **The Images Window:** As you read through the images window, you will focus on all of the images in the graphic novel. When selecting images for the images window, it would be a good idea to recall the different types of panels and gutters that occur between them. In short, if you understand what is happening in the panels and in their gutters, you will make wise decisions about the images window.

**3.** **The Words and Images Window:** As you read through the words and images window, you will consider how the images and the words in the graphic novel work together to tell the story. This consideration should hopefully remind you of the critical-reading partnerships possible between words and images in graphic novels.

Note: Putting together a combination of the responses you had for the words window and the images window could also work here.

**Directions:** On this first handout, and the accompanying other two handouts, you will find a story map. Your goal is to read the assigned section of the graphic novel (in our case, the opening pages of *Chiggers*), look through the window assigned to each handout, and fill out the story map accordingly.

# COMPREHENDING GRAPHIC NOVELS THROUGH THE WORDS WINDOW

*** For this window, please use words to fill in your map. ***

**Map Panel 1:**
Characters

**Map Panel 2:**
Setting

**Map Panel 3:**
Problem/Conflict(s) in the Story

**Map Panel 4:**
Story Event

**Map Panel 5:**
Story Event

**Map Panel 6:**
Story Event

**Map Panel 7:**
Story Event

**Map Panel 8:**
Story Event

**Map Panel 9:**
Prediction: What do you think will happen next?
If this is the end of the graphic novel, how was the problem solved?

1. ABBY AND HER MOM
2. ABBY'S ROOM
3. ABBY NEEDS TO HURRY UP AND GET READY
4. ABBY IS FOLDING HER SHIRT
5. ABBY IS PACKING HER SUITCASE
6. ABBY'S MOM TELLS HER TO HURRY UP
7. ABBY REPLIES THAT SHE'S COMING
8. ABBY ZIPS UP HER SUITCASE
9. ABBY IS GOING SOMEWHERE AND MUST HURRY UP

**Figure 2.5: Handout #2—Comprehending Graphic Novels through the Images Window (Middle School)**

Name: _____

# COMPREHENDING GRAPHIC NOVELS THROUGH THE IMAGES WINDOW

*** For this reading window, please use images to fill in your map. You can reference Hope's drawings and then draw your own depictions of the story. ***

**Map Panel 1:**
Characters

**Map Panel 2:**
Setting

**Map Panel 3:**
Problem/Conflict(s) in the Story

**Map Panel 4:**
Story Event

**Map Panel 5:**
Story Event

**Map Panel 6:**
Story Event

**Map Panel 7:**
Story Event

**Map Panel 8:**
Story Event

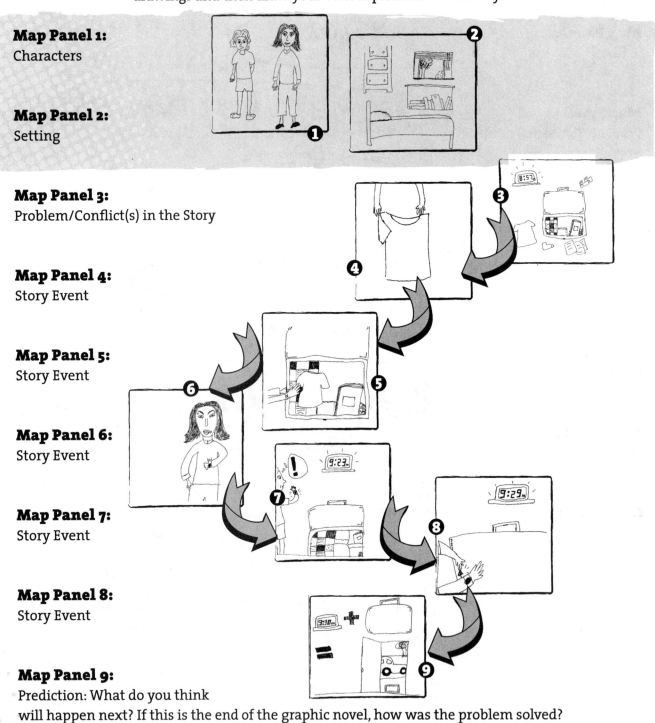

**Map Panel 9:**
Prediction: What do you think
will happen next? If this is the end of the graphic novel, how was the problem solved?

**Figure 2.6: Handout #3—Comprehending Graphic Novels through the Words and Images Window (Middle School)**

Name: _____

# COMPREHENDING GRAPHIC NOVELS THROUGH THE WORDS AND IMAGES WINDOW

*** For this reading window, please use images and words to fill in your map. ***

**Map Panel 1:**
Characters

ABBY'S ROOM ②

ABBY AND HER MOM ①

**Map Panel 2:**
Setting

ABBY NEEDS TO HURRY UP AND GET READY ③

ABBY IS FOLDING HER SHIRT ④

**Map Panel 3:**
Problem/Conflict(s) in the Story

ABBY IS PACKING HER SUITCASE ⑤

**Map Panel 4:**
Story Event

**Map Panel 5:**
Story Event

**Map Panel 6:**
Story Event

ABBY ZIPS UP HER SUITCASE ⑧

ABBY'S MOM TELLS HER TO HURRY UP ⑥

**Map Panel 7:**
Story Event

ABBY REPLIES THAT SHE'S COMING ⑦

**Map Panel 8:**
Story Event

ABBY IS GOING SOMEWHERE AND MUST HURRY UP ⑨

**Map Panel 9:**
Prediction: What do you think will happen next?
If this is the end of the graphic novel, how was the problem solved?

Now that we have an understanding of how story maps can be used to teach graphic novel reading comprehension in middle school, we can next look at teaching this topic in high school ELA. For high school readers, we will build upon the story map reading strategy by adding a second story map to each handout. Just like middle school readers, high school readers will be asked to look through the three windows of reader access, but they will also be asked to fill in two story maps: a retell story map and a text potential story map.

## TEACHING READING COMPREHENSION WITH GRAPHIC NOVELS IN HIGH SCHOOL ELA

During the 2003-2004 school year, I taught high school ELA at Columbus Torah Academy (CTA) in Columbus, Ohio. At CTA, I met many students who were visual learners, but two of them stand out predominantly in my memory.

While I knew that Mikala could demonstrate comprehension by drawing her responses to literature, Alec simply surprised me one day by randomly starting to draw his responses as well. Because I did not know any better at the time, and was still defining reading through a print-text literacy perspective only, I discouraged both of them. But, upon further thought, I changed my mind, rescinded my red-light hold on drawing, and instead offered Mikala and Alec a green light on drawing. Mikala and Alec's drawings were not only extremely articulate, but also A-level responses. These two students taught me that while some students were gifted with print-text literacies, others were just as gifted with visual literacies. I began to ask myself, "Why shouldn't all students be allowed to use their literacy strength, whatever that may be?"

With readers like Alec and Mikala in mind, I suggest that when we teach graphic novel reading comprehension in high school ELA, we build upon the story map reading strategy and add a second visual component.

Specifically, we will add *text potential story maps*. Originally written about in the mid-1980s, text potential stresses the relationship between the text and the individual reader. In other words, text potential sees each reader as a unique person who comes to the reading experience with his or her own background, culture, and history in mind. With him- or herself in focus, the reader then forms a unique relationship with the text (Harste, Woodward, & Burke, 1984). The unique meanings created between the text and the individual reader are called text potentials.

Text potential will appear on each of the three handouts for teaching reading comprehension in high school ELA. Students, in short, will be offered two story maps per window of reader access. For example, on the words window handout, there will be two story maps, dividing the page into two columns. On the left side of the handout, the reader will be asked to fill in a retell story map, a summary of the story. On the right side of the handout, the reader will be asked to fill in a text potential story map. The same format will appear on each of the two other handouts as well.

The two-story map reading strategy will then call on high school readers to relate—and comprehend—the story on two levels: as a summarizer (retell) and as an individual (text potential). Readers will comprehend the graphic novel's main idea when filling out the retell story map, and they will comprehend their own, personal connection to the graphic novel when they fill out the text potential story map.

In fact, opposed to a singular strategy in middle school ELA, the high school reading standards stress that students use a variety of strategies—such as two different story maps—to comprehend literary texts.

**Figure 2.7: Example of a high school reading comprehension standard**

## HIGH SCHOOL READING COMPREHENSION STANDARD

The student will be able to use a variety or combination of reading comprehension strategies to comprehend (nurture/foster) grade-level text.

By asking students to think through two very different story maps, this dual-story-map reading strategy is a strong step toward teaching the *variety* or *combination* of reading strategies the high school ELA standard calls for.

Before we continue, however, let's take a closer look at how the text potential story map will work together with the three windows of reader access.

**Figure 2.8: The three windows of reader access and their relationship to the text potential story map**

1. **Words Window and Text Potential:** The potential to **personally** enter the graphic novel and comprehend its story by relating to the **words**.

2. **Images Window and Text Potential:** The potential to **personally** enter the graphic novel and comprehend its story by relating to the **images**.

3. **Words and Images Window and Text Potential:** The potential to **personally** enter the graphic novel and comprehend its story by relating to the words and the images together.

When students read graphic novels with text potential in mind, they will look through each window of reader access and determine how they, as individual readers, personally relate to the story through words, images, or words and images together.

With our new understanding of text potential in mind, and how students will use it to look through the three windows of reader access found in graphic novels, we can now look at Lesson Idea 2.B. This lesson outlines and suggests a plan of action for ELA teachers to take when teaching the dual-story-map reading strategy with high school graphic novel readers.

# LESSON IDEA 2.B: TEACHING READING COMPREHENSION IN HIGH SCHOOL ELA

**The graphic novel:** Graphic novel of your choice; in the example that will follow, we will use Appollo and Trondheim's *Bourbon Island: 1730*.

**The Standard:** Reading Comprehension in high school ELA

**The Reading Strategy:** the graphic novel's 3 windows of reader access in combination with two story maps (retell and text potential)

**Steps for Teaching High School Reading Comprehension with Graphic Novels**

1. First, students need to understand the terms *retell* and *text potential*. Most likely, students will understand what it means to retell. So please ask them to suggest ideas for this term first (and list them on the board). Things like *summary*, *paraphrase*, and *list of events* will probably appear on the board.

2. Next, it is time to ask students to think about text potential. The most success I have had introducing text potential is with picture books. Thus, I suggest that you choose a picture book that is thematically similar to the graphic novel being taught. Since we are using *Bourbon Island 1730* in this example, I recommend any picture book about social justice, multiculturalism, or even pirates.

3. Once you have chosen a picture book, ask the students to brainstorm what they think text potential might mean. Following this discussion, ask students to share their thoughts and create a second list of text potential ideas, perhaps in a second column next to the retell list.

   - Retell: To summarize, paraphrase, tell again, chronicle, and/or list the details or events of a story. Note: In a retell, the reader is neutral and conveys NO personal relationship with the text. The retell focuses solely on the details of the story.
   - Text potential: A unique reading relationship between the reader and the text which relates how the reader and the text have come together to create a unique, specific meaning.

## TEXT POTENTIAL VISUAL

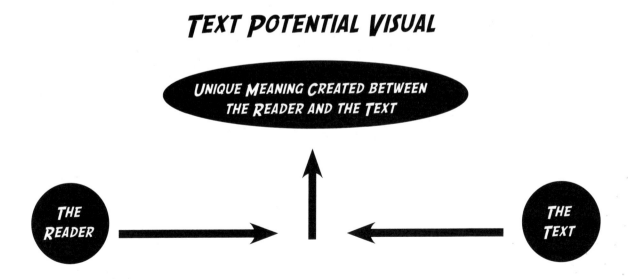

**4.** After discussing the students' ideas and offering the aforementioned definition for text potential, draw the text potential visual on the board. Discuss the visual along with the class' thoughts on text potential.

**5.** Now you are ready to read the picture book with the students. At this point, you should tell students that you will read them the picture book, and, when finished, you will ask them to both retell and offer text potentials.

**6.** After reading the picture book, ask students to retell and then offer text potentials. Make another two-column list on the board for their retell responses and their text potential responses.

**7.** Now that students understand retell and text potential, it is time to introduce them to the two types of story maps, the retell story map and the text potential story map.

**Note 1:** Before going directly to the maps, however, first discuss the top of Handout #1, which outlines the three windows of reading access with graphic novels: words window, images window, and words and images window.

**Note 2:** After discussing the windows of reader access, you are ready to discuss the two types of story maps. Inform students about the purpose of reading with two story maps: to comprehend the story on two levels. Students are able to summarize and personally relate to the graphic novel. The combination of both strengthens their ability to understand the text.

**8.** At this point, you have a number of choices for how you facilitate your movement through the graphic novel and how students will utilize the handouts. The two most obvious movements are to distribute the three handouts for each chapter, asking students to complete the handouts after they finish each chapter, or to divide the graphic novel up (perhaps as a whole text or as a section of pages at a time) and ask students to fill out the handouts accordingly, giving them as many copies of the handouts as they will need to match the way in which you divided the graphic novel.

The three handouts that accompany this dual-story-map reading strategy are on the next few pages. **Appendix C** offers blank templates of these three handouts and is intended for your classroom use. For illustrative purposes, *Teaching Graphic Novels* will use Appollo and Trondheim's graphic novel *Bourbon Island 1730* as an example. The following three example handouts are filled out assuming that readers were assigned the first chapter of *Bourbon Island 1730*, entitled "The Birds."

## Figure 2.9: Appollo and Trondheim's *Bourbon Island 1730* (First Second Books, 2008)

### Summary

An intense historical drama, *Bourbon Island 1730* captures the intriguing time in world history when the golden age of piracy began to fade and, in its fading, found itself colliding with the growing slave trade. Set on an island near Mauritius in the Indian Ocean, readers will find a cast of characters who are all racing to find a hidden treasure. In their haste, however, this diverse cast of characters also reveals their inner, true selves. Rich in issues of freedom, equality, gender, and cultural exploration, *Bourbon Island 1730* contains a treasure chest of discussion points for high school ELA teachers and their students.

### Creator: Appollo (1969-present) and Creator/Illustrator: Lewis Trondheim (1964-present)

Both Lewis Trondheim and Appollo are French comic creators, and *Bourbon Island 1730* is their first collaborative project. While Trondheim offers his sketch-like drawing style, Appollo offers his enchanting storytelling techniques. Together, they create a mesmerizing collage of images and words that entice the reader from beginning to end; many of the high school readers I have interviewed have stated that this graphic novel is extremely challenging to put down, especially due to its intense action and engaging characters.

Further, one of Trondheim's latest projects, entitled *Shampooing*, is a comic creation for all ages. Trondheim has also been nominated for an Eisner Award in the category of Best Writer/Artist Humor for his children's graphic novel *A.L.I.E.E.N.* (2006), also published by First Second Books.

### Interesting Information

- Trondheim's wife is a comics colorist, and they have two children.
- Appollo lives on a small island in France called The Meeting.
- Both Appollo and Trondheim were born in the 1960s.
- When Trondheim draws himself, he always draws himself with a beak, similar to the characters in *Bourbon Island 1730*.

### From Lewis Trondheim

"We can do everything in comics, even things that haven't been done yet. It's a wide-open playing field."

"Drawing is writing and hypnotizing."

Assuming students have been assigned the first chapter of *Bourbon Island 1730*, Figures 2.10-2.12 offer teachers examples of how students may fill out the three handouts for teaching graphic novel reading comprehension in high school ELA. Please note that, once again, on Handout #1, you will find references to the essential terminology for reading graphic novels discussed in Chapter 1, the terminology students need to know in order to learn to read graphic novels.

Name: _____

# COMPREHENDING GRAPHIC NOVELS IN HIGH SCHOOL ELA

There are three windows to look through when reading a graphic novel.

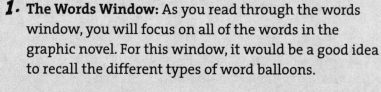

**1.** **The Words Window:** As you read through the words window, you will focus on all of the words in the graphic novel. For this window, it would be a good idea to recall the different types of word balloons.

**2.** **The Images Window:** As you read through the images window, you will focus on all of the images in the graphic novel. When selecting images for the images window, it would be a good idea to recall the different types of panels and gutters that occur between them. In short, if you understand what is happening in the panels and in their gutters, you will make wise decisions about the images window.

**3.** **The Words and Images Window:** As you read through the words and images window, you will consider how the images and the words in the graphic novel work together to tell the story. This consideration should hopefully remind you of the critical-reading partnerships possible between words and images in graphic novels.

Note: Putting together a combination of the responses you had for the words window and the images window could also work here.

**Directions:** On this first handout, and the accompanying other two handouts, you will find two story maps. Your goal is to read the assigned section of the graphic novel, look through the window assigned to each handout, and fill out the two story maps accordingly. In the example that follows, *Teaching Graphic Novels* uses Chapter 1 of *Bourbon Island*, entitled "The Birds."

# COMPREHENDING GRAPHIC NOVELS THROUGH THE WORDS WINDOW

*** For this window, please use words to fill in your map. ***

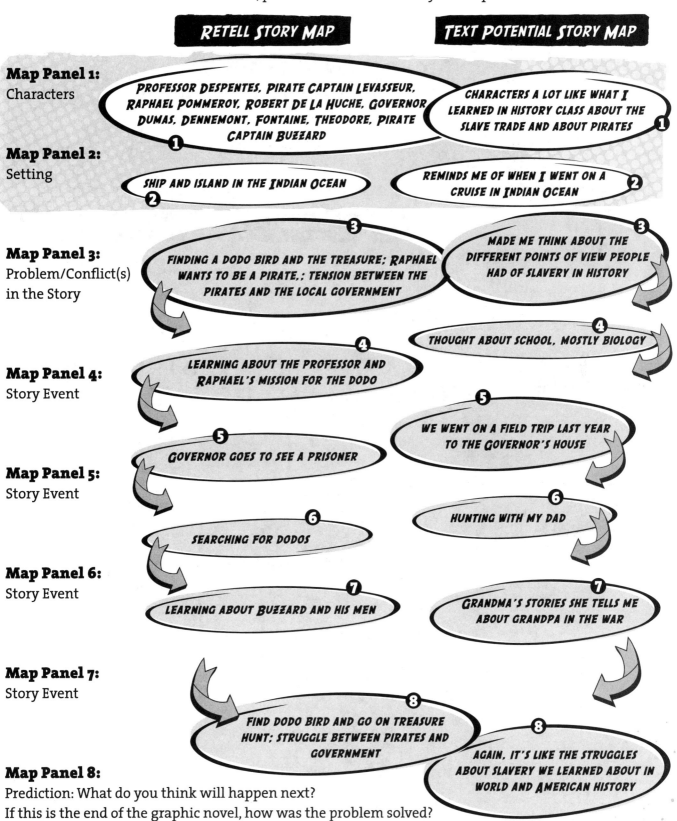

**RETELL STORY MAP**

**TEXT POTENTIAL STORY MAP**

**Map Panel 1:**
Characters

PROFESSOR DESPENTES, PIRATE CAPTAIN LEVASSEUR, RAPHAEL POMMEROY, ROBERT DE LA HUCHE, GOVERNOR DUMAS, DENNEMONT, FONTAINE, THEODORE, PIRATE CAPTAIN BUZZARD **1**

CHARACTERS A LOT LIKE WHAT I LEARNED IN HISTORY CLASS ABOUT THE SLAVE TRADE AND ABOUT PIRATES **1**

**Map Panel 2:**
Setting

SHIP AND ISLAND IN THE INDIAN OCEAN **2**

REMINDS ME OF WHEN I WENT ON A CRUISE IN INDIAN OCEAN **2**

**Map Panel 3:**
Problem/Conflict(s)
in the Story

**3** FINDING A DODO BIRD AND THE TREASURE; RAPHAEL WANTS TO BE A PIRATE,; TENSION BETWEEN THE PIRATES AND THE LOCAL GOVERNMENT

**3** MADE ME THINK ABOUT THE DIFFERENT POINTS OF VIEW PEOPLE HAD OF SLAVERY IN HISTORY

**4** THOUGHT ABOUT SCHOOL, MOSTLY BIOLOGY

**Map Panel 4:**
Story Event

**4** LEARNING ABOUT THE PROFESSOR AND RAPHAEL'S MISSION FOR THE DODO

**5** WE WENT ON A FIELD TRIP LAST YEAR TO THE GOVERNOR'S HOUSE

**5** GOVERNOR GOES TO SEE A PRISONER

**Map Panel 5:**
Story Event

**6** HUNTING WITH MY DAD

**6** SEARCHING FOR DODOS

**Map Panel 6:**
Story Event

**7** LEARNING ABOUT BUZZARD AND HIS MEN

**7** GRANDMA'S STORIES SHE TELLS ME ABOUT GRANDPA IN THE WAR

**Map Panel 7:**
Story Event

**8** FIND DODO BIRD AND GO ON TREASURE HUNT; STRUGGLE BETWEEN PIRATES AND GOVERNMENT

**8** AGAIN, IT'S LIKE THE STRUGGLES ABOUT SLAVERY WE LEARNED ABOUT IN WORLD AND AMERICAN HISTORY

**Map Panel 8:**
Prediction: What do you think will happen next?
If this is the end of the graphic novel, how was the problem solved?

**Figure 2.11: Handout #2—Comprehending Graphic Novels through the Images Window (High School)**

Name: _____

# COMPREHENDING GRAPHIC NOVELS THROUGH THE IMAGES WINDOW

*** For this reading window, please use your own drawings/images to fill in your maps ***

Note: Retell story map panels from *Bourbon Island 1730* reprinted with permission from First Second Books

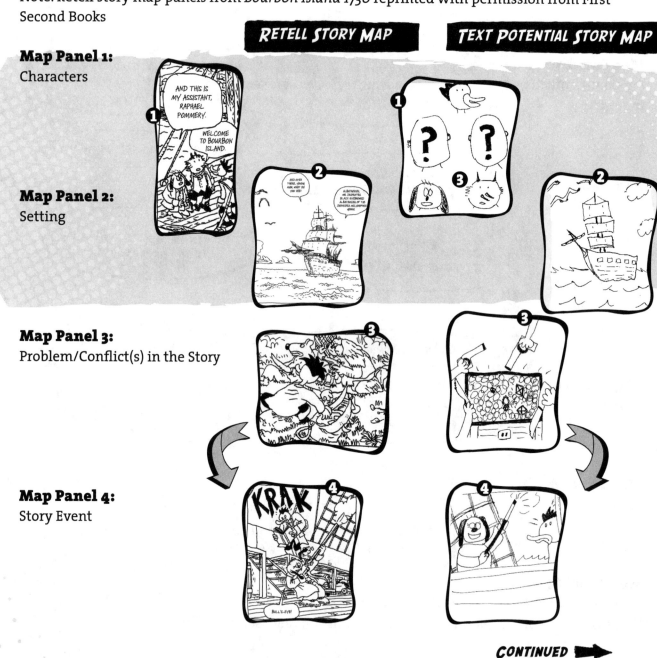

**Map Panel 1:**
Characters

**Map Panel 2:**
Setting

**Map Panel 3:**
Problem/Conflict(s) in the Story

**Map Panel 4:**
Story Event

CONTINUED ➡

**Figure 2.11: Handout #2—Comprehending Graphic Novels through the Images Window (High School)**

# COMPREHENDING GRAPHIC NOVELS THROUGH THE IMAGES WINDOW (CONT'D.)

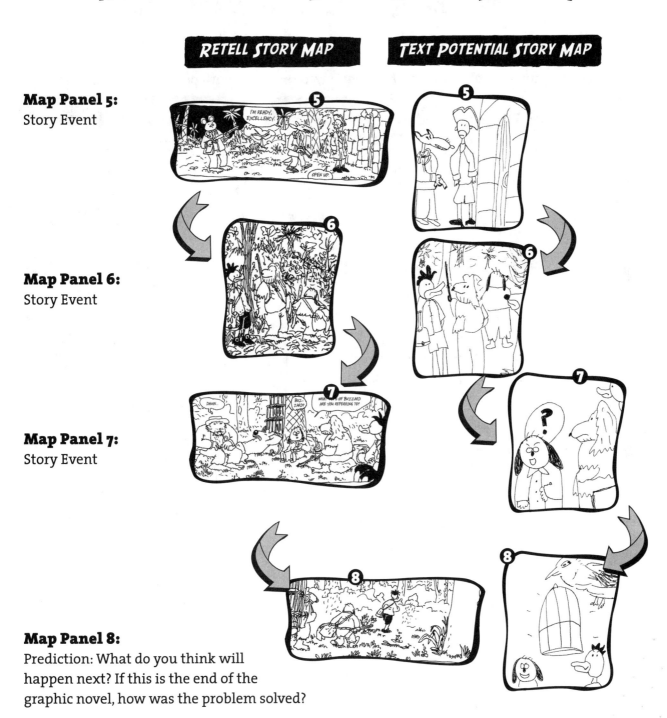

**RETELL STORY MAP**

**TEXT POTENTIAL STORY MAP**

**Map Panel 5:**
Story Event

**Map Panel 6:**
Story Event

**Map Panel 7:**
Story Event

**Map Panel 8:**
Prediction: What do you think will happen next? If this is the end of the graphic novel, how was the problem solved?

Name: _____

# COMPREHENDING GRAPHIC NOVELS
# THROUGH THE WORDS AND IMAGES WINDOW

*** For this reading window, please use images and words to fill in your maps. ***

Note: Retell story map panels from *Bourbon Island 1730* reprinted with permission from First Second Books

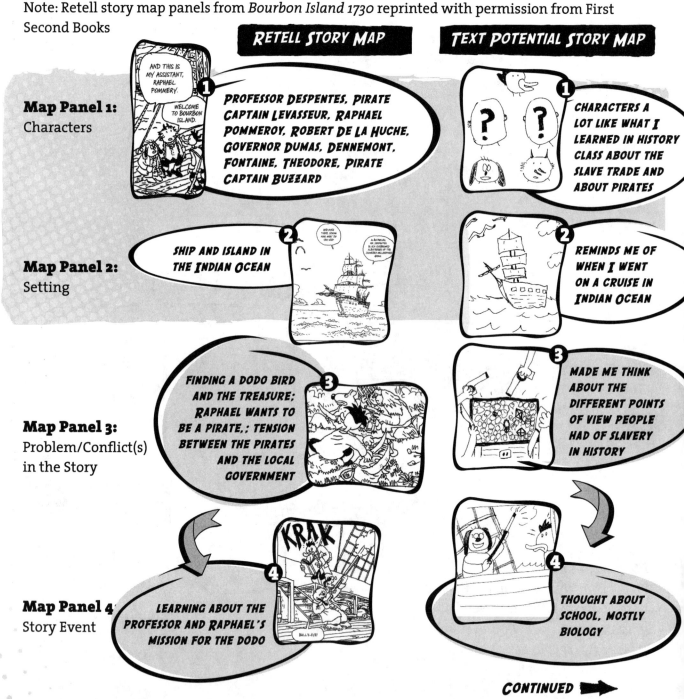

CONTINUED ➡

# COMPREHENDING GRAPHIC NOVELS
## THROUGH THE WORDS AND IMAGES WINDOW (CONT'D.)

*** For this reading window, please use images and words to fill in your maps. ***

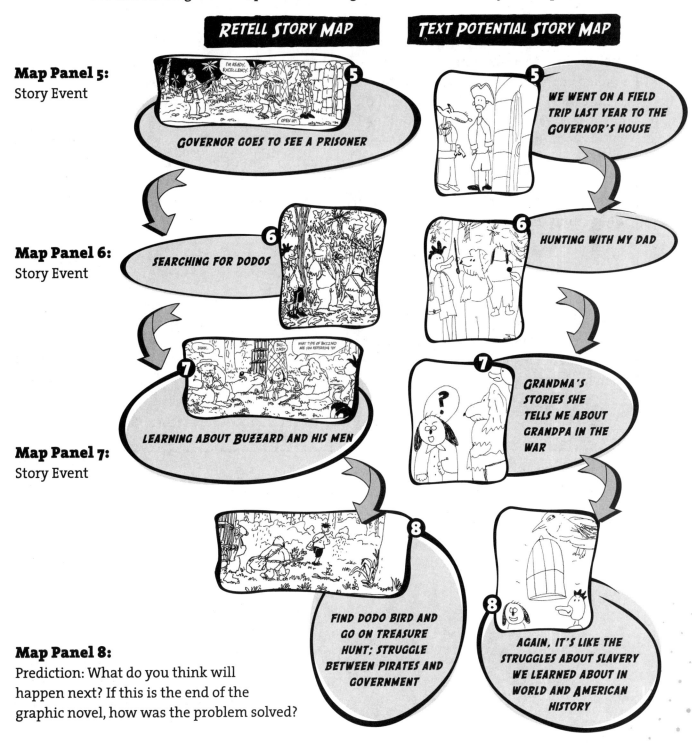

**RETELL STORY MAP**

**TEXT POTENTIAL STORY MAP**

**Map Panel 5:**
Story Event

GOVERNOR GOES TO SEE A PRISONER

WE WENT ON A FIELD TRIP LAST YEAR TO THE GOVERNOR'S HOUSE

**Map Panel 6:**
Story Event

SEARCHING FOR DODOS

HUNTING WITH MY DAD

LEARNING ABOUT BUZZARD AND HIS MEN

GRANDMA'S STORIES SHE TELLS ME ABOUT GRANDPA IN THE WAR

**Map Panel 7:**
Story Event

**Map Panel 8:**
Prediction: What do you think will happen next? If this is the end of the graphic novel, how was the problem solved?

FIND DODO BIRD AND GO ON TREASURE HUNT; STRUGGLE BETWEEN PIRATES AND GOVERNMENT

AGAIN, IT'S LIKE THE STRUGGLES ABOUT SLAVERY WE LEARNED ABOUT IN WORLD AND AMERICAN HISTORY

# YOUR STUDENTS WILL TALK...

About a year ago, one of my graduate students shared a memorable anecdote about teaching with these three handouts.

As we move through *Teaching Graphic Novels*, it is ever present and continuously important that we remember stories like this one, stories that highlight the importance of involving modern students not only in visual or image-based storytelling, but also in personal reflection with graphic novels.

Since I was a sub, I think, the students started class by talking louder than I did. "Just a sub!" seemed to be flashing in neon colors, right above their heads or something. When I pulled out a graphic novel, though, they at least looked at me. Probably because of the pictures. So I started to talk and got out the handouts. Maybe the pictures again, but they talked less. Venturing forward, I explained retell.

Someone even asked a question: "Summarize! What do I care? Has nothing to do with me?"

I explained text potential. A young man raised his hand next: "You really want to know what I think about the book?"

"Yes!"

The air shifted and everyone wanted to talk. But they talked about the graphic novel! These kids who seemed to not care about reading—some even proudly saying that they didn't like to read—were, in fact, not poor readers. Unmotivated readers, I began to think. But not poor readers. The text potential story map encouraged them to want to summarize and then relate the story to themselves. It had worked!

–Twelfth-grade ELA substitute teacher, Cleveland, Ohio

In the next chapter, we will further add to what we have learned in this chapter and in Chapter 1 by considering how graphic novel vocabulary and reading comprehension both influence the teaching of graphic novel works of fiction in ELA.

## CHAPTER 2 HIGHLIGHTS

In this chapter, we focused on teaching reading comprehension with graphic novels in middle and high school.

- The three windows of reader access possible with graphic novels: words window, images window, and words and images window.

- Teaching middle school ELA reading comprehension with the story map reading strategy and the three windows of reader access. Example graphic novel: Hope Larson's *Chiggers*.

- Teaching high school ELA reading comprehension with the three windows of reader access and a dual-story-map reading strategy. Example graphic novel: Appollo and Lewis Trondheim's *Bourbon Island 1730*.

- Terms: Words window, images window, words and images window, retell story map, and text potential story map

# CHAPTER 3

## TEACHING GRAPHIC NOVEL FICTION

"WHAT IS PAST IS PROLOGUE."
- United States Archives Building, Washington, DC -

The beginning of this chapter was challenging to write. In fact, I had to come back and rewrite it. Here is why.

For years now I have thought and rethought about how complex it is to ask teachers to take something they know (teaching print-text literary fiction) and begin again, anew, with something they do not necessarily know (teaching graphic novel literary fiction).

So, during a particularly frustrating morning of trying to express my sentiments on this topic, I wrote and deleted several different openings to this chapter. On the fifth draft, I realized I should probably just take a walk and think it through a little more. So, grumbling to myself, I set off.

I had only to walk down the hall to find some unplanned inspiration. Hanging on my colleague's office door was a new quotation.

"What is past is prologue," I read.

And then I began to repeat, "What is past is . . . . YES! That's it!"

What is past (teaching print-text literary fiction) is prologue (a starting point) for what is to come (teaching graphic novel literary fiction).

During this new media age, print-text works of literary fiction and graphic novel works of literary fiction share the stage. They are, as I mentioned in the Introduction, co-stars. Thus, in this chapter, I will discuss how what we already know about teaching print-text literary fiction can serve as a prologue for teaching graphic novel literary fiction.

With an eye on how we have traditionally taught fiction in ELA, this chapter will address the teaching of graphic novel works of literary fiction in middle school and then in high school. For both grade ranges, we will use the same graphic novel example, *American Born Chinese* by

Gene Yang (2006). *American Born Chinese* is appropriate for both grade ranges because it can address middle school students' understandings of the elements of story and their own personal responses to those elements. And, for high school students, it can address both a more detailed listing of the elements of story and the adoption of critical-reading lenses.

Before we focus on each grade range, however, let me first outline the familiar pedagogical insight that will guide us through the teaching of graphic novel works of literary fiction. Mentored by the idea that what is past is prologue, I recommend that ELA teachers pair graphic novel works of literary fiction with print-text works of literary fiction. This pairing approach will help students make connections between the two formats—a skill that is also mentioned in the benchmarks for teaching fiction in middle school and in high school ELA. When we pair traditional print-text literature with modern graphic novel literature, we are showing students the literacy revolution currently at play during their own time and place in history.

To help paint this current literacy climate for our students, this chapter will specifically pair middle school ELA students' readings of *American Born Chinese* with S.E. Hinton's *The Outsiders*. And, for high school ELA students, this chapter will pair *American Born Chinese* with Chaim Potok's *The Chosen*.

## TEACHING GRAPHIC NOVEL FICTION IN MIDDLE SCHOOL ELA

When I taught middle school ELA, I read more fiction than I have ever read in my life. Why? My students were constantly recommending their favorite novels. They were amazing, motivated young readers, and they taught me an important lesson that continues to influence my reading choices each and every day. They taught me that young adult fiction is perhaps the most rewarding fiction to read, for young adult writers seem to put extra effort into writing quality stories that will appeal to energetic, and sometimes moody, readers.

For instance, my students explained that, while their parents often continued to read any book of fiction they started, they did not. Many of them stated that fiction needs "to capture" them. I remember one student saying, "Fiction needs to keep me in the story, not because I tell myself to stay there, but because I am just there."

With these young adults' zest for life and for choosing quality fiction in mind, pairing Yang's *American Born Chinese* with S.E. Hinton's *The Outsiders* was a logical choice.

I have chosen these two texts because: 1. Both have been extremely well received by teachers and readers over time, and 2. Both have received literary acclaim and acknowledgement, earning them lasting and strong reputations among teachers, parents, students, and the general reading community at large. But, before we move on, I wish to once again stress that *Teaching Graphic Novels* is written with lesson ideas and reading strategies that may apply to any graphic novel— and, in this chapter, its accompanying print-text work of literary fiction. So, I will leave my fiction recommendations as they are for now, and we will begin our discussion by taking a closer look at the suggested lesson ideas and reading strategies for teaching middle school graphic novel fiction.

The standard for teaching fiction in middle school ELA addresses students' abilities to identify, analyze, and apply their knowledge of fiction into thoughtful literary responses.

**Figure 3.1: ELA middle school fiction standard**

## STANDARD FOR TEACHING MIDDLE SCHOOL FICTION

Students are able to identify, analyze, and apply their knowledge of various types of fictional texts, and, moreover, develop thoughtful, literary responses to those texts.

If we break this standard into steps, we will see that ELA teachers are asked to make three pedagogical movements when teaching fiction in middle school ELA:

1. Students need to be able to identify and apply the elements of fiction;

2. Students need to be able to work with a variety of fictional texts; and

3. Students need to be able to use their knowledge of a variety of fictional texts (such as a print-text work of literary fiction and a graphic novel work of literary fiction) to develop their own, personal responses.

The reading strategy that best fits these three steps is a graphic organizer I call the Literate Eye (see figure 3.2).

The first of the three movements with the Literate Eye reading strategy addresses the elements of story. Figure 3.2 shows the Literate Eye handout. When copying for student use (**Appendix D**), please copy twice as a front-and-back handout. On the front of the handout, students are to think about and label the elements of story; on the back of the handout, students are to think about their own unique responses to those elements of story. See Figure 3.5 for a filled-out example of both sides.

**Figure 3.2: The Literate Eye reading strategy for middle school ELA students**

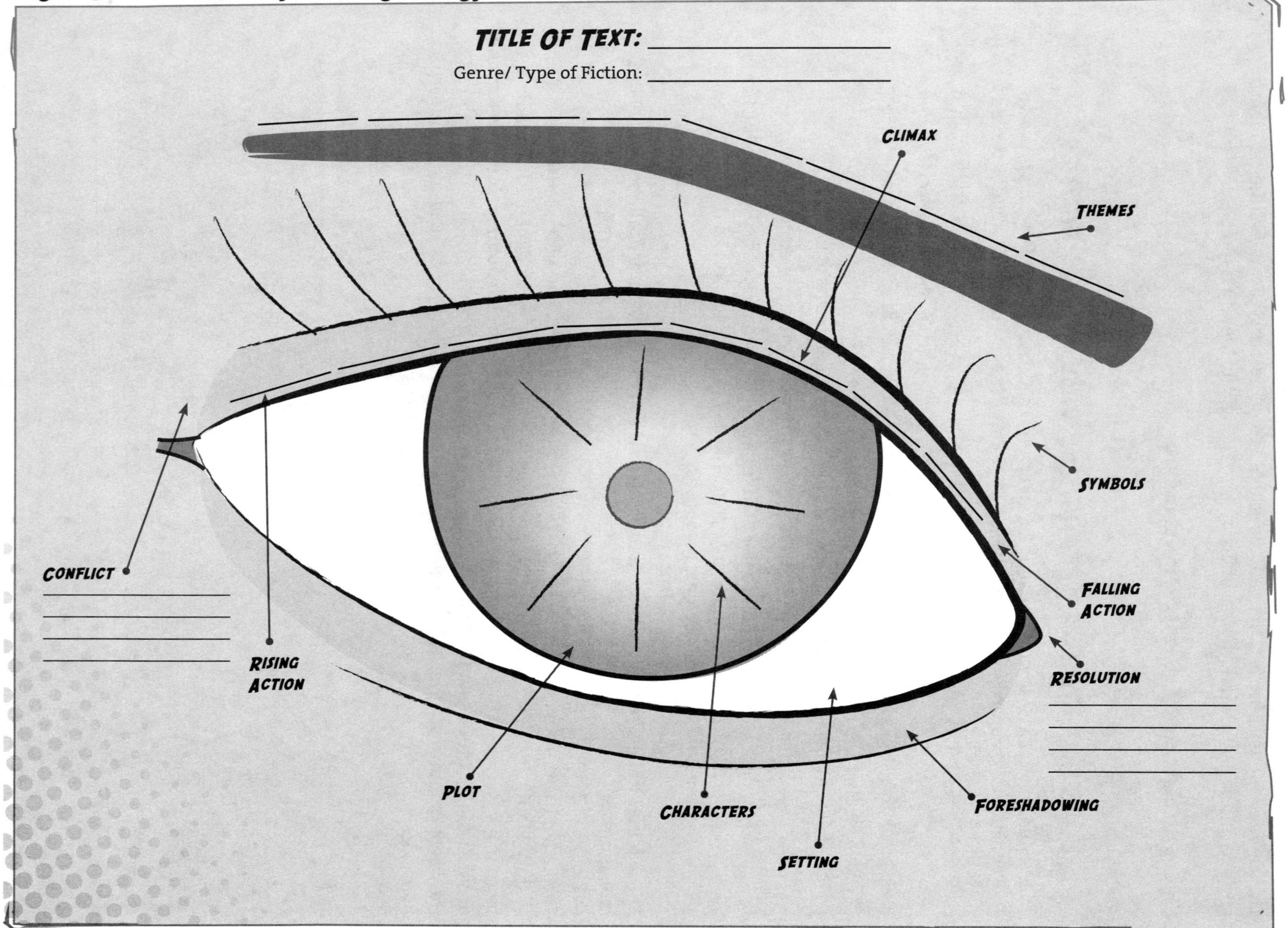

*TITLE OF TEXT:* _____ _____

Genre/Type of Fiction: _____

THEMES

SYMBOLS

FALLING ACTION

RESOLUTION

FORESHADOWING

CLIMAX

SETTING

CHARACTERS

PLOT

RISING ACTION

CONFLICT

To begin, students should receive a copy of **Appendix E**, which lists the elements of story they will be asked to know: plot, characters, setting, conflict, rising action, climax, falling action, resolution, symbols, theme, and foreshadowing. This information is also included below.

Next, students should be given two copies of the Literate Eye (**Appendix D**)—one for the print-text work of fiction and one for the graphic novel work of fiction.

Explained further in Lesson Idea 3.A, on the front side of the Literate Eye, above each eye, students will fill in the titles of the two works of fiction. If students are reading the two fiction selections recommended earlier for middle school, they would write *American Born Chinese* on one handout and *The Outsiders* on the other handout. Below that space, students will also write the type of format for each work of fiction. Again, given the two fiction examples *Teaching Graphic Novels* has suggested, students would write print "print-text fiction" below *The Outsiders* and "graphic novel fiction" below *American Born Chinese*.

Lesson Ideas 3.A and 3.B will provide further directions for using the Literate Eye reading strategy in middle and high school.

### Appendix E: The Literate Eye reading strategy for middle school ELA students

*PLOT* — the primary sequence of events that setup or tell a story

*CHARACTER* — a person, persona, or identity within a fiction story

*SETTING* — where the events of the story take place

*CONFLICT* — the tension, disagreement, or discord that occurs in a story

*RISING ACTION* — the action or events in the story that stem from the primary conflict and lead to the climax

*CLIMAX* — the point of greatest intensity in a story, a culminating point, usually led up to by rising action and followed by a resolution

*RESOLUTION* — the final outcome to solve or address the conflict

*SYMBOLS* — an iconic representation that stands for something larger than itself

*THEME* — a main idea or emphasized aspect of a story

*FORESHADOWING* — a moment in the story when the reader feels like something to happen later in the story is alluded to or referenced

# LESSON IDEA 3.A: TEACHING GRAPHIC NOVEL FICTION IN MIDDLE SCHOOL ELA

**The graphic novel:** Fiction graphic novel and print-text work of fiction of your choice; in the example that follows, Yang's *American Born Chinese* is paired with Hinton's *The Outsiders*.
**The Standard:** Middle school fiction
**The Reading Strategy:** The Literate Eye

### Steps for Teaching Middle School Fiction with Graphic Novels

*1.* First, students need to be introduced to the elements of story (see **Appendix E**).

*2.* After reading through and discussing these terms, it is a good idea to ask students to write and draw their own explanations for these terms and definitions. Space is provided below each term. Please note that this space is divided into two sides. On one side, students should write out their own definitions for each term. On the other side, students should illustrate their definitions.

*3.* After understanding the terms and their definitions, teachers should pass out the two Literate Eye handouts and ask students to fill in the titles of the two works of fiction and their format types (i.e., print-text fiction, graphic novel fiction).

*4.* Reminding students to think first about the elements of story and second about their own responses to those elements, assign the students certain chapters or sections from the two works of fiction.

Note: The Literate Eye reading strategy works best if students read both works of fiction alongside each other, continuously (instead of one complete work of fiction and then the other work of fiction). Reading the two works of fiction alongside each other supports better fluency and stronger cross-text connections for students (intertextuality). Further, for each assigned section or chapter of reading, students should fill out a Literate Eye. This way, students have an entire chronicle of the elements of story and their own responses to those elements for both works of fiction.

*5.* Once students have read their first set of assigned reading sections or chapters from the two works of fiction, ask them to think about the elements of story and label the eyes on the front of the handouts.

*6.* After students fill out the eyes on the front of the handouts, ask them to: "Take a moment and think about how you, personally, feel about the elements of story within the two works of fiction. If you could respond to the author about each of these elements, what would you say?" Or, "What were you thinking about the elements of story when you read? On the back of the handout, on the second eye, write your responses to the elements of story for each work of fiction."

**Figure 3.3: Gene Yang's *American Born Chinese* (First Second Books, 2006)**

**Summary**

In this coming-of-age graphic novel, readers follow what at first seems like three unrelated tales. As the story moves on, however, Yang masterfully merges the tales of Jin Wang, the Monkey King, and Chin-Kee together, prompting young adult readers to think about a variety of pertinent and age-appropriate social issues: identity, difference, tradition, stereotypes, young love, friendship, and, most importantly, self-acceptance.

**Creator: Gene Yang (1973-present)**

Hailed as a beacon of light in the graphic novel world, Yang has received tremendous acclaim for *American Born Chinese*. The first graphic novel nominated for the prestigious National Book Award, *American Born Chinese* was also the first graphic novel to win the American Library Association's acclaimed Printz Award for young adult literature.

So, why might Yang be such a talented young adult writer? Just like you, he works with young adults each and every day. He is a computer science teacher at a high school in the San Francisco Bay Area. He and his wife also have a young son named Kolbe.

**Interesting Information**

- Yang maintains his own website about graphic novels and even concentrates on graphic novels in education. His website is www.humblecomics.com, and it offers links for teachers and/or students who are interested in creating their own comics or graphic novels.

- Yang often states that *American Born Chinese* is generated from his experiences as a young Asian-American student.

- Yang maintains a website dedicated to one of the main characters in *American Born Chinese* as well. Readers can learn more about the Monkey King by going to www.humblecomics.com/monkey/.

**From Gene Yang**

"The way I see it, the medium of comics is a multimedia medium. It combines two distinct media, still images and text, into a single unified reading experience. I don't think it's a coincidence that the revival of interest in graphic novels is occurring simultaneously with the rise of the World Wide Web. The Web is multimedia, and Web users are used to that sort of content. As a cartoonist, my deep hope is that academic and critical interest in comics will bring about more literary graphic novels, and vice versa—that it will be a big, beautiful, self-feeding cycle."

**Figure 3.4: S.E. Hinton's *The Outsiders* (Puffin Books, 1967)**

**Summary**
From Ponyboy's point of view, there are two types of people: socs and greasers. Short for "social," a soc has money and can get away with anything. Known for their greasy hair, greasers do not have money and cannot get away with anything. A greaser is an outsider and needs to watch his back. Through Ponyboy's perspective, Hinton offers readers a story about what can happen when two groups, who think they are so different, break out in violent feud and find, in the end, more similarities than differences.

**Author: S.E. Hinton (1950-present)**
Susan Eloise Hinton was born and raised in Tulsa, Oklahoma. Often noted for stating that there was not much for a young adult to do in Tulsa, Hinton turned to reading and writing at a young age. Her passion for the two subjects was further strengthened when, during her junior high school years, she used the two interests to help deal with her father's cancer. Since writing perhaps her most famous novel, *The Outsiders*, Hinton has written a number of other fiction titles as well: *Rumble Fish*; *That Was Then, This is Now*; *Tex, Taming the Star Runner*; *Hawk's Harbor*; *Tim's Stories*; *Big David, Little David*; and *The Puppy Sister*.

**Interesting Information**

- Hinton was 17 when she wrote and published *The Outsiders*.
- *The Outsiders* is actually based on rival gangs from Hinton's own high school.
- Hinton's hobby is horseback riding.
- When writing, Hinton says that she first writes long-hand and then types on the computer.

**From S.E. Hinton**
"It's okay. We aren't in the same class. Just don't forget that some of us watch the sunset too."
–Ponyboy, *The Outsiders*

Now that we have a better understanding of these two works of fiction and their authors, let's look at the Literate Eye reading strategy. A teacher-friendly version of this reading strategy can be found in **Appendix D**.

**Figures 3.5-3.6: The Literate Eye reading strategy**
As we move from teaching graphic novel fiction in middle school to teaching graphic novel fiction in high school, we will continue to rely on the Literate Eye reading strategy. For high school ELA, however, we will add a more in-depth list of the elements of story, and we will also add a critical component to our students' personal responses by asking students to not only think about their own personal responses to the two works of fiction, but also to choose a critical-reading lens through which to filter those responses.

**Figure 3.5: The Literate Eye reading strategy for middle school ELA students (American Born Chinese)**

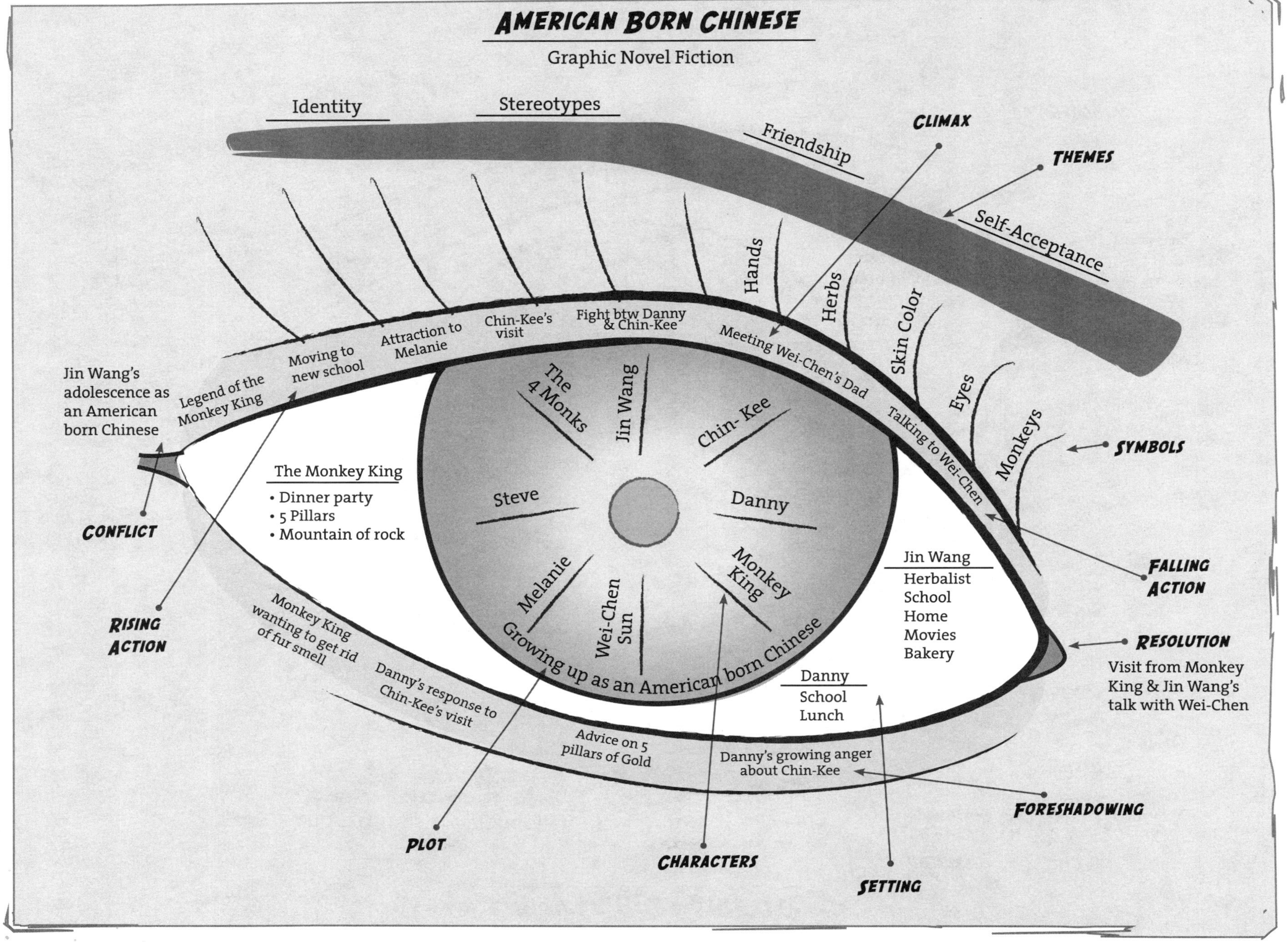

## AMERICAN BORN CHINESE

Graphic Novel Fiction

THEMES

Identity

Stereotypes

Self-Acceptance

Friendship

CLIMAX

Meeting Wei-Chen's Dad

Hands

Herbs

Skin Color

Eyes

Monkeys

SYMBOLS

Talking to Wei-Chen

FALLING ACTION

RESOLUTION

Visit from Monkey King & Jin Wang's talk with Wei-Chen

Jin Wang
Herbalist
School
Home
Movies
Bakery

Danny
School
Lunch

Danny's growing anger about Chin-Kee

FORESHADOWING

SETTING

Chin-Kee
Danny
Monkey King
Jin Wang
Wei-Chen Sun
Steve
Melanie
The 4 Monks

Growing up as an American born Chinese

Advice on 5 pillars of Gold

CHARACTERS

Fight btw Danny & Chin-Kee

Chin-Kee's visit

Attraction to Melanie

Moving to new school

Legend of the Monkey King

Jin Wang's adolescence as an American born Chinese

The Monkey King
• Dinner party
• 5 Pillars
• Mountain of rock

Monkey King wanting to get rid of fur smell

Danny's response to Chin-Kee's visit

PLOT

CONFLICT

RISING ACTION

# Figure 3.5: The Literate Eye reading strategy for middle school ELA students (*American Born Chinese*)

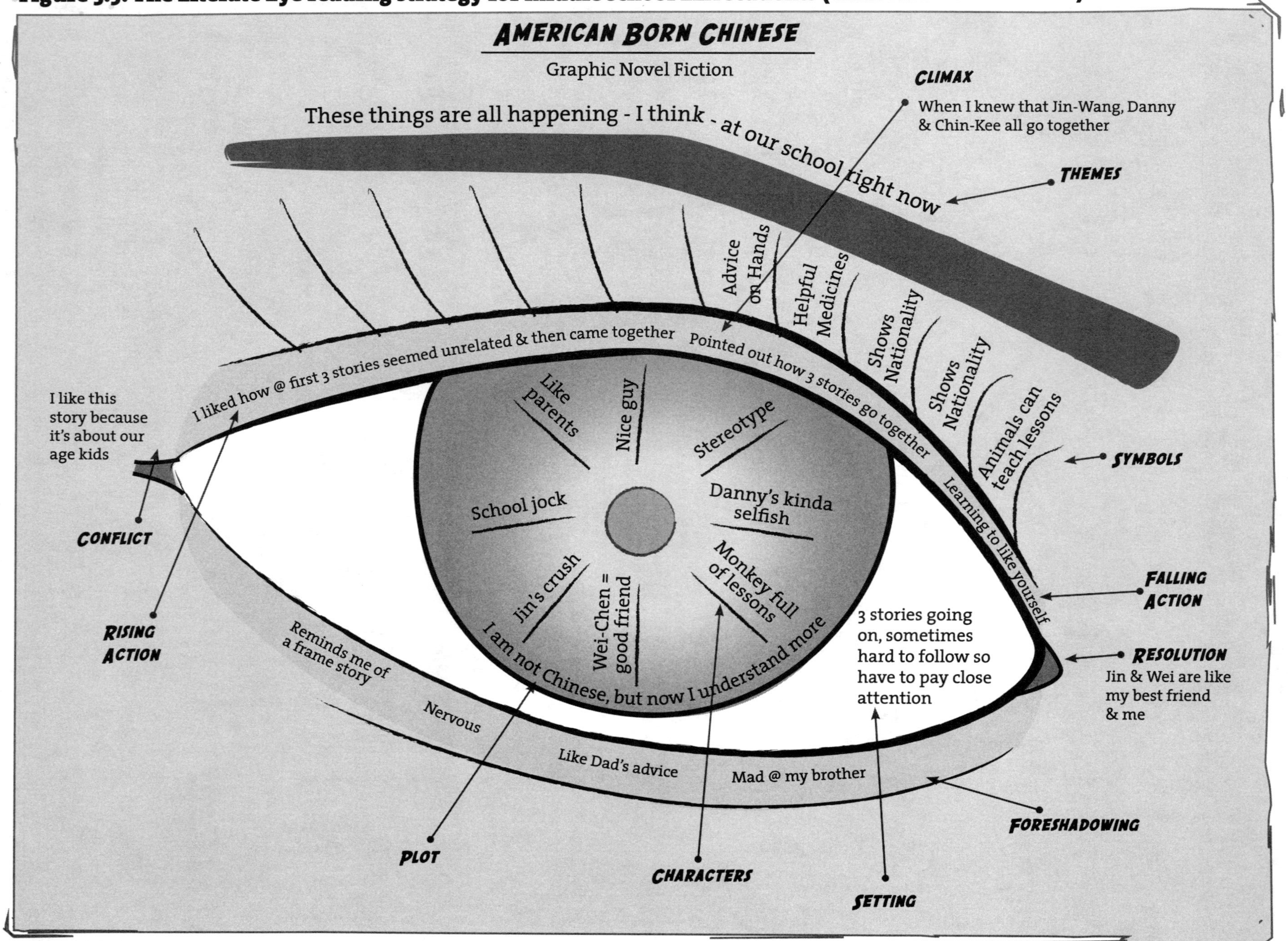

## AMERICAN BORN CHINESE

Graphic Novel Fiction

**CLIMAX**
When I knew that Jin-Wang, Danny & Chin-Kee all go together

**THEMES**
These things are all happening - I think - at our school right now

**SYMBOLS**
Animals can teach lessons

**FALLING ACTION**

**RESOLUTION**
Jin & Wei are like my best friend & me

**FORESHADOWING**

Learning to like yourself

Shows Nationality
Shows Nationality
Helpful Medicines
Advice on Hands
Pointed out how 3 stories go together

3 stories going on, sometimes hard to follow so have to pay close attention

Mad @ my brother

**SETTING**

Danny's kinda selfish

Monkey full of lessons

Stereotype

Nice guy

Wei-Chen = good friend

Like parents

School jock

Jin's crush

**CHARACTERS**

Like Dad's advice

I am not Chinese, but now I understand more

I liked how @ first 3 stories seemed unrelated & then came together

Reminds me of a frame story

Nervous

**PLOT**

I like this story because it's about our age kids

**CONFLICT**

**RISING ACTION**

# Figure 3.6: The Literate Eye reading strategy for middle school ELA students (*The Outsiders*)

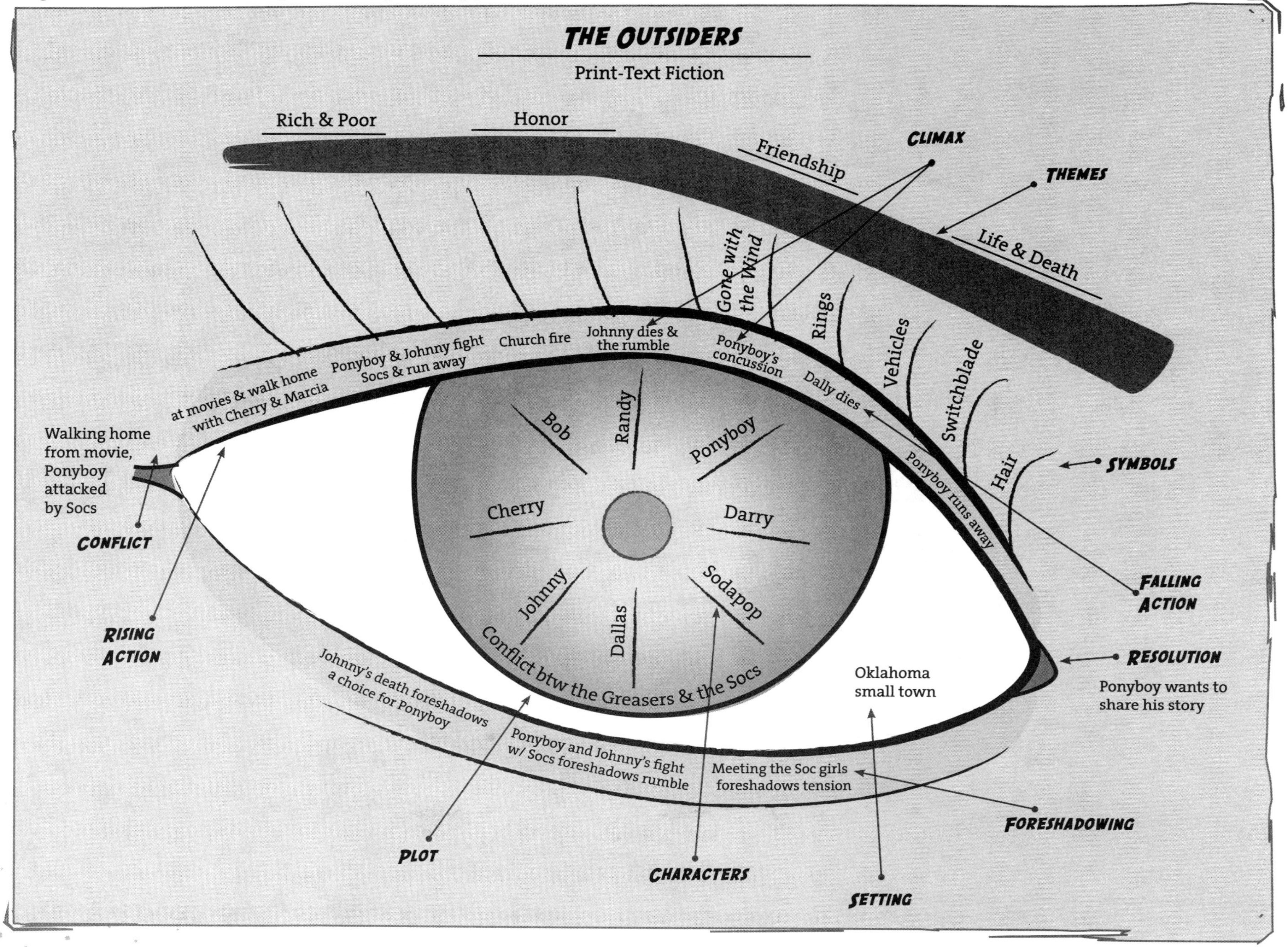

**THE OUTSIDERS**

Print-Text Fiction

**THEMES**

Life & Death

Honor

Rich & Poor

Friendship

**CLIMAX**

Gone with the Wind

Ponyboy's concussion

Johnny dies & the rumble

Church fire

Ponyboy & Johnny fight Socs & run away

at movies & walk home with Cherry & Marcia

Walking home from movie, Ponyboy attacked by Socs

**CONFLICT**

**RISING ACTION**

**SYMBOLS**

Hair

Switchblade

Vehicles

Rings

**FALLING ACTION**

Dally dies

Ponyboy runs away

**RESOLUTION**

Ponyboy wants to share his story

**FORESHADOWING**

Oklahoma small town

Meeting the Soc girls foreshadows tension

**SETTING**

Ponyboy and Johnny's fight w/ Socs foreshadows rumble

Conflict btw the Greasers & the Socs

**CHARACTERS**

Darry

Ponyboy

Sodapop

Randy

Dallas

Bob

Cherry

Johnny

Johnny's death foreshadows a choice for Ponyboy

**PLOT**

**Figure 3.6: The Literate Eye reading strategy for middle school ELA students (*The Outsiders*)**

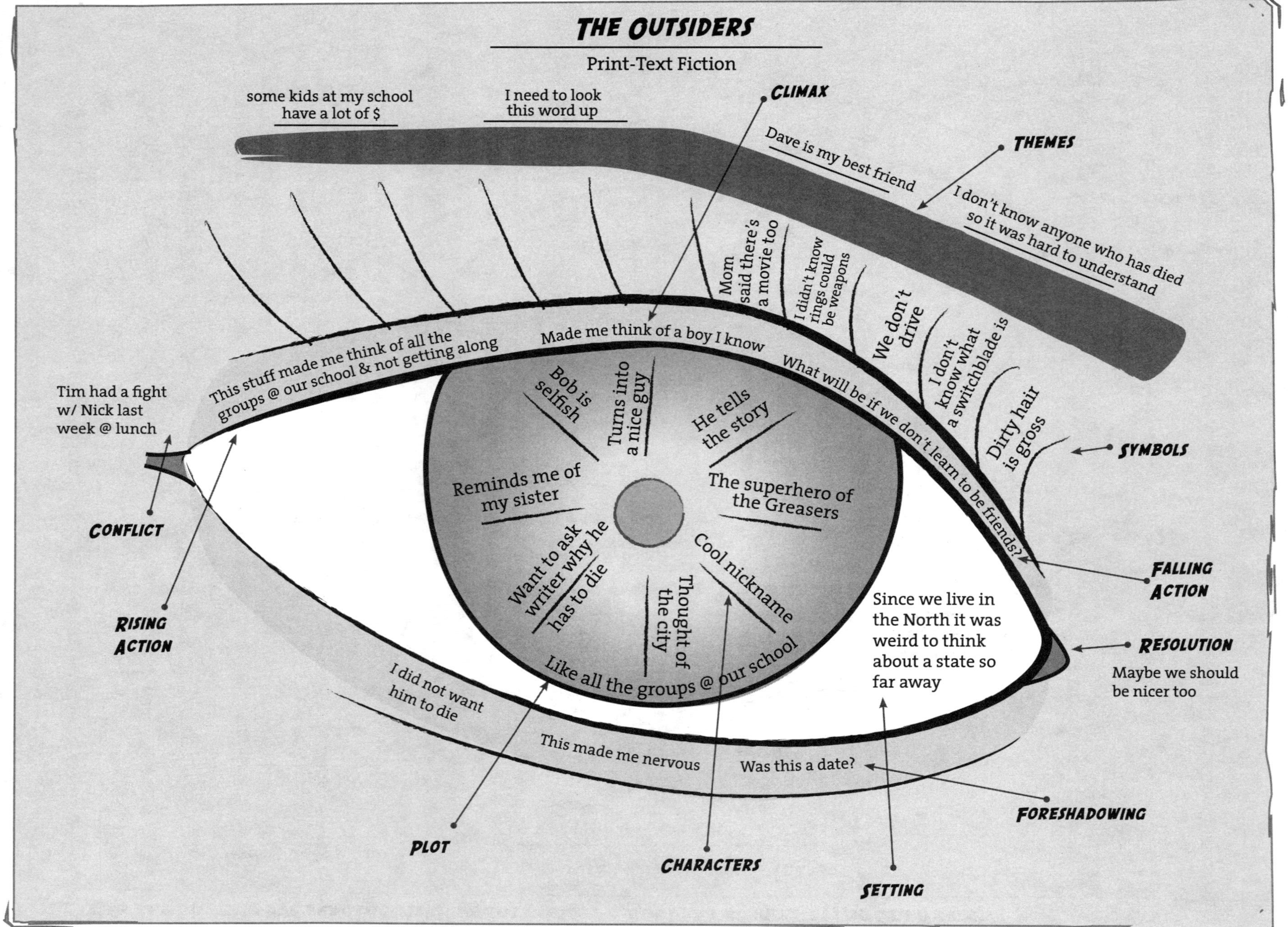

THE OUTSIDERS

Print-Text Fiction

THEMES

I don't know anyone who has died so it was hard to understand

Dave is my best friend

CLIMAX

I need to look this word up

some kids at my school have a lot of $

SYMBOLS

Dirty hair is gross

I don't know what a switchblade is

We don't drive

FALLING ACTION

RESOLUTION

Maybe we should be nicer too

What will be if we don't learn to be friends?

I didn't know rings could be weapons

FORESHADOWING

Mom said there's a movie too

Since we live in the North it was weird to think about a state so far away

Made me think of a boy I know

SETTING

He tells the story

The superhero of the Greasers

Was this a date?

Cool nickname

Thought of the city

Turns into a nice guy

Like all the groups @ our school

This made me nervous

Bob is selfish

Want to ask writer why he has to die

CHARACTERS

Reminds me of my sister

I did not want him to die

PLOT

This stuff made me think of all the groups @ our school & not getting along

RISING ACTION

Tim had a fight w/ Nick last week @ lunch

CONFLICT

# TEACHING GRAPHIC NOVEL FICTION IN HIGH SCHOOL ELA

There are two popular trends currently taking place with high school graphic novel fiction. First, as we already know, graphic novel fiction is being published on a literary level that is equal to that of traditional print-text literature and can be taught as such. Second, there are many high-school-level graphic novel adaptations of traditional literature (one of the best and most recent I have read is an adaptation of F. Scott Fitzgerald's *The Curious Case of Benjamin Button*, which has also been made into a movie). **Appendix F** offers a further list of graphic novel adaptations of traditional print-text literature.

No matter what current trend you choose for your high schoolers , however, the Literate Eye reading strategy will work. The Literate Eye will allow you to pair graphic novel fiction with either its original print-text version or with an entirely separate work of print-text fiction.

In terms of *Teaching Graphic Novels*, we will look at a graphic novel work of fiction and a separate piece of traditional print-text fiction. For high school readers, *Teaching Graphic Novels* recommends pairing *American Born Chinese* with Chaim Potok's *The Chosen*.

Just like the middle school ELA standard for teaching fiction, the high school standard also stresses the same three pedagogical steps. ELA teachers need to make sure that their students are able to understand, analyze, and apply the elements of fiction to a variety of fiction texts while developing their own, thoughtful response.

Although the wording may be similar, the teaching of fiction texts in high school ELA must be more in-depth and more critical than its middle school counterpart. Thus, with depth and critical analysis in mind, I suggest that high school teachers use a more advanced version of the Literate Eye. In the high school version, there is a more detailed listing of the elements of story and, along with that more detailed list, students will be asked to adopt a critical-reading lens. The high school ELA version of the Literate Eye is found in Figure 3.7, and a teacher-friendly version is found in **Appendix G**.

**Figure 3.7: The Literate Eye reading strategy for high school ELA students**

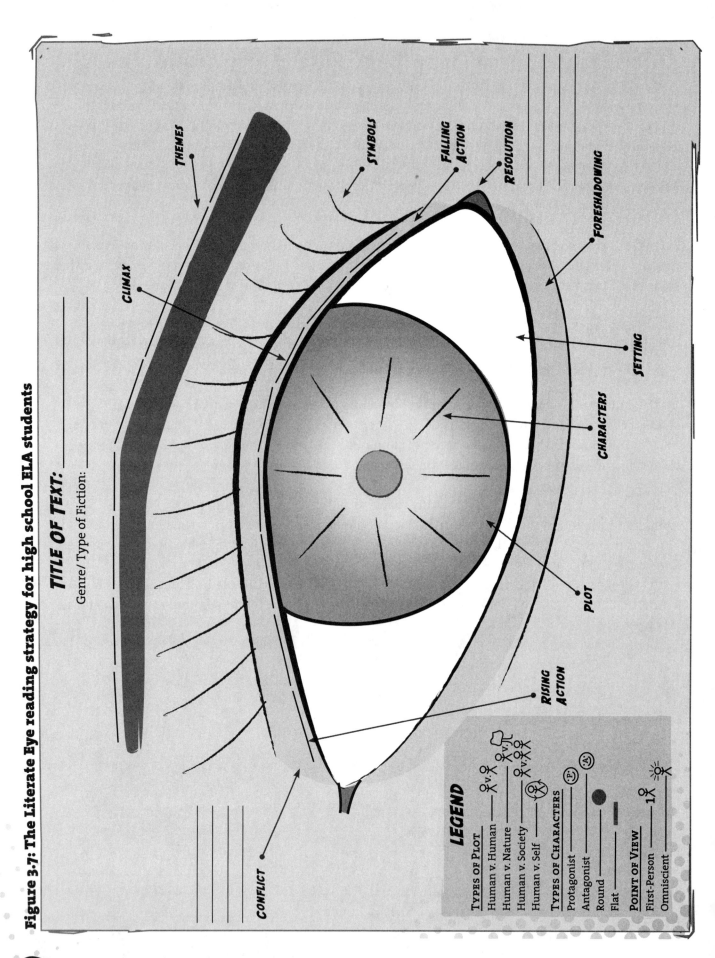

*TITLE OF TEXT:* _____

Genre/Type of Fiction: _____

THEMES

SYMBOLS

FALLING ACTION

RESOLUTION

FORESHADOWING

CLIMAX

SETTING

CHARACTERS

PLOT

RISING ACTION

CONFLICT

**LEGEND**

TYPES OF PLOT
Human v. Human
Human v. Nature
Human v. Society
Human v. Self

TYPES OF CHARACTERS
Protagonist
Antagonist
Round
Flat

POINT OF VIEW
First-Person
Omniscient

Similar to the middle school lesson, the high school version of the Literate Eye also has a supplemental handout. The high school handout contains an updated list of the elements of story and a listing of the four critical-reading lenses, as noted in Figure 3.8 (see **Appendix H** for a copy-friendly version).

**Figure 3.8: Updated list of the elements of story for high school graphic novel readers of fiction and the four critical-reading lenses that accompany the Literate Eye reading strategy**

# ELEMENTS OF STORY

Directions: Please discuss the elements of fiction, and rewrite the definitions in your own words and in your own illustrations.

Plot—the primary sequence of events that setup or tell a story
- Types of plot
    1. Human vs. human—the sequence of events sets up a conflict between two or more characters
    2. Human vs. nature—the primary conflict in this sequence of events is between a character (or characters) and the natural environment
    3. Human vs. society—one or more of the characters experiences a sequence of events that places him (or them) at odds with the larger community
    4. Human vs. self—in this sequence of events, a character struggles with him- or herself

Characters—a person, persona, or identity within a fiction story
- Types of characters
    1. Protagonist—typically the main character, the protagonist is usually the character highlighted in the story, the character whom the plot revolves around
    2. Antagonist—the source of conflict for the protagonist
    3. Round—full, well-developed character
    4. Flat—dull, poorly developed character

Point of view (POV)—the perspective from which the story is told

- Types of POV
    1. First-person—the narrator speaks from an "I" perspective
    2. Omniscient—either the writer is all-knowing about all of the characters and the plot that involves them, or the writer chooses one character to be the main source of information to the reader, thus making him or her all knowing.
    3. Objective—the writer is a detached observer who tells what happens without disclosing what characters think or feel
    4. Third-person—the narrator is an outside voice who tells how the characters feel but does not participate in the action of the story

**SETTING** — where the events of the story take place

**CONFLICT** — the tension, disagreement, or discord that occurs in a story

**RISING ACTION** — the action or events in the story that stem from the primary conflict and lead to the climax

**CLIMAX** — the point of greatest intensity in a story, a culminating point, usually led up to by rising action and followed by a resolution

**RESOLUTION** — the final outcome to solve or address the conflict

**SYMBOL** — an iconic representation that stands for something larger than itself

**THEME** — a main idea or emphasized aspect of a story

**FORESHADOWING** — a moment in the story when the reader feels like something to happen later in the story is alluded to or referenced

# CRITICAL-READING LENSES FOR HIGH SCHOOL READERS OF GRAPHIC NOVEL FICTION

Directions: Please discuss the critical-reading lenses listed below. Under each lens, please explain the term and its meaning in your own words (you may either write or draw).

1. **Reader Response Lens:** Through this lens, you will pay particular attention to your own reaction to the text. What do you think about when you are reading? Why? Try to connect your thoughts to the elements of fiction. Why does a certain element make you think _____?

2. **Marxist Lens:** Similar to the feminist lens, the Marxist lens asks you to think about the political and historical context the author is writing from. Specifically, Marxism seeks to foster questions about how texts are socially constructed. Who has power? Who does not? Why? Which social classes are represented? Which are not? Why? Essentially, you are to read through this lens with a mind for thinking about how society is constructed in the text and what the author is trying to say about society—during that time and place in history—as a result of the text's social constructions. When filling out the Literate Eye with a Marxist lens, you might ask yourself: "How do the elements of style reflect decisions of social construction?"

3. **Feminist Lens:** Just like the Marxist lens, the Feminist lens is also very political and social in nature. The major emphasis for the Feminist lens, however, rests on power. The questions that guide the Feminist lens are: Who has power? Who does not? What is being said about gender? What is considered masculine? Feminine? Who has a voice? Who does not? Overall, what is being said about males and about females in this text? How do the elements of style illustrate this point?

4. **Cultural Lens:** When you look through the cultural lens, you will want to think about how different types of people and their histories and/or backgrounds are represented. Who is visible? Who is not? Does a certain group hold any sort of power? How so? Who makes up the majority? The minority? In the end, you are reading with an eye toward different cultural backgrounds and experiences, paying particular attention to issues of diversity in the text, and how the elements of style highlight or shun those issues.

# LESSON IDEA 3.B: TEACHING GRAPHIC NOVEL FICTION IN HIGH SCHOOL ELA

**The graphic novel:** Fiction graphic novel and print-text work of fiction of your choice; *Teaching Graphic Novels* recommends Yang's *American Born Chinese* and Potok's *The Chosen*
**The Standard:** High school fiction
**The Reading Strategy:** The Literate Eye, an updated list of the elements of story, and the four critical-reading lenses

**Steps for Teaching High School Fiction with Graphic Novels**

*1.* First, students need to be introduced to **Appendix H**, the terms and definitions for the elements of story in high school ELA. After discussing the terms, ask students to notice the spaces provided below each term, divided into two sides. On one side, students should use their own words to define the terms. On the other side, students can draw their definitions.

*2.* With an understanding of the elements of story underway, it is now time to introduce students to the four critical-reading lenses.
Note: Since critical theory can be exciting and yet also challenging for students, I find that it is best to introduce critical theory with picture books. Picture books provide a scaffold for students before they approach larger works of fiction. Below is a suggested list of picture books that can be paired to each critical-reading lens.

  *A)* Reader Response Lens—*Penguin* by Polly Dunbar, *The Cat in the Hat* by Dr. Seuss, *Tuesday* by David Wiesner
  *B)* Marxist Lens—*Horton Hears a Who* by Dr. Seuss, *Share and Take Turns* by Cheri J. Meiners, *The Human Race* by Jamie Lee Curtis
  *C)* Feminist Lens—*The Sissy Duckling* by Harvey Fierstein, *Beauty and the Beast* by Marianna Mayer, *Stories for Little Girls* by Lesley Sims
  *D)* Cultural Lens—*Grandfather's Journey* by Allen Say, *Heather Has Two Mommies* by Leslea Newman, *Abuela* by Arthor Dorres, *Halmoni's Day* by Edna Coe Bercaw, *I Love My Hair* by Natasha Anastasia Tarpley

*3.* You can divide up the teaching of the four critical-reading lenses a number of ways: all four in one day, one each day for four days, et cetera. The choice is up to you. However, I recommend that, after you acquaint students with a particular lens, you read a complementary picture book. Lens by lens, you will discuss the definition, the picture book, and then have students expand upon and support their own definitions/versions of that lens as they make notes on the handout.

**4.** Once students have an understanding of the elements of fiction and the four critical-reading lenses, it is time to acquaint them with the Literate Eye reading strategy (**Appendix G**). Remember to have students label the handout with the title of the work of fiction and its format/type. They should also note which critical-reading lens they will be using.

Note: The high school version of the Literate Eye contains a legend with the updated list of the elements of story. Allow students to choose where they would like to place the symbols for each element.

**5.** Remembering that it is best for students to read the graphic novel and the print-text novel simultaneously, divide the reading however you would like. Be sure to give students two handouts of the Literate Eye for each section of the reading you assign, one for each text. If they have a Literate Eye for each section, they will have an entire chronicle of the elements of story and their own critical-reading lens experiences; perhaps, for high school readers, you could even ask them to fill out a culminating, final Literate Eye that looks back over all their previous Literate Eyes and pulls out only the main ideas.

## Figure 3.9: Chaim Potok's *The Chosen* (Simon & Schuster, 1967)

### Summary
Another coming-of-age novel, *The Chosen* is about two young Jewish boys who are raised by extremely different, yet faithful, Jewish fathers. While Danny's father is a vocal, domineering Hasidic rabbi who expects his son to follow in his footsteps, Reuven's father is a gentle, kind-hearted scholar and an Orthodox Jew. Thus, when Danny's inner angst at his father's dominance and expectations causes him to explosively and traumatically injure Reuven during a parochial school baseball game, the two young boys at first seem like unlikely friends. Yet, despite their familial traditions and their fathers' dreams for their futures, the two boys slowly become friends and together begin to question themselves, each other, and the greater world around them. Some of the many themes that align this print-text piece of literature with *American Born Chinese* are: identity, difference, tradition, stereotypes, friendship, and, most importantly, self-acceptance.

### Author: Chaim Potok (1929-2002)
Born in the year of the Great Depression (1929) in New York City, Potok is often acknowledged for his many different passions in life. Potok is known as a novelist, a philosopher, a historian, a theologian, a playwright, an artist, and an editor. In terms of writing fiction, Potok's first work was authored when he was sixteen. His first submission for publication, however, was at age 17 to *Atlantic Monthly*. In order to support his diversity of interests, Potok received his Ph.D. in philosophy in 1965 (two years before the publication of *The Chosen*), his masters of theology in 1954, and his bachelors in English literature in 1950.

### Interesting Information
- Potok's wife, Adena, was a psychiatric social worker.
- While he and his brother both became rabbis, his sisters married rabbis.
- Potok is also the author of three books for children: *The Tree of Here* (1993), *The Sky of Now* (1995), and *Zebra and Other Stories* (1998).
- *The Chosen* was turned into a play and debuted in New York City in 1988.
- A great teacher resource for teaching Potok and his work can be found at http://potoklasierra.edu/Potok.teachers.html.

### From Chaim Potok
"What does it mean to have to suffer so much if our lives are nothing more than the blink of an eye? I learned a long time ago, Reuven, that a blink of an eye in itself is nothing. But the eye that blinks, that is something. A span of life is nothing. But the man who lives that span, he is something."
–*The Chosen*

# Figure 3.10: The Literate Eye reading strategy for high school ELA students (*American Born Chinese*)

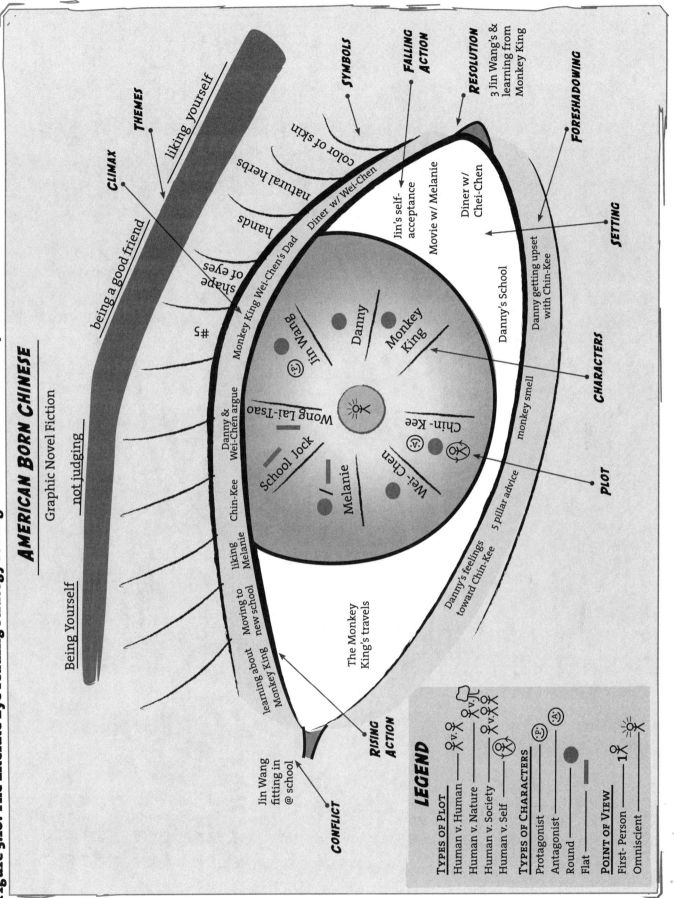

**Figure 3.10: The Literate Eye reading strategy for high school ELA students (American Born Chinese)**

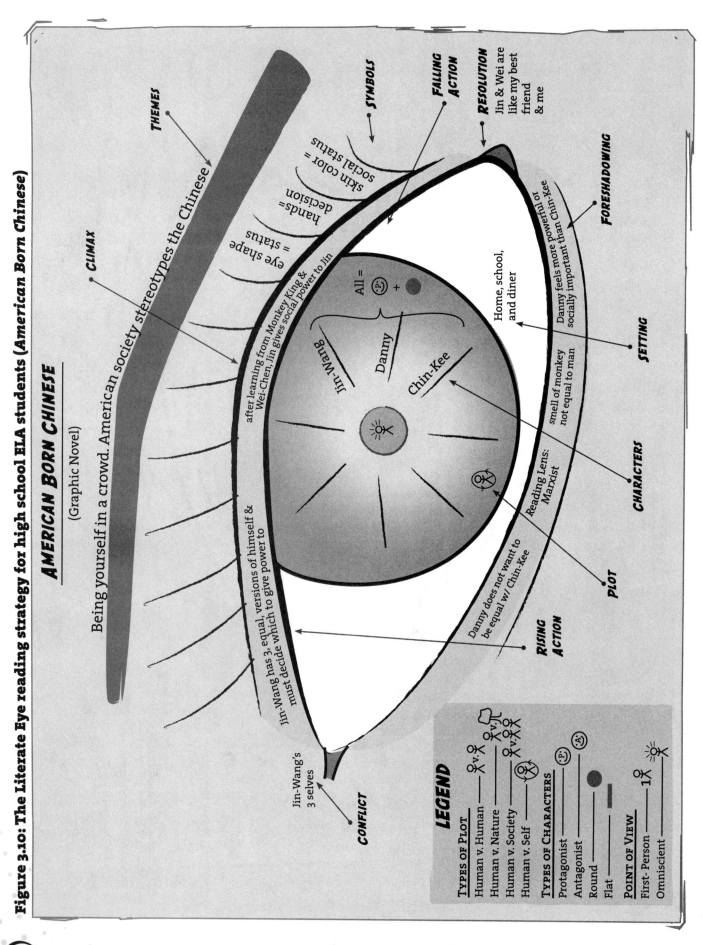

# Figure 3.11: The Literate Eye reading strategy for high school ELA students (*The Chosen*)

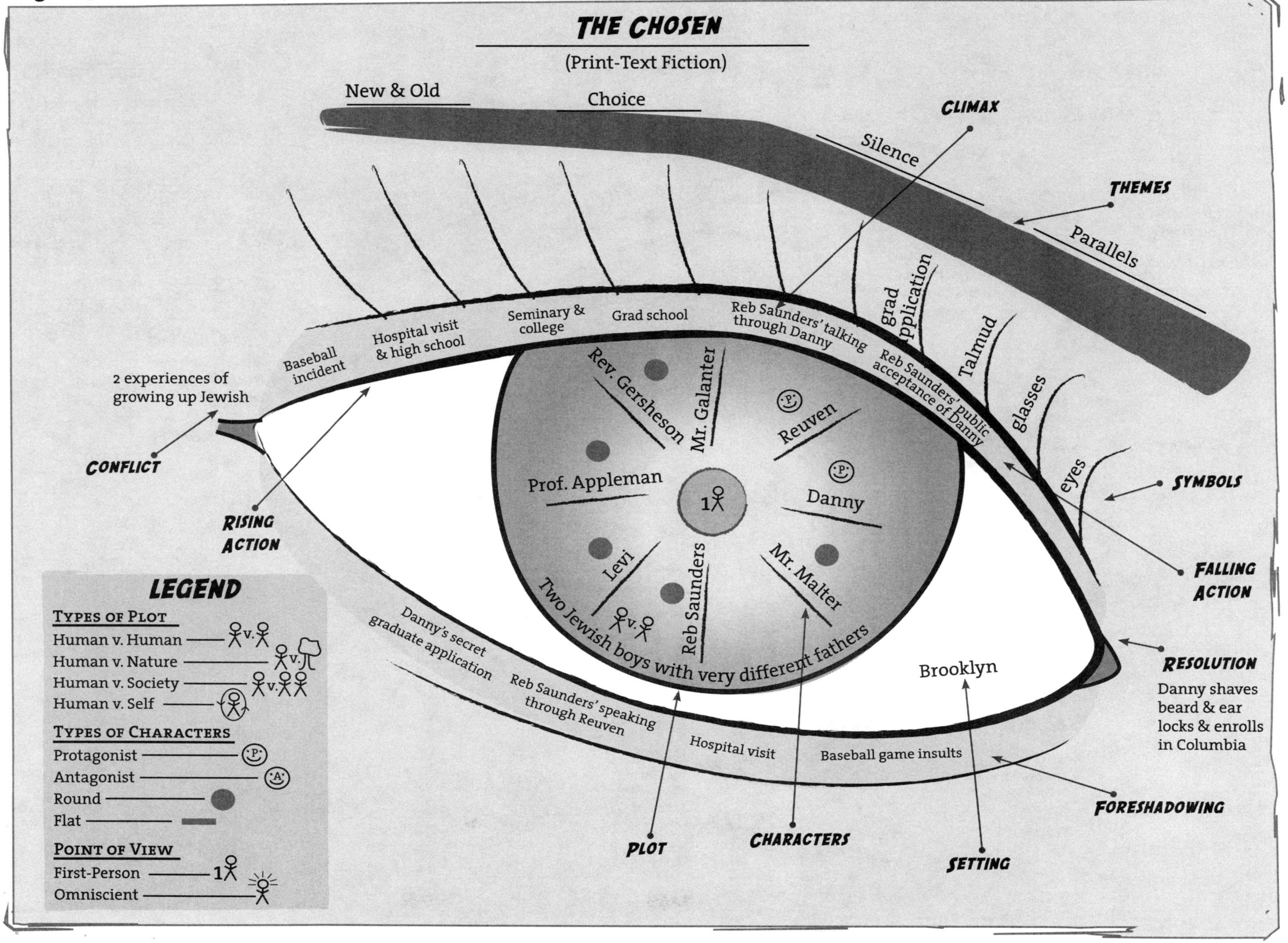

## THE CHOSEN
(Print-Text Fiction)

**THEMES**
- Parallels
- Choice
- New & Old

**CLIMAX** — Silence

**SYMBOLS**
- glasses
- eyes
- Talmud

**FALLING ACTION**
- grad application
- Reb Saunders' public acceptance of Danny

**RESOLUTION** — Danny shaves beard & ear locks & enrolls in Columbia

**FORESHADOWING**
- Brooklyn
- Baseball game insults

**SETTING** — Brooklyn

Reb Saunders' talking through Danny

**CHARACTERS**
- Reuven (P.)
- Danny (P.)
- Mr. Malter
- Mr. Galanter
- Rev. Gersheson
- Reb Saunders
- Levi
- Prof. Appleman

1人

Two Jewish boys with very different fathers

Hospital visit

**PLOT**
- Danny's secret graduate application
- Reb Saunders's speaking through Reuven

Seminary & college

Grad school

Hospital visit & high school

Baseball incident

**RISING ACTION**

2 experiences of growing up Jewish

**CONFLICT**

## LEGEND

### TYPES OF PLOT
- Human v. Human
- Human v. Nature
- Human v. Society
- Human v. Self

### TYPES OF CHARACTERS
- Protagonist (P.)
- Antagonist (A.)
- Round
- Flat

### POINT OF VIEW
- First-Person — 1人
- Omniscient

# Figure 3.11: The Literate Eye reading strategy for high school ELA students (*The Chosen*)

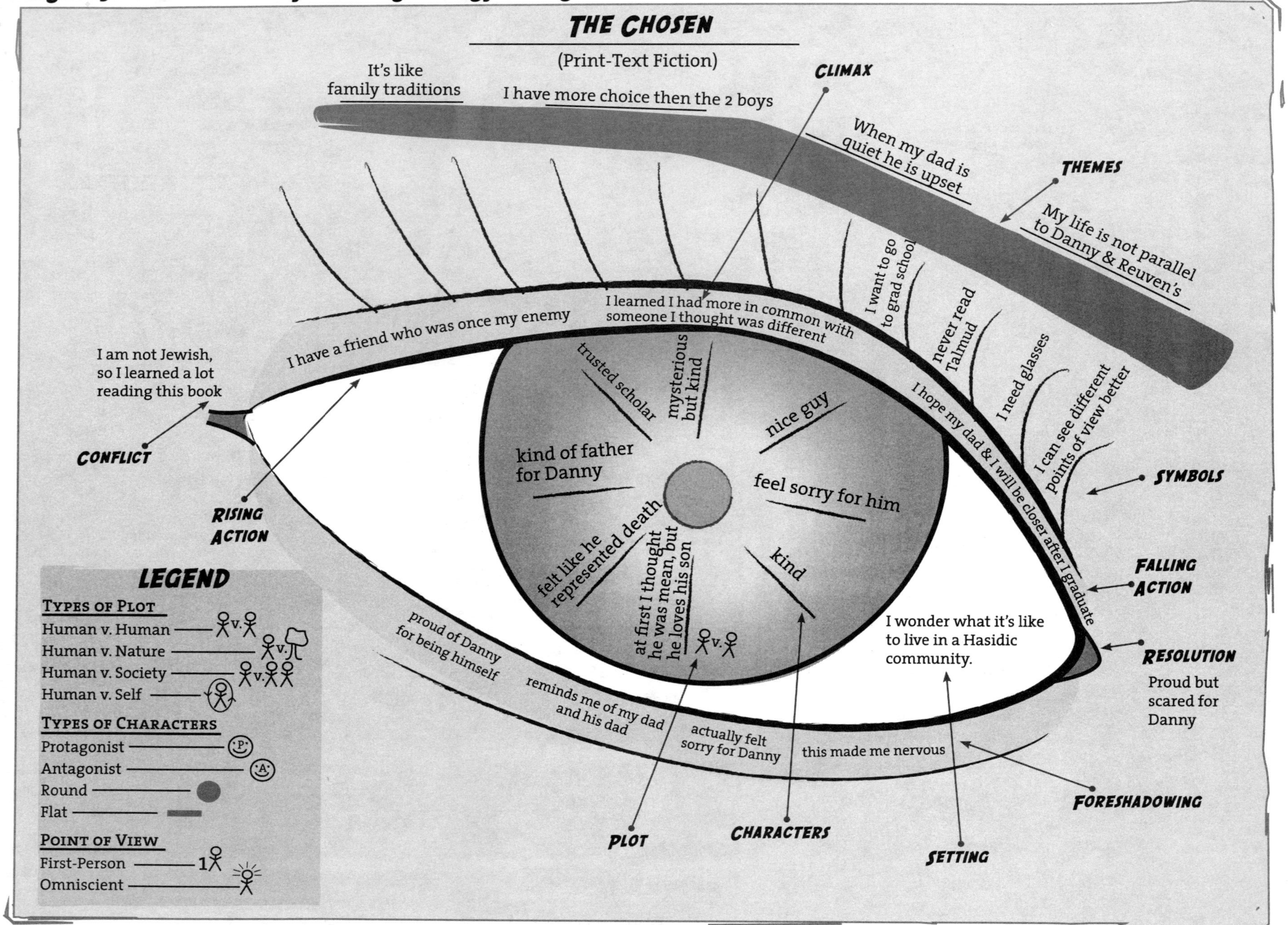

## THE CHOSEN

(Print-Text Fiction)

I have more choice then the 2 boys

**THEMES**

My life is not parallel to Danny & Reuven's

When my dad is quiet he is upset

I want to go to grad school

never read Talmud

I need glasses

I can see different points of view better

I hope my dad & I will be closer after I graduate

**SYMBOLS**

**FALLING ACTION**

**RESOLUTION**

Proud but scared for Danny

**FORESHADOWING**

I wonder what it's like to live in a Hasidic community.

this made me nervous

**SETTING**

**CLIMAX**

I learned I had more in common with someone I thought was different

nice guy

feel sorry for him

kind

mysterious but kind

trusted scholar

kind of father for Danny

felt like he represented death

at first I thought he was mean, but he loves his son

actually felt sorry for Danny

reminds me of my dad and his dad

**CHARACTERS**

**PLOT**

proud of Danny for being himself

It's like family traditions

I have a friend who was once my enemy

**RISING ACTION**

I am not Jewish, so I learned a lot reading this book

**CONFLICT**

## LEGEND

**TYPES OF PLOT**
Human v. Human
Human v. Nature
Human v. Society
Human v. Self

**TYPES OF CHARACTERS**
Protagonist
Antagonist
Round
Flat

**POINT OF VIEW**
First-Person
Omniscient

Each time I use the Literate Eye reading strategy, my students react the same way. At first, they are excited to fill out something so visual; somehow, they get the impression that it might be "easier." As you may notice with your own students, however, filling out the Literate Eye is a lot of hard work. And students typically start to couple their excitement with comments about how hard work can sometimes be enjoyable, especially when it's visual. As one student recently explained, "It's hard work that I kinda like. The picture of the eye is sorta glued in my head. I see it and know the pieces without looking."

## BRINGING IT ALL TOGETHER: BRIDGING THE READING-WRITING LINK WITH GRAPHIC NOVEL FICTION

In this chapter and those that follow, you will not only find reading strategies for teaching graphic novels, but also culminating writing activities (or assessments). After all, reading and writing are reciprocal processes, and graphic novels can be used to teach and reinforce both.

As we learned in this chapter, the standard for teaching fiction in middle and high school ELA both stress the elements of story, the students' abilities to read different formats of fictional representation, and, also, have a personal response to those formats. After they have completed the Literate Eye, students have a chronicle of their reading experiences with the two works of fiction that can serve as a scaffold for their writing. The writing standard that most logically aligns with the Literate Eye is the one for persuasive writing (see Figure 3.11).

## TEACHING GRAPHIC NOVEL FICTION IN MIDDLE SCHOOL ELA: A WRITING ACTIVITY

**Figure 3.11: Standard for teaching middle school persuasive writing**

### STANDARD FOR TEACHING MIDDLE SCHOOL FICTION

Students are able to identify, analyze, and apply their knowledge of various types of fictional texts, and, moreover, develop thoughtful, literary responses to those texts.

Since the middle school version of the Literate Eye has already prepared students to think about the various elements of story found in the two works of fiction and their own responses to those elements, students' work on the Literate Eye can easily lend itself to the writing of a compare and/or contrast essay. When they are asked to persuasively write in a way that will influence the reader, students can look back at their work on the Literate Eye and use it as a source for their writing.

With this documentation in hand, teachers can then formulate a writing prompt that asks students to filter their reading experiences with the Literate Eye into a persuasive, written expression. Figure 3.12 offers an example writing prompt.

**Figure 3.12: Example writing prompt for scaffolding middle school ELA students' reading experiences with the Literate Eye into a persuasive essay**

### Directions

Now that you have documented your reading experiences with the two works of fiction using the Literate Eye, it is time to think about writing. Using your filled-out Literate Eye as a source, write a persuasive essay that compares and/or contrasts the elements of story in the two works of fiction. You can choose to concentrate on the elements of story and/or on your own responses to those elements. Either way, your goal is to influence the reader to understand your point of view.

It is VERY important that you list specific, detailed reasons for your comparisons and/or contrasts, for the reader will understand you better—and ultimately feel influenced by your writing—when you offer specific details or examples to support your thoughts.

Thinking about the above writing assignment, your essay might be formatted in the following manner:

**A)** Introduction: what you will compare and/or contrast about the two works of fiction

**B)** Body paragraph 1: the first item you will compare and/or contrast from the elements of story

**C)** Body paragraph 2: the second item you will compare and/or contrast from the elements of story

**D)** Body paragraph 3: the third item you will compare and/or contrast from the elements of story

**E)** Conclusion

Note: Your essay does NOT have to follow this format. This is only an example. You may find that you want to choose to compare and/or contrast four elements of story. The amount of comparisons and contrasts is up to you. Just remember when making your choices, however, that your ultimate goal is to influence the reader.

## TEACHING GRAPHIC NOVEL FICTION IN HIGH SCHOOL ELA: A WRITING ACTIVITY

Since our teaching of the high school standard for teaching fiction is similar to its middle school counterpart, it can be coupled with the standard for persuasive writing as well. In high school ELA, however, we added more elements of story and the four critical-reading lenses to our students' reading of fiction. Thus, our writing prompt must also consider these additions. The high school standard for teaching persuasive writing is found in Figure 3.13.

**Figure 3.13: Standard for teaching high school persuasive writing**

## HIGH SCHOOL PERSUASIVE WRITING

Students should be able to write in order to influence the reader.

The writing prompt for the high school compare/contrast essay takes into consideration the two additions to the Literate Eye for high school readers—more elements of story and the four critical-reading lenses. See Figure 3.14.

**Figure 3.14: Example writing prompt for scaffolding high school ELA students' reading experiences with the Literate Eye into a persuasive essay**

### Directions

Now that you have documented your reading experiences with the two works of fiction using the Literate Eye, it is time to think about writing. Using the Literate Eye as a source, write a persuasive essay that compares and/or contrasts the elements of story in the two works of fiction. Specifically, when detailing your comparisons and/or contrasts, your essay needs to consider: 1. The elements of story (front side of the Literate Eye), and 2. The critical-reading lens(es) you used to respond to each work of fiction.

It is VERY important that you list specific, detailed reasons for your comparisons and/or contrasts, for the reader will understand you better—and ultimately feel influenced by your writing—when you offer specific details or examples to support your thoughts.

Thinking about the above writing assignment, your essay might be formatted in the following manner:

**A)** Introduction: what you will compare and/or contrast about the two works of fiction

**B)** Body paragraph 1: the first item you will compare and/or contrast from the elements of story

**C)** Body paragraph 2: the second item you will compare and/or contrast from the elements of story

**D)** Body paragraph 3: the first item you will compare and/or contrast from your critical-reading lenses

**E)** Body paragraph 4: the second item you will compare and/or contrast from your critical-reading lenses

**F)** Conclusion

Note: Your essay does NOT have to follow this format. This is only an example. You may find that you want to choose to compare and/or contrast three elements of story and three critical-reading lenses. The amount of comparisons and contrasts is up to you. Just remember when making your choices, however, that your ultimate goal is to influence the reader.

Before we move on to teaching graphic novel nonfiction, let's look at one more resource. Cross-indexes 1 and 2, located at the back of this book, provide references for teachers who wish to further explore the pairing of graphic novel fiction with traditional print-text fiction using thematic graphic novel topics as guides.

## CHAPTER 3 HIGHLIGHTS

Chapter 3 focused on teaching graphic novel fiction in middle and high school ELA classrooms.

- The Literate Eye reading strategy asks students to label the elements of fiction on one side and consider their own responses to those elements on the other side.

- When teaching graphic novel fiction in middle school ELA, we used the following two example texts: *American Born Chinese* by Yang and *The Outsiders* by Hinton.

- When teaching graphic novel fiction in high school ELA, we once again used *American Born Chinese*, but this time we coupled it with Potok's *The Chosen*.

- For high school graphic novel readers, we extended our listing of the elements of story, and we also introduced critical-reading lenses, such as reader response, Feminist, Marxist, and cultural. High school students were then encouraged not only to respond to the two works of fiction, but also to respond while looking through one of these critical-reading lenses.

- To bridge the reading and writing link, we reviewed sample writing prompts for bringing the teaching of graphic novel fiction together with the teaching of persuasive writing.

- Finally, Cross-indexes 1 and 2 present thematic listings of graphic novel fiction appropriate for middle and high school ELA, respectively.

# CHAPTER 4

## TEACHING GRAPHIC NOVEL NONFICTION

"IT'S NOT THE YEARS IN YOUR LIFE THAT COUNT. IT'S THE LIFE IN YOUR YEARS."
- Abraham Lincoln -

*T*he first and only graphic novel to win a Pulitzer Prize is a work of nonfiction. And, believe it or not, it won the Pulitzer Prize almost twenty years ago.

*Maus I* (1986) and the Pulitzer Prize-winning *Maus II* (1991) document the experiences of Art Spiegelman's father during the Holocaust. Probably the most well-known graphic novels in middle and high school social studies classrooms, *Maus I* and *Maus II* are often taught with an historical emphasis on World War II and the Holocaust. Such graphic novel works of nonfiction also belong in the ELA classroom, specifically as texts that align to the standard for teaching nonfiction.

### Figure 4.1: Two types of graphic novel nonfiction

**Informational Nonfiction Graphic Novel**—an informational graphic novel is expository and attempts to strictly convey or explain only factual information, with very little creator involvement.

**Creative Nonfiction Graphic Novel**—a creative nonfiction graphic novel focuses on factually accurate events, people, places and/or times AND the author's use of creative license (or storytelling).

In fact, there are two types of graphic novel nonfiction that can be taught in ELA. While *Maus I* and *Maus II* fall under the category of creative nonfiction, other graphic novel nonfiction, such as C.M. Butzer's *Gettysburg: The Graphic Novel* (2008), fall under the category of informational nonfiction. Figure 4.1 defines the two different types of graphic novel nonfiction.

The main difference between the creative nonfiction graphic novel and the informational nonfiction graphic novel is the creator's level of involvement. While the creative nonfiction graphic novel allows room for authors to explore creative license, informational nonfiction graphic novels stress that the author pay strict attention to fact. In terms of a creative nonfiction graphic novel, authors explore creative license in regards to the author's use and interpretation of words and images that appear in the panels and between the gutters.

Before we look at the two types of nonfiction graphic novels any further, let's first look at the standard for teaching nonfiction in middle and high school ELA, for they are often worded similarly. Figure 4.2 presents the key ideas.

**Figure 4.2: Standard for teaching middle and high school nonfiction**

## *MIDDLE AND HIGH SCHOOL NONFICTION*

Students should be able to identify, analyze, and apply their knowledge of a variety of nonfiction texts in order to demonstrate an understanding of the information presented.

The overall goal of the nonfiction standard is for students to be able to work with and understand a variety of nonfiction texts. Thus, the two different types of graphic novel nonfiction fit well within this standard.

Beyond a stress on the two different types of nonfiction graphic novels, we can also see that the standard for teaching nonfiction emphasizes three main ideas:

*1.* Students should be able to identify the elements of nonfiction.

*2.* Students should be able to analyze the elements of nonfiction.

*3.* Students should be able to apply the elements of nonfiction.

The reading strategy that best suits teaching nonfiction graphic novels with these three main ideas is called Nonfiction Collaboration.

Depending on the type of graphic novel you choose—informational or creative—you will work with one of two different versions of the Nonfiction Collaboration reading strategy: the Nonfiction Collaboration Journey or the Nonfiction Collaboration Stair-Step. While the Nonfiction Collaboration Journey focuses on the path students take as they read a creative nonfiction graphic novel, the Nonfiction Collaboration Stair-Step focuses on the ordering of information students receive as they read an informational nonfiction graphic novel. In short, the key words are: journey and stair-step. A *journey* focuses on what one learns along a certain path (in this case, a reading path). A *stair-step*, on the other hand, focuses on the steps one takes when climbing.

# TEACHING GRAPHIC NOVEL NONFICTION IN MIDDLE SCHOOL

Since we are already familiar with the standard for teaching nonfiction graphic novels, let's jump right into a discussion of the two different versions of the Nonfiction Collaboration reading strategy in middle school ELA.

## NONFICTION COLLABORATION STAIR-STEP: INFORMATIONAL NONFICTION GRAPHIC NOVELS

Because it stresses order, the Nonfiction Collaboration Stair-Step is most often used with an informational nonfiction graphic novel. In other words, since the informational nonfiction graphic novel is concerned with sequencing, it fits well alongside a reading strategy that offers students a chance to climb a virtual staircase (see Figures 4.3 and 4.4 or **Appendices I and J** for copy-friendly versions of the Nonfiction Collaboration Stair-Step).

As you can see in Figures 4.3 and 4.4, there are two handouts that accompany the Nonfiction Collaboration Stair-Step reading strategy. In Figure 4.3, readers are presented with the initial steps for climbing the stairs. In Figure 4.4, readers are presented with supplemental stairs for lengthier climbs (i.e., reading assignments). Because this reading strategy is so visual in nature, some teachers have even asked students to fill out numerous supplemental stairs and, once the graphic novel and the staircase are both completed, have then displayed the students' various staircase responses around the classroom.

**Figure 4.3: The Nonfiction Collaboration Stair-Step reading strategy for middle school readers**

# NONFICTION COLLABORATION STAIR-STEP

NAME: _____

READING ASSIGNMENT: _____

MIDDLE SCHOOL ELA

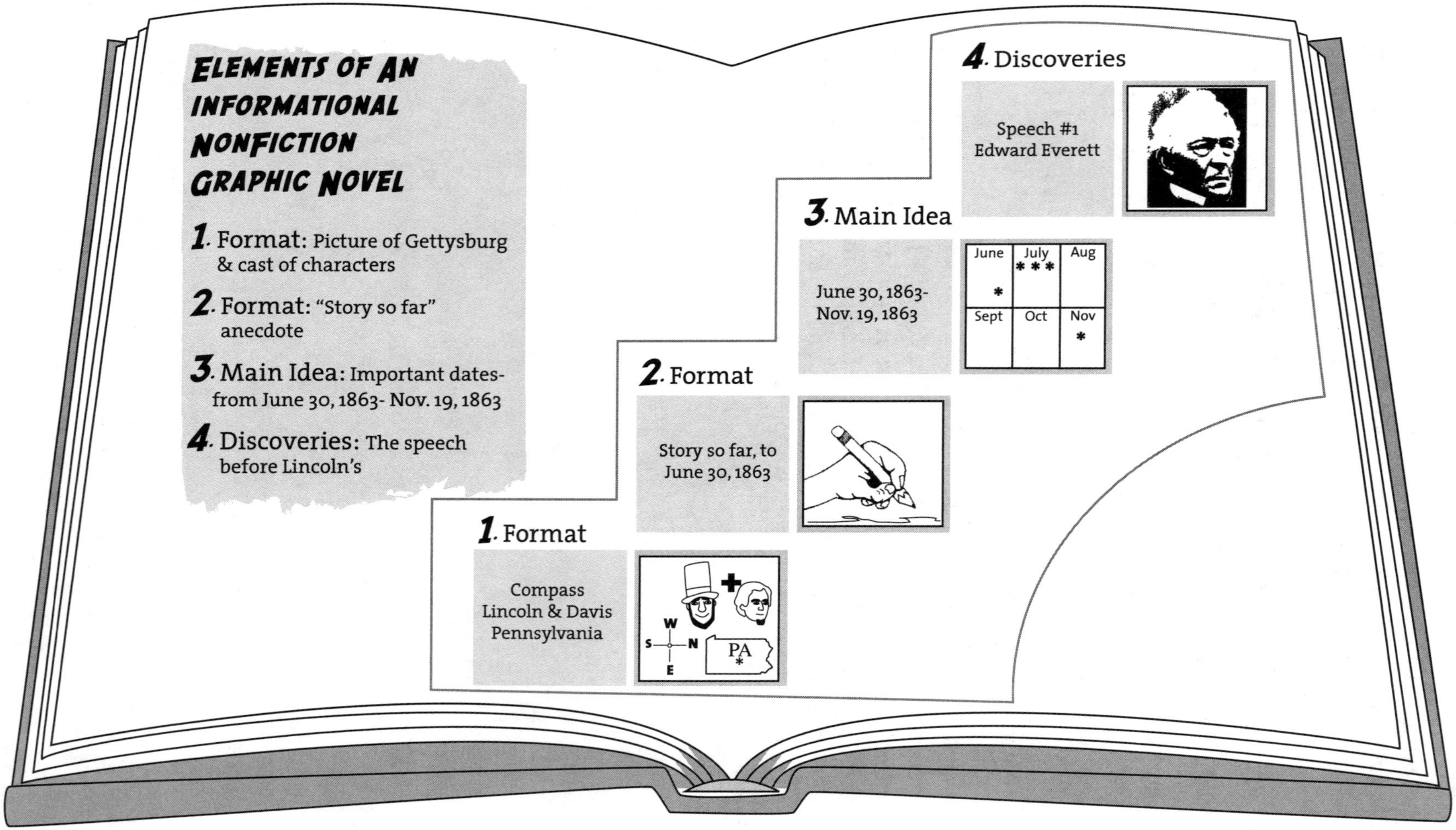

**ELEMENTS OF AN INFORMATIONAL NONFICTION GRAPHIC NOVEL**

**1** Format: Picture of Gettysburg & cast of characters

**2** Format: "story so far" anecdote

**3** Main Idea: Important dates- from June 30, 1863- Nov. 19, 1863

**4** Discoveries: The speech before Lincoln's

**4.** Discoveries

Speech #1
Edward Everett

| June | July | Aug |
|------|------|-----|
|      | ***  | *   |
| Sept | Oct  | Nov |
| *    |      | *   |

**3.** Main Idea

June 30, 1863-
Nov. 19, 1863

**2.** Format

Story so far, to
June 30, 1863

**1.** Format

Compass
Lincoln & Davis
Pennsylvania

**Figure 4.4: Supplemental stairs for the Nonfiction Collaboration Stair-Step reading strategy (middle school or high school)school)**

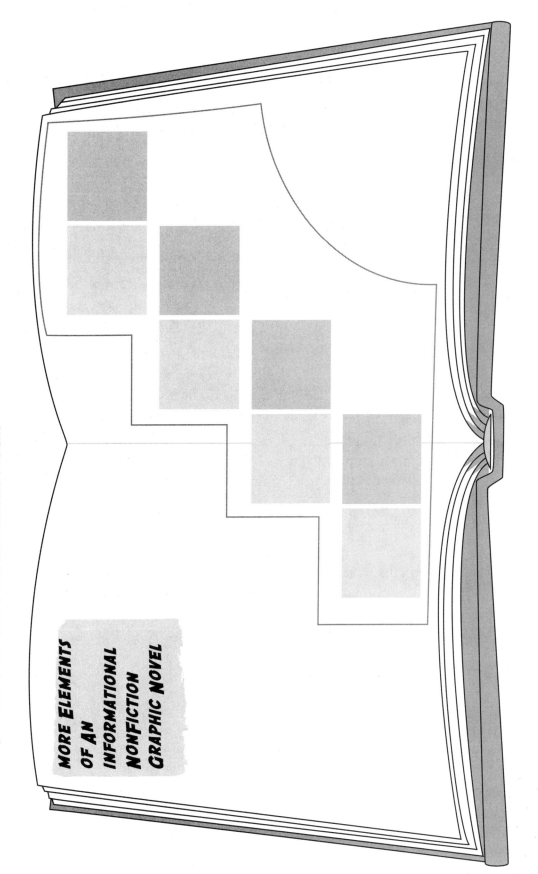

IF TEACHERS WANT TO CONTINUE THE STAIR-STEP FOR LONGER READING ASSIGNMENTS, THESE ARE THE SUPPLEMENTAL STAIRS

MORE ELEMENTS OF AN INFORMATIONAL NONFICTION GRAPHIC NOVEL

Now that we have looked at the Nonfiction Collaboration Stair-Step, we can next discuss how to teach this reading strategy to middle school ELA students. Lesson Idea 4.A walks us through this process.

# LESSON IDEA 4.A: TEACHING INFORMATIONAL NONFICTION GRAPHIC NOVELS IN MIDDLE SCHOOL ELA

**The Graphic Novel:** Informational nonfiction graphic novel; suggested informational nonfiction graphic novel: C.M. Butzer's (2009) *Gettysburg: The Graphic Novel*
**The Standard:** Middle school nonfiction
**The Reading Strategy:** Nonfiction Collaboration Stair-Step

**Steps for Teaching Middle School Informational Nonfiction Graphic Novels**

1. In order to engage students with a reading strategy, it is typically wise to build their schema. Thus, the Nonfiction Collaboration Stair-Step is best taught by first asking students to discuss what happens when they climb a flight of stairs.

2. After discussing what happens when going up a flight of stairs, students are ready to be introduced to the Nonfiction Collaboration Stair-Step reading strategy.

3. The directions for the Nonfiction Collaboration Stair-Step (below and in **Appendix I**) state that students will work through the following steps:

   A. **Step 1: Identification.** For this reading strategy, you will first identify the elements of an informational nonfiction graphic novel. You will find a box for listing these elements on the front of your handout. They are: format, discoveries, and main idea.

      - **Format:** Format relates to organization or sequencing of information. For example, are there chapter titles, subtitles, headings, subheadings, bold-faced words, lists, charts, figures, pictures, anecdotes, quotations, and so on?

      - **Discoveries:** Discoveries relate to all of the interesting and/or fun facts, curious information, significant details, or new knowledge gained from reading the informational nonfiction graphic novel.

      - **Main Idea:** The main idea is the key piece (or pieces) of information the creator is trying to convey.

   B. **Step 2: Organization.** After identifying the elements of nonfiction in the box on the front side of the Nonfiction Collaboration Stair-Step, you can now start to organize these elements on the stairs.

   Note: Above each stair, identify an element of the informational nonfiction graphic novel, in order.

**C.** **Step 3: Analyze.** Just like a graphic novel, this reading strategy asks you to next think in terms of words and images.

- Each stair is divided into two. On each stair, you are to put both the words and the images that help explain that element of nonfiction. On the left, you will write the words. On the right, you will draw the images.

- In short, you are to ask yourself: "What are the words that remind me of this element of nonfiction and, further, what are the images that remind me of this element of nonfiction?"

**4.** When you finish reading these directions to students, it is a good idea to once again point out the shape and division of each stair on the front of the handout. Each stair is divided in two. On the left side, students are to use words to explain each element of nonfiction. On the right side, students are to use images to explain each element of nonfiction.

Note: Before giving students their reading assignment, remind them about the styles and conventions of graphic novels (Chapter 1) as well. Our pedagogical approach in teaching graphic novels should always match the styles and conventions found in graphic novels. Thus, in order to best comprehend nonfiction graphic novels, it becomes critical that students think about the significance of what is found in the panels and in the gutters, in the word balloons and in the critical partnerships between words and images.

**5.** It is now time to offer students their first reading assignment. There are two ways you can assign reading with the Nonfiction Collaboration Stair-Step.

**A.** You can assign students to read only a section or chapter of reading and give them a single version of the Nonfiction Collaboration Stair Step (**Appendix I**), or

**B.** You can assign students a lengthy section of reading and give them both **Appendix I** and **Appendix J** (depending on the length of the reading, even multiple copies of **Appendix J**).

One excellent middle-school-level informational nonfiction graphic novel is *Gettysburg: The Graphic Novel* by C.M. Butzer (2009).

## Figure 4.5: Butzer's *Gettysburg: The Graphic Novel* (HarperCollins, 2009)

**Summary**

*Gettysburg: The Graphic Novel* uses primary sources (letters, diaries, speeches, and so on) to retell two of the most defining moments in American History, the battle of Gettysburg and Lincoln's Gettysburg Address. Brilliantly invoking the visual and verbal literacy skills critical to graphic novel reading, Butzer inspires modern readers to once again think about the sacrifices of those who fought for democracy in nineteenth-century America. The result is a striking work of graphic novel nonfiction that takes a fresh, modern look at this momentous time in history and the people who lived through it.

**Creator: C.M. Butzer (1974-present)**

C.M. Butzer grew up in Portland, Oregon and refers to his childhood as very Huck Finn-like, filled with activities like camping, fishing, and a little mischief here and there (for good measure). After this Huck Finn-like childhood and graduation from high school, Butzer attended Cornish College of the Arts and earned a B.F.A. in illustration. In 1997 Butzer found himself moving to Florence, Italy, where he became a Renaissance tour guide. After six years in Italy, in 2003, Butzer moved back to the U.S, to New York City. In New York City he attended the School of Visual Arts and earned his M.F.A. in illustration, graduating in 2005. Along with his latest publication, *Gettysburg: The Graphic Novel*, Butzer is also known for his work with Paul Hoppe on the *Rabid Rabbit* comic anthology.

**Interesting Information**

- Butzer used primary sources in *Gettysburg: The Graphic Novel*, drawing on speeches, letters, diaries, and even Lincoln's writing of the address.
- To see more of Butzer's work or to learn more about him, go to www.cmbutzer.com.
- Butzer lives and works in Brooklyn.
- The *Rabid Rabbit* comic anthology can be found at www.rabidrabbit.org and has won numerous awards.

**From C.M. Butzer**

"Comics must be considered equal to other forms of literature within the classroom. Only then can they start to be taught to the fullest potential . . . . With the understanding that comics [are] a unique form of literature, I think teachers will find them as dynamic as any other form."
–C.M. Butzer

# TEACHING THE INFORMATIONAL NONFICTION GRAPHIC NOVEL IN MIDDLE SCHOOL ELA: A WRITING ACTIVITY

Since the Nonfiction Collaboration Stair-Step already offers middle school readers a well-organized structure, it is relatively simple to transition this reading strategy into a writing activity. The writing standard that best complements the Nonfiction Collaboration Stair-Step is the informational writing standard (seen Figure 4.6).

**Figure 4.6: Middle school ELA standard for informational writing**

## MIDDLE SCHOOL INFORMATIONAL WRITING

Students should be able to demonstrate technical writing that offers information to the reader about real-world topics.

One of the most practical and real-world informative writing tasks that students will encounter in the future is summary writing. A summary writing assignment asks students to consider what they have read and then paraphrase it. Directions for this informational writing assignment can be found below.

**Directions**

Now that you have recorded what you have learned from this informational nonfiction graphic novel, it is time to share this knowledge with others. For this writing assignment, you will write a summary about the informational nonfiction graphic novel.

In order to write this summary, you should first consider the overall topic of the informational nonfiction graphic novel. Then, you should consider each of your stair-steps. Each stair-step represents a new piece of knowledge that you read about. Thus, each stair-step can become its own body paragraph that explains the overall topic. If, however, you have many stair-steps (perhaps for longer reading assignments), you might want to thematically or sequentially combine stair-steps together into paragraphs.

After you have introduced your topic and discussed each of its stair-steps, it is now time to close your essay. A proper summary closing for informational writing is simply a restatement of the overall topic and its supporting elements.

The organization of your informational summary essay might look like this:
A. Introduction (overall topic)
B. First stair-step (be sure to consider the images and the words you used to document each element when writing these paragraphs)
C. Second stair-step (be sure to consider the images and the words you used to document each element when writing these paragraphs)
D. Third stair-step (be sure to consider the images and the words you used to document each element when writing these paragraphs)
E. Fourth stair-step (be sure to consider the images and the words you used to document each element when writing these paragraphs)
F. Conclusion (restatement of overall topic and supporting elements)

# NONFICTION COLLABORATION JOURNEY: CREATIVE NONFICTION GRAPHIC NOVELS IN MIDDLE SCHOOL

Unlike the Nonfiction Collaboration Stair-Step, the Nonfiction Collaboration Journey works best with creative nonfiction graphic novels. As previously noted, a creative nonfiction graphic novel performs two tasks: first, it bases itself in factually accurate events, people, places and/or times and, second, it allows the author to use creative license to tell the story. The creative nonfiction graphic novel is not only based on real events, people, places, and/or times, but is also based on the author's interpretation of those events, people, places, and/or times.

With a combination of historical fact and author imagination, readers are then embarking on a journey of understanding when they read a creative nonfiction graphic novel. Thus, when we think about a reading strategy that would be a good fit for a creative nonfiction graphic novel, we want to focus on the journey the reader takes as he or she reads through the combination of factual information and author storytelling. One reading strategy that suits this journey-like reading experience is the Nonfiction Collaboration Journey. (See Figure 4.7; for a copy-friendly version of this reading strategy, see **Appendix K**).

**Figure 4.7: The Nonfiction Collaboration Journey reading strategy for middle school**

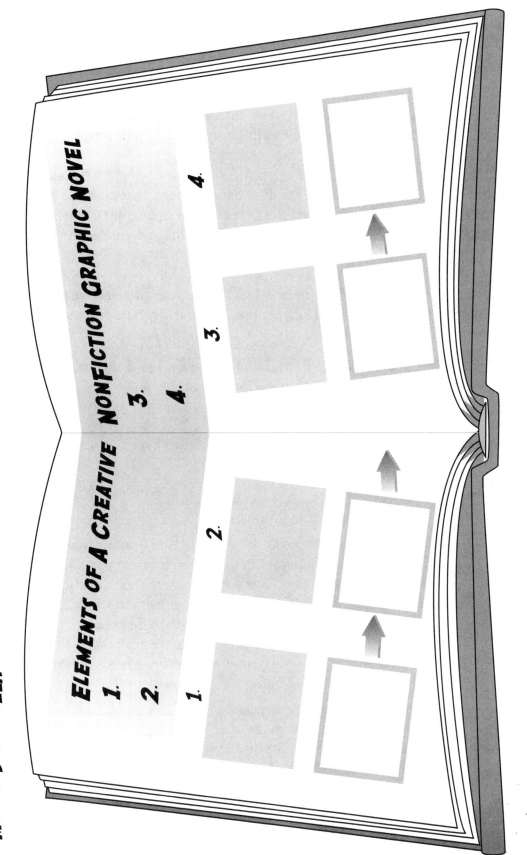

## NONFICTION COLLABORATION JOURNEY

NAME: _____

READING ASSIGNMENT: _____

MIDDLE SCHOOL ELA

ELEMENTS OF A CREATIVE NONFICTION GRAPHIC NOVEL

1.
2.
3.
4.

1.

2.

3.

4.

To begin, students can start to organize the elements of a creative nonfiction graphic novel by writing them, in the order that they appear in the graphic novel, on the arrow-lines. The rectangles that appear above and below the arrows can then be filled out in the following manner:

- The rectangles above the arrow should be filled out with words that represent the identified element of the creative nonfiction graphic novel.

- The rectangles below the arrow should be filled out with the reader's illustration of the identified element of the creative nonfiction graphic novel.

Just like the Nonfiction Collaboration Stair-Step, the Nonfiction Collaboration Journey also asks the reader to think in terms of the dominant literacies that make up a graphic novel: print-text literacies and image literacies. As we know from Chapter 1, when students are able to simultaneously think in terms of print-text and image literacies, they become stronger readers of graphic novels.

Lesson Idea 4.B further explains how ELA teachers can use creative nonfiction graphic novels with the Nonfiction Collaboration Journey reading strategy in middle school ELA classrooms.

# LESSON IDEA 4.B: TEACHING CREATIVE NONFICTION GRAPHIC NOVELS IN MIDDLE SCHOOL ELA

**The Graphic Novel:** Creative nonfiction graphic novel; suggested creative nonfiction graphic novel: Abadzis' (2007) *Laika*
**The Standard:** Middle school nonfiction
**The Reading Strategy:** Nonfiction Collaboration Journey

**Steps for Teaching Middle School Creative Nonfiction Graphic Novels**

1. Many students are familiar with film adaptations of popular nonfiction texts. For example, many states require that middle school students learn about the Civil War, an event with many, many film adaptations. Thus, in order to build schema to help students understand a creative nonfiction graphic novel, it is wise to first show a film. Just like a creative nonfiction graphic novel, a film provides its creator's take—the director's, in the case of a film—on real events, people, places, and/or times. It is a combination, in short, of factual history and creative storytelling.

2. ELA teachers can start the discussion about creative nonfiction by asking students to first complete a KWL (know-wonder-learn) chart (Ogle, 1986) about the chosen topic (the film and the graphic novel should be focused on the same topic). KWL charts ask the following: "What do students **KNOW** about the topic?"; "What do students **WONDER** about the topic?"; and, finally, "What do students want to **LEARN** about the topic?" Each letter has its own column. Charts can be drawn on the board or on poster paper.
Note: Students can complete the KWL chart either on their own and then have a class discussion, or they can fill out the chart as a class.

| KNOW | WONDER | LEARN |
|------|--------|-------|
|      |        |       |

3. Following this discussion of the KWL chart, it is time to show students a film clip. After the clip, ask students to compare and/or contrast their KWL thoughts with what they saw in the film. Then, pushing their analysis a bit further, ask them, "What do you think the director of the film wanted you to KNOW, WONDER, and/or LEARN about this film?" And, then, preparing students to think even more analytically, ask them the following questions:

  • Can you explain the journey that the director of this film clip took you on?

  • Are you able to identify historical fact from the director's creative interpretation of events, people, places, and/or times?

  • How? What indications—or elements of the film—gave you these clues?

Note: It will probably take a full class period to work through these first few steps. But, since creative nonfiction is such a new format of expression (the first Ph.D. to be issued in creative nonfiction was in 1983), it is wise to take extra time when presenting this genre.

4. Once you have built your students' schemas about creative nonfiction, you can now distribute the creative nonfiction graphic novel. After a brief review of your film-based KWL work (probably the following class session), tell students that they are now going to think about the same creative nonfiction topic but, this time, everyone will be reading a creative nonfiction graphic novel. Instead of seeing moving images, like in a film, students will need to read stationary images, like in a graphic novel. At this point, if you have not already done so, introduce students to the terminology for reading graphic novels found in Chapter 1.

**5.** With the creative nonfiction graphic novel in hand, you can now discuss what students will need to do in order to complete the Nonfiction Collaboration Journey (directions found on the back of the **Appendix K**):

**A.** **Step 1: Identification.** For this reading strategy, you will first identify the elements of a creative nonfiction graphic novel. You will find a box for listing these elements on the front of your handout. They are:

- **Element of Historical Fact:** Historical fact is the information in the graphic novel that is accurate and factual. The element of historical fact can be broken down into the following identifying categories:

**1)** Factual event: historically accurate and known event

**2)** Factual people: historically real person/people

**3)** Factual time: historically accurate time period or moment in time

**4)** Factual place: historically accurate place or location

**5)** Factual artifact: historically accurate, existent document or artifact

- **Element of Author Storytelling:** The author's storytelling is the creative technique(s) the author uses to help shape the story he or she wishes to tell about the nonfiction event, people, place, and/or time. Author storytelling can be broken down into the following identifying categories:

**1)** Creator's voice: The author's own voice/tone used to influence the story

**2)** Creator's style: How the words or images influence the story being told

**3)** Creator's device: A situation, person, place, event, or artifact the author creates for his or her own storytelling purposes

**B.** **Step 2: Application/Organization.** After identifying the elements of a creative nonfiction graphic novel and listing them in the box on the front of the handout, you can now start to organize these elements. On each arrow, write the name of the identified element (the more specific—what type/category of historical element or author storytelling element—the better!).

**C.** **Step 3: Analyze.** Just like a graphic novel, this reading strategy then asks you to think in terms of words and images. Above and below each arrow, you will find a rectangle.

- The rectangles above the arrow should be filled out with words that represent that element and category of the creative nonfiction graphic novel. **Try asking yourself: "Which words in this creative nonfiction graphic novel remind me of this element and category?"**

- The rectangle below the arrow should be filled out with illustrations that represent that element and category of the creative nonfiction graphic novel. **Try asking yourself: "Which images in this creative nonfiction graphic novel remind me of this element and category?"**

*6.* It is now time to offer students their first reading assignment. There are two ways you can assign reading with the Nonfiction Collaboration Journey.

*A.* You can assign students to read only a section or chapter and give them a single version of the Nonfiction Collaboration Journey (**Appendix K**); or

*B.* You can assign students a lengthy section and give them both **Appendix K** and **Appendix L**, a supplemental handout that lengthens the students' Nonfiction Collaboration Journeys (depending on the length of the reading, you might even need multiple copies of **Appendix L**).

One of the most engaging creative nonfiction graphic novels I have recently read, and recommend to you, is Nick Abadzis' (2007) *Laika*.

## Figure 4.8: Abadzis' *Laika* (First Second Books, 2007)

**Summary**

The dog, Laika, was the first living creature on earth to be sent into orbit. She was sent into orbit, however, with no plan for her return. More than fifty years later, Abadzis retells Laika's story by weaving together historical fact and creative storytelling, ultimately spinning a fascinating historical account of this dog, her journey, and the people who both cared for her and sent her into orbit. When asked about how he created a historically accurate, yet creative, graphic novel, Abadzis says, "I could've taken an entirely documentary approach, but I felt that dramatizing it and saying, okay, maybe this is how it *could* have happened gave me more scope to explore all the characters. Although I was pretty rigorous in all the reading and research I did, ultimately I'm a storyteller."

**Creator: Nick Abadzis (1965-present)**

Born in Sweden to Greek and English parents, Nick Abadzis grew up in both Switzerland and England. Known worldwide for his work with children's books, comics, and graphic novels, today he refers to himself as "a writer and artist who likes comics." In order to write and illustrate *Laika*, a story that had intrigued him since childhood, Abadzis spent years doing research on the Soviet space program, the Cosmodog program, and the people of the Soviet Union. He even traveled to Moscow.

**Interesting Information**

- Today, Abadzis lives in London with his wife and daughter.

- To learn more about Abadzis or Laika go to www.nickabadzis.com.

- The following is a list of awards for *Laika*:

  *1.* **2008 Awards:** Eisner Awards—Best Teen Graphic Novel; nominated for Best Reality-based Work; nominated for a National Cartoonists Society Division Award; nominated for a Harvey Award for Best Original Graphic Album

  *2.* **2007 Awards:** *Publisher's Weekly* Best Book of the Year; *Kirkus Review* Best Young Adult Book of the Year; YALSA Top Ten Graphic Novel; YALSA Great Graphic Novel; NYPL Book for the Teen Age; nominated for a Cybil Award for Best Young Adult Graphic Novel

**From Nick Abadzis**

"The graphic novel . . . . is an arena where storytelling is evolving, undergoing current, rapid change. I'm excited that the language of comics has colonized education, too, and I'm excited that my own graphic novel *Laika* was chosen by Katie Monnin to be a part of this book. Comics, as a medium, if it's in the right hands, is capable of incredibly subtle and nuanced storytelling and the graphic novel seems to me to be one of the best means by which to explore those areas of expression. It's therefore important to encourage new storytellers and interest in the medium, as it will become one of the primary places where our children articulate themselves and invent, express, and define new ideas."

–Nick Abadzis

# NONFICTION COLLABORATION JOURNEY

## ELEMENTS OF A CREATIVE NONFICTION GRAPHIC NOVEL

1. Historical Fact: early story of chief designer
2. Author Storytelling: Kudryavka as a puppy
3. Author Storytelling: Mikhail and Kudryavka
4. Author Storytelling: dog catchers get Kudryavka

**1.**

Chief designer

Historical person

**2.**

puppy

Author device

**3.**

Mikhail doesn't take good care of her

Author style

**4.**

Dog Catchers

Author device

# TEACHING THE CREATIVE NONFICTION GRAPHIC NOVEL IN MIDDLE SCHOOL ELA: A WRITING ACTIVITY

Because of the creative nonfiction graphic novel's emphasis on factual information and on creative storytelling, ELA teachers can bring the standards for informational writing and creative writing together for this writing assignment. When we bring these two standards together, we are able to ask students to not only identify the elements of a creative nonfiction graphic novel, but also creatively analyze those elements.

As mentioned earlier, when discussing the informational nonfiction graphic novel, the standard for middle school informational writing states that students will be able to demonstrate and develop technical writing related to real-world, information-based tasks.

**Figure 4.9: Middle school ELA standard for creative writing**

## MIDDLE SCHOOL CREATIVE WRITING
Students should be able to develop skills in creative writing.

If we combine the standard for informational writing with the standard for creative writing, we can draw a parallel between the format the graphic novelist used to create the graphic novel and the writing format the students will follow to write their own papers. In essence, we are asking students to think primarily about the two identifying elements that compose creative nonfiction graphic novels:

- The element of historical fact
- The element of author storytelling

Since students have already identified and organized these elements on their Nonfiction Collaboration Journey handout, this reading strategy can now serve as a springboard for their writing.

The directions read: "Choosing a character from the creative nonfiction graphic novel, retell the story through that character's perspective. In this retelling, you will need to base your ideas in historical truth and in creative storytelling; in other words, you will need to demonstrate an understanding of how to tell a story using both creative storytelling techniques and factual information. For this writing assignment, you will be working with both of the elements of a creative nonfiction graphic novel . This time, however, you will not be reading the text but instead writing the text."

These directions can also be found in **Appendix K**.

# TEACHING GRAPHIC NOVEL NONFICTION IN HIGH SCHOOL

Even though the standard for teaching nonfiction in high school ELA is often comparable to the standard for teaching nonfiction in middle school ELA, the teaching of nonfiction in high school is more complex. High school ELA students should be asked to engage in a more dynamic, multi-faceted consideration of the three aspects of nonfiction: identification, application/organization, and analysis. The Nonfiction Collaboration Stair-Step and the Nonfiction Collaboration Journey that follow will embrace these higher levels of reading engagement with nonfiction graphic novels.

# NONFICTION COLLABORATION STAIR-STEP: INFORMATIONAL NONFICTION GRAPHIC NOVELS

As we learned when discussing informational nonfiction graphic novels for middle school ELA, the Nonfiction Collaboration Stair-Step reading strategy helps students to: 1. Identify the elements of an informational nonfiction graphic novel; 2. Apply (or organize) the elements of an informational nonfiction graphic novel; and 3. Analyze the elements of an informational nonfiction graphic novel. For high school readers, however, each of these steps will be intensified.

For example, when identifying the elements of an informational nonfiction graphic novel, high school readers will need to consider a more in-depth list of possibilities. This in-depth list will include the elements given to middle school readers (format, discoveries, and style), but it will also add *style*, *tone*, and *validity* to the list. Figure 4.10 offers definitions for the elements of nonfiction found in high-school-level informational nonfiction graphic novels.

**Figure 4.10: Definitions of elements for high-school-level informational nonfiction graphic novels**

**FORMAT.** The organization of the writing. For example, are there chapter titles, subtitles, headings, subheadings, bold-faced words, lists, charts, figures, pictures, anecdotes, quotations, and so on? Panels and gutters (terms defined in Chapter 1) are key here, too, for they can really help readers identify how the creator has formatted the text.

**DISCOVERIES.** Interesting facts, curious information, significant details, and/or new knowledge gained from reading the informational nonfiction graphic novel.

**MAIN IDEA.** The key piece (or pieces) of information the creator is trying to convey.

**STYLE.** Word choice and writing techniques used in the text. In a work of nonfiction, the style should hold the reader's attention. It should read smoothly, going from one idea to the next idea with grace.

**TONE.** The creator's attitude toward the subject and audience. The tone of a work of nonfiction should be reader-friendly and invite you into the text.

**VALIDITY.** The soundness of a creator's claims. High school readers need to be ready to validate the information that they find in informational texts of any kid. Thus, testing for validity asks them to research the elements the creator sees as legitimate and, in doing so, either confirm or reject the validity of the creator's claims. This element will be further highlighted in the writing assignment that follows.

Since there are more elements of informational nonfiction graphic novels for high school readers to consider, the Nonfiction Collaboration Stair-Step for high school readers offers more opportunities to record this information. (See Figure 4.11 and **Appendix M**.)

**Figure 4.11: Nonfiction Collaboration Stair-Step for high school readers**

# NONFICTION COLLABORATION STAIR-STEP

NAME:

READING ASSIGNMENT:

HIGH SCHOOL ELA

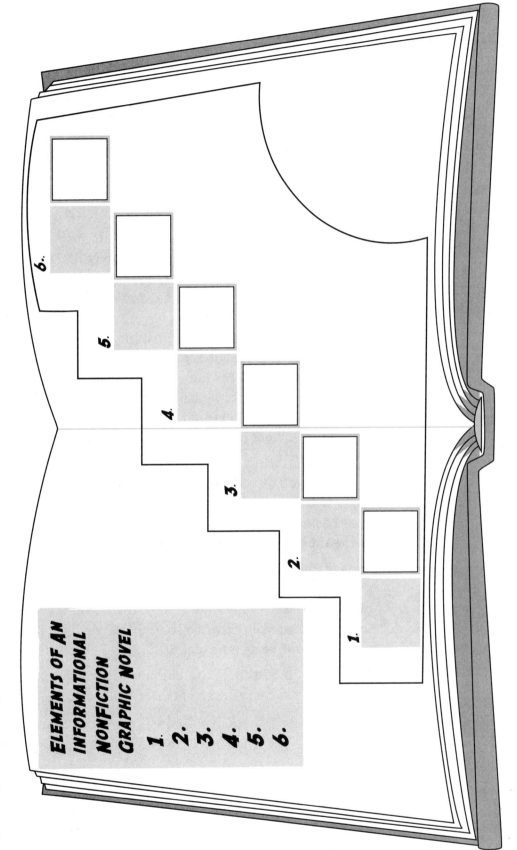

ELEMENTS OF AN INFORMATIONAL NONFICTION GRAPHIC NOVEL

1.
2.
3.
4.
5.
6.

# LESSON IDEA 4.C: TEACHING INFORMATIONAL NONFICTION GRAPHIC NOVELS IN HIGH SCHOOL ELA

**The Graphic Novel:** Informational nonfiction graphic novel; suggested informational graphic novel for high school readers: Jacobson & Colón's (2006) *The 9/11 Report*
**The Standard:** High school nonfiction
**The Reading Strategy:** Nonfiction Collaboration Stair-Step

**Steps for Teaching High School Informational Nonfiction Graphic Novels**

1. Because high school readers need to consider a more in-depth listing of the elements contained within informational nonfiction graphic novels, I suggest you start your lesson planning with an introduction to these elements. You can begin by handing out the Nonfiction Collaboration Stair-Step (**Appendix M**) and asking students to work in small groups to fill out the back of the handout. Here students will find the elements of an informational nonfiction graphic novel. Instruct students that they are to activate their own schema while also consulting a variety of resources made available to them around the classroom (dictionaries, online computers, ELA textbooks, and yourself) to define the elements found in an informational nonfiction graphic novel. If you prefer, you could ask students to work at stations (you being one of the stations) for certain time periods, or you could ask them to work in small groups, sending representatives to retrieve (or interview, if they want to consult you) various resources when they need them.

2. After this activity, you can take time to further explore the appropriate definitions for the elements of an informational nonfiction graphic novel by writing each term—one by one—on the board or on chart paper. Once the class has discussed their findings, you can write the definitions from this book alongside those of the class.

   A. **Format.** The organization of the writing. For example, are there chapter titles, subtitles, headings, subheadings, bold-faced words, lists, charts, figures, pictures, anecdotes, quotations, and so on? Panels and gutters (terms defined in Chapter 1) are key here, too, for they can really help readers identify how the creator has formatted the text.

   B. **Discoveries.** Interesting facts, curious information, significant details, and/or new knowledge gained from reading the informational nonfiction graphic novel.

   C. **Main Idea.** The key piece (or pieces) of information the creator is trying to convey.

   D. **Style.** Word choice and writing techniques used in the text. In a work of nonfiction, the style should hold the reader's attention. It should read smoothly, going from one idea to the next idea with grace.

   E. **Tone.** The creator's attitude toward the subject and audience. The tone of a work of nonfiction should be reader-friendly and invite you into the text.

**F. Validity.** The soundness of a creator's claims. High school readers need to be ready to validate the information that they find in informational texts of any kid. Thus, testing for validity asks them to research the elements the creator sees as legitimate and, in doing so, either confirm or reject the validity of the creator's claims. This element will be further highlighted in the writing assignment that follows.

Note: Having taught in both middle and high school ELA classrooms, I am a strong proponent of asking students to put definitions of key terms into their own words. In my experience, students are more likely to be engaged and remember the terms and their definitions if time is spent honoring their thoughts and ideas.

**3.** Now that the class understands the definitions of the elements found within an informational nonfiction graphic novel, it is time to look at the front of **Appendix M**. Here students will find a visual depiction of stairs, with lines above each stair and an identification box. The directions are as follows:

You will complete three steps in order to fill out the Nonfiction Collaboration Stair-Step:

**1.** You will identify and pull out the elements of nonfiction from the informational nonfiction graphic novel and write each of these elements in the identification box labeled "elements."

**2.** Next, you will need to place the elements on the stairs, appropriately, in order of their appearance. Lines are provided above each stair.

Note: Since there are multiple steps to these directions, I suggest that ELA teachers also write these steps on the board.

**3.** Finally, just like a graphic novel, this reading strategy asks you to next think in terms of words and images. Each stair is divided into two. On each stair, you are to put both the words and the images that help explain that element of nonfiction. On the left, you will write the words. On the right, you will draw the images.

Note: Teachers, it is now time to think about the reading assignment. Once again, this reading assignment can take different structures. It could be a short reading assignment, where ELA teachers only need to distribute one copy of the Nonfiction Collaboration Stair-Step for high school readers. Or, it could be a longer reading assignment, and teachers could offer students copies of the Nonfiction Collaboration Stair-Step and its supplemental handout (**Appendix J**).

An excellent informational nonfiction graphic novel for high school readers is *The 9/11 Report: A Graphic Adaptation* by Sid Jacobson and Ernie Colón. This graphic novel offers readers a 130-page nonfiction adaptation of the 9/11 Commission's 600-page report. The chair and the vice-chair of the 9/11 Commission were so impressed with the authenticity of this informational nonfiction graphic novel that they even wrote supportive forewords as introductions to the book.

## Figure 4.12: Sid Jacobson and Ernie Colón's *The 9/11 Report: A Graphic Adaptation* (Hill and Wang, 2006)

### Summary

*The 9/11 Report: A Graphic Adaptation* has gone to extraordinary lengths—both visually and verbally—to respect the 9/11 Commission's print-text report. In fact, the creators of this informational nonfiction graphic novel have stated that it was imperative to them to leave their own political opinions out of the graphic adaptation. Colón claimed that all quotations from prominent individuals in the retelling were exact, literal quotations. On the back cover, famed comic creator Stan Lee speaks directly to the authenticity of this work of nonfiction: "Never before have I seen a nonfiction book as beautifully and compellingly written and illustrated . . . . I cannot recommend it too highly . . . . [it] should be required reading in every home, school, and library."

### Authors: Sid Jacobson (1929-present) and Ernie Colón (1931-present)

Sid Jacobson and Ernie Colón met at Harvey Comics in the 1950s. With Jacobson as editor and Colón as illustrator, they worked together on projects such as *Casper the Friendly Ghost* and *Richie Rich*. In 2004, when the *9/11 Commission Report* was published, Colón felt that the text could be made accessible to the average reader, so he called his good friend Jacobson. Over the next year, Colón and Jacobson adapted the print-text report into a graphic novel. Along with gaining kudos from the commission members themselves, *The 9/11 Report: A Graphic Adaptation* also earned Jacobson and Colón a spot on *The New York Times* Best-Seller List.

### Interesting Information

- When speaking about the audience for this graphic novel, Jacobson says, "I don't think we kept in mind children per se. We wanted to do it for all people, for young and old."
- Since Jacobson lives in Los Angeles and Colón lives in New York City, both creators state that the graphic novel was created using the Internet to accommodate for the distance.
- Colón's favorite comic character is Richie Rich.
- In 2008, Jacobson and Colón published *After 9/11: America's War on Terror*.
- Due to their level of research and an adherence to a strict translation of the *9/11 Commission Report*, Jacobson and Colón sometimes call this informational nonfiction graphic novel "graphic journalism."

### From Ernie Colón:

In an interview about *9/11: The Graphic Adaptation*, Colón explains how important it was to be as authentic as possible when interpreting the *9/11 Commission Report*: "We wanted to remain faithful to what the report had to say and not inject any aspects of our own opinions into it. It had to be a completely faithful adaptation of the report."

(Source: Newsrama.com, August, 25, 2006, interviewed by Daniel Robert Epstein)

# NONFICTION COLLABORATION STAIR-STEP

**NAME:** _____

**READING ASSIGNMENT:**
**HIGH SCHOOL ELA**

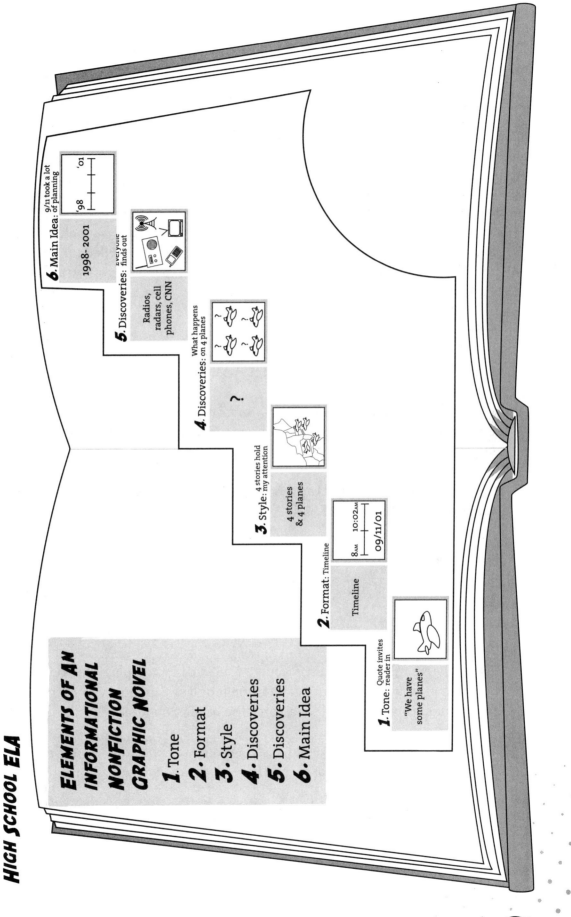

**ELEMENTS OF AN INFORMATIONAL NONFICTION GRAPHIC NOVEL**

1. Tone
2. Format
3. Style
4. Discoveries
5. Discoveries
6. Main Idea

1. Tone: Quote invites reader in — "We have some planes"

2. Format: Timeline — Timeline — 8 AM 10:02 AM — 09/11/01

3. Style: 4 stories hold my attention — 4 stories & 4 planes

4. Discoveries: What happens on 4 planes — ~.

5. Discoveries: everyone finds out — Radios, radars, cell phones, CNN

6. Main Idea: 9/11 took a lot of planning — 1998-2001 — '98  '01

Whenever I have taught *The 9/11 Report: A Graphic Adaptation*, I have had tremendously rewarding teaching experiences. Grant it, I would like to think that I have always taught nonfiction well, no matter what the text or the topic. And I might have taught well, but I have never taught any other nonfiction text that has generated more classroom energy than *The 9/11 Report*. For that reason, I would like to cater this particular writing assignment to this informational nonfiction graphic novel; please remember, however, that *Teaching Graphic Novels* encourages ELA teachers to revise these writing assignments to suit their own needs, those of their students, and those of their selected graphic novel.

For two reasons, students seem to be highly engaged readers of this particular informational nonfiction graphic novel. First, most students have concrete, almost tangible, memories of 9/11. Second, based on their experiences, students often feel like this graphic novel invites them into an historical take on the behind-the-scenes events that paralleled their own lives. Students can, in other words, draw parallels between their own experiences on 9/11 and those chronicled in *The 9/11 Report: A Graphic Adaptation*. The reader, in essence, becomes a virtual participant in the text.

In terms of a writing assignment, ELA teachers can build a bridge between students' memories of 9/11 and those chronicled within *The 9/11 Report: A Graphic Adaptation* by focusing on the standard for teaching informational or expository writing in high school ELA.

Typically, the standards for teaching informational or expository writing both stress that students develop and demonstrate writing that provides information related to real-world events or tasks. (See Figure 4.13.)

**Figure 4.13: Typical wording found in informational and expository writing standards in high school ELA**

## INFORMATIONAL OR EXPOSITORY WRITING

Students should be able to develop and demonstrate writing about real-world tasks or events.

ELA teachers can also bring the standard for research into play. Thinking and writing beyond their own memories and experiences, and those found within the informational nonfiction graphic novel, students can be asked to research the nonfiction topic as well.

In order to write a research-based, informational or expository essay, students should think about three areas of writing development. These areas are highlighted in Figure 4.14 and can be found for your use in **Appendix M**.

**Figure 4.14: Directions and organization for high school ELA writers of a research-based, informational or expository essay on an informational nonfiction graphic novel**

### Directions

For this writing assignment, you will write a research-based, informational or expository essay. Your topic will be the same topic found in our informational nonfiction graphic novel (topic: _____). When you write your essay, you will need to consider three sources of information. They are:

*1.* The topic of the informational nonfiction graphic novel

*2.* Your own experiences/feelings about this topic

*3.* Research you find on this topic

With these three topics in mind, your essay will then be organized as follows:

*A)* Introduction to topic: Develop an engaging highlight of everything your essay will discuss

*B)* Information about the informational nonfiction graphic novel

*C)* Information about your own experiences/feelings on this topic

*D)* Information you have researched on this topic

*E)* Conclusion: Find a way to bring all three areas of information together and close your thoughts for the reader, who has now learned about the graphic novel, you, and the research you found.*

*Note: Your essay does NOT have to follow this format. This is only an example.

ELA teachers are encouraged to see this example as one among a possible many. I encourage you to share your new and engaging alternative thoughts about reading or writing with graphic novels on the Teaching Graphic Novels blog, http://teachinggraphicnovels.blogspot.com/, so that we may all contribute and grow together in teaching the graphic novel in ELA.

## NONFICTION COLLABORATION JOURNEY: CREATIVE NONFICTION GRAPHIC NOVELS IN HIGH SCHOOL

Just like in middle school ELA, creative nonfiction graphic novels for high school readers also perform two main tasks. First, creative nonfiction graphic novels are based on factually accurate events, people, places, and/or times, and, second, they allow the author to use creative license to enhance the story.

Through this combination of historical fact and creative storytelling, the reader of a creative nonfiction graphic novel embarks on a journey of understanding. Hence, the reading strategy that best suits this type of graphic novel is once again the Nonfiction Collaboration Journey. (See Figure 4.15 and **Appendix N**.)

Figure 4.15: The Nonfiction Collaboration Journey reading strategy for high school

# NONFICTION COLLABORATION JOURNEY

NAME: _____
READING ASSIGNMENT: _____
HIGH SCHOOL ELA

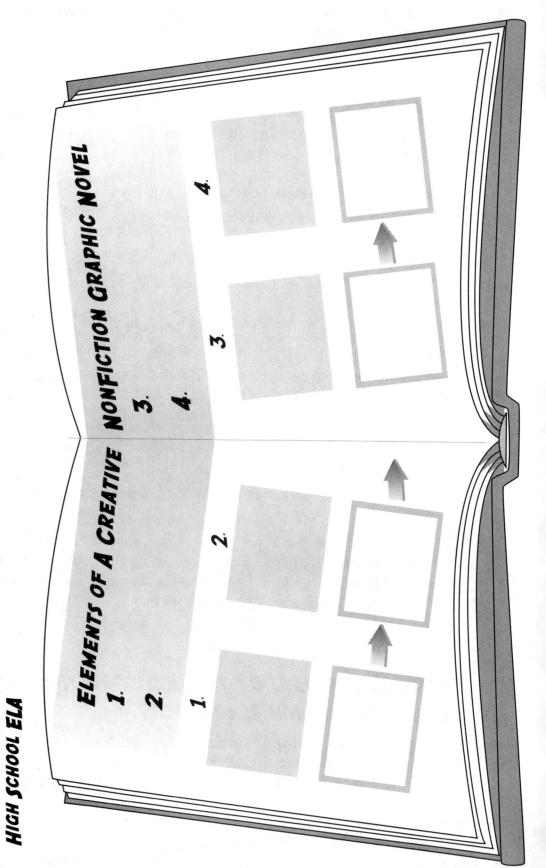

ELEMENTS OF A CREATIVE NONFICTION GRAPHIC NOVEL

1.
2.
3.
4.

1.

2.

3.

4.

Ultimately, students will fill out the Nonfiction Collaboration Journey reading strategy as follows:

- First, students need to identify the elements of the creative nonfiction graphic novel and list them in the elements box.

- Second, on each arrow-line, students need to organize the elements by writing them in the order that they appear in the creative nonfiction graphic novel.

- The rectangles above the arrows should be filled out with words that represent the identified element of a creative nonfiction graphic novel.

- The rectangles below the arrows should be filled out with images that the reader feels depict that element of a creative nonfiction graphic novel.

Once students understand the directions for filling out the Nonfiction Collaboration Journey (which are found in **Appendix N**), it is time to remind them of the lessons from Chapter 1 of *Teaching Graphic Novels*. As stated earlier, it is strongly suggested that, before teaching any specific type of graphic novel, students be introduced to the vocabulary and terminology for reading with image literacies and print-text literacies found in graphic novels.

Reading strategy 4.D will further explain how teachers can use the Nonfiction Collaboration Journey to help high school students read a creative nonfiction graphic novel.

## LESSON IDEA 4.D: TEACHING CREATIVE NONFICTION GRAPHIC NOVELS IN HIGH SCHOOL ELA

**The Graphic Novel:** Creative nonfiction graphic novel; suggested graphic novel: Emmanuel Guibert's (2008) *Alan's War: The Memories of G.I. Alan Cope*
**The Standard:** High school nonfiction
**The Reading Strategy:** Nonfiction Collaboration Journey

**Steps for Teaching High School Creative Nonfiction Graphic Novels**

*1.* In order to build schema experiences that will help students understand the elements of a creative nonfiction graphic novel, I recommend beginning with a film adaptation (a clip) of a nonfiction event, person, place and/or time. Just like a creative nonfiction graphic novel, film provides its creator's take—the director, in this case—on real events, people, places and/or times. It is a combination, in short, of factual information and creative storytelling.

*2.* Instead of a KWL chart, as was suggested for middle school readers of creative nonfiction graphic novels, high school readers are asked to take general notes on the film clip. After taking notes, break students into small groups of three or four. In these small groups, ask students to share their notes on one piece of paper and place their information into one of two categories: fact or creative storytelling. While students are working together, you can write these categories in column format on the board.

| FACT | CREATIVE STORYTELLING |
|---|---|
| | |

**3.** Before collecting these group lists of notes, work through the same process as an entire class. As you do so, please ask students to explain, in detail, why they placed something in the fact column or in the creative storytelling column.

**4.** Next, pass out the Nonfiction Collaboration Journey handout (**Appendix N**). This is also a good time to pass out the creative nonfiction graphic novel of your choice. Referencing the examples students just gave, review the directions on the back of the Nonfiction Collaboration Journey. They read as follows:

**A.** **Step 1: Identification.** For this reading strategy, you will first need to identify the elements of a creative nonfiction graphic novel. You will find a box for listing these elements on the front of your handout. There are two main elements found in a creative nonfiction graphic novel:

- **The Element of Historical Fact:** Historical fact is the information in the graphic novel that is accurate and factual. The elements of historical fact fall into the following categories:

    **1)** Factual event: historically accurate and known event

    **2)** Factual people: historically real person/people

    **3)** Factual time: historically accurate time period or moment in time

    **4)** Factual place: historically accurate place or location

    **5)** Factual artifact: historically accurate, existent document or artifact

- **The Element of Author Storytelling:** The author's storytelling is the creative technique(s) the author uses to help shape the story he or she wishes to tell about the nonfiction event, people, place, and/or time. The elements of author storytelling fall into the following categories:

    **1)** Creator's voice: The author's own voice/tone used to influence the story

    **2)** Creator's style: How the words or images influence the story being told

    **3)** Creator's device: A situation, person, place, event, or artifact the author creates for his or her own storytelling purposes.

**B.** **Step 2: Application/Organization.** After identifying the elements of a creative nonfiction graphic novel and listing them on the front of the handout (in the elements box), you can now start to organize those elements. On each arrow, and in order of their appearance, write the name of the identified elements (the more specific the category—historical fact element or author element—the better!).

**C.** **Step 3: Analyze.** Just like a graphic novel, this reading strategy then asks you to think in terms of words and images. Above and below each arrow you will find a rectangle:

- The rectangles above the arrow should be filled out with words that represent that element and category of the creative nonfiction graphic novel.

- The rectangles below the arrow should be filled out with your own drawings/ images that you feel best represent that element and category.

- In order to help fill out each of the rectangles, try asking yourself: "What are the words in this creative nonfiction graphic novel that remind me of this element and category, and, further, what are the images that remind me of this element and category?"

**D.** **Step 4: Reflection.** After you have identified, organized, and analyzed the elements and categories of a creative nonfiction graphic novel, you will next need to reflect on your reasons for choosing each element and category. In short, you will need to write explanations for your choices in paragraph form.

- Try asking yourself: "Given the definitions for each element and category, what made me select this element and category? Why did I choose these words or these images to represent this element and category?"

- Please write these paragraph reflections on your own paper and staple your paper to your Nonfiction Collaboration Journey handout when you turn it in.

**5.** Depending on the length of the reading assignment you have in mind for the creative nonfiction graphic novel, students can fill out **Appendix N** (if reading a short section). Or, if they are reading the entire graphic novel or a longer section, you can offer them as many copies of the supplemental handout for the Nonfiction Collaboration Journey (**Appendix L**) that they may need.

Before discussing the writing activity, however, let's take a closer look at one of my favorite creative nonfiction graphic novels, *Alan's War* by Emmanuel Guibert.

**Figure 4.16: Emmanuel Guibert's *Alan's War: The Memories of G.I. Alan Cope* (First Second, 2008)**

### Summary

It was merely by chance in 1994, while asking for directions, that Emmanuel Guibert met Alan Cope on a small island off the Atlantic coast of France. Through this chance encounter, however, a significant friendship blossomed, and Guibert found himself listening to Cope's stories about World War II. Together, they both agreed that Cope's stories might interest others, especially readers who had learned about World War II only through history textbooks and who might not have had the chance to learn about World War II through one American G.I.'s perspective. Thus, while Cope told Guibert about his experiences in World War II, a cassette player recorded his narrative. *Alan's War*, then, is the result of a creative collaboration between Cope's memories and Guibert's drawings.

### Creator: Emmanuel Guibert (1964-present)

Emmanuel Guibert was born in Paris, France. His first comic, *Brune*, appeared in 1992. It tells the story of the rise of fascism in Germany during the 1930s. Two years after this publication, Guibert met Alan Cope, whose life not only touched Guibert personally, but also lead to the publication of one of his most significant graphic novels, *Alan's War*. Published by First Second Books and showered with awards, Guibert's graphic novel once again uses nonfiction as a stepping-stone for creating a moving story. In *The Photographer*, Guibert focuses on the mission of Doctors Without Borders in 1980s Afghanistan.

### Interesting Information
- Guibert has collaborated on other successful graphic novel projects with the famed graphic novelist Joann Sfar.
- Today, he lives in Paris with his wife and daughter.
- One of Guibert's artistic techniques for illustrating *Alan's War* was to draw with water.
- Guibert plans on following *Alan's War* with another graphic novel entitled *Alan's Youth*.

### From Emmanuel Guibert

When asked about why his graphic novels often have a nonfiction emphasis, Guibert frequently cites that he owns a "top secret" time machine.

## TEACHING THE CREATIVE NONFICTION GRAPHIC NOVEL IN HIGH SCHOOL ELA: A WRITING ACTIVITY

Since high school readers of a creative nonfiction graphic novel are asked to not only identify, apply, and analyze the elements of a creative nonfiction graphic novel, but also reflect on those elements in writing, they have already performed a pre-writing activity; as a result, their reflections meet the standard not only for reading nonfiction in high school ELA, but also for pre-writing in high school ELA.

With the standard for pre-writing already performed, ELA teachers can next bring the standard for persuasive writing to the table. Figure 4.18 highlights these two writing standards.

**Figure 4.17: Nonfiction Collaboration Journey reading strategy for high school**

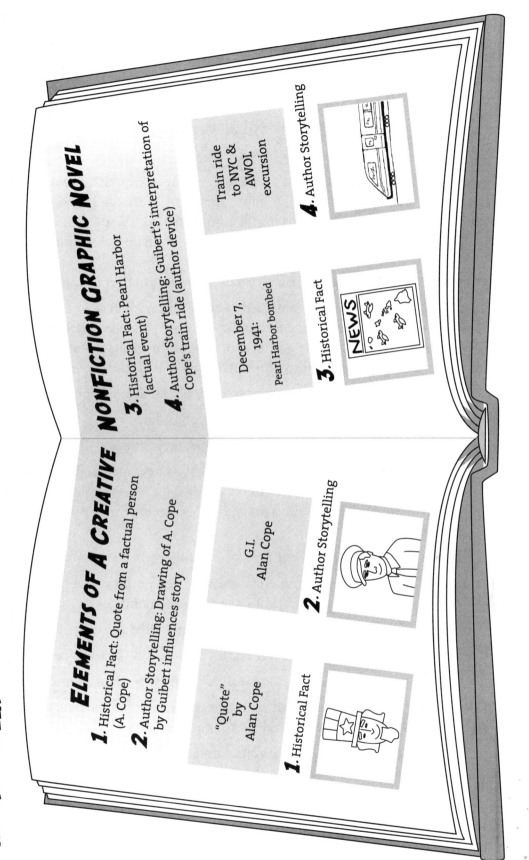

# NONFICTION COLLABORATION JOURNEY

NAME: _____

READING ASSIGNMENT: _____

HIGH SCHOOL ELA

## ELEMENTS OF A CREATIVE NONFICTION GRAPHIC NOVEL

*1.* Historical Fact: Quote from a factual person (A. Cope)

*2.* Author Storytelling: Drawing of A. Cope by Guibert influences story

*3.* Historical Fact: Pearl Harbor (actual event)

*4.* Author Storytelling: Guibert's interpretation of Cope's train ride (author device)

"Quote" by Alan Cope

*1.* Historical Fact

G.I. Alan Cope

*2.* Author Storytelling

December 7, 1941: Pearl Harbor bombed

NEWS

*3.* Historical Fact

Train ride to NYC & AWOL excursion

*4.* Author Storytelling

**Figure 4.18: High school pre-writing and persuasive writing standards**

# PRE-WRITING AND PERSUASIVE WRITING

**Pre-writing:** Students will be able to develop a plan for writing.

**Persuasive:** Students will be able to use their writing skills to influence the reader.

When we ask students to persuade a reader, we are asking them to use their writing to influence the reader's opinion. The reader, in short, should be persuaded to see the writer's point of view. With this in mind, the directions for the high school ELA writing activity with creative nonfiction graphic novels reads as follows (and can also be found on the second page of **Appendix N**):

**Pre-writing and Persuasive Writing for Creative Nonfiction Graphic Novels in High School**

1. **Step 1: Research.** First, you need to engage in some research on our nonfiction topic. After you research the topic and consult your own reflection paragraphs, decide whether or not you agree with the author's interpretation of the events, places, people, and/or times. Decide whether you think the author did one of three things:

   **A)** Used his or her storytelling to stray too far away from the truth

   **B)** Used an appropriate balance of fact and storytelling

   **C)** Used too much fact and not enough storytelling

2. **Step 2: Persuasive Writing.** Once you have performed your research and know how you personally feel about the author's use of the elements of a creative nonfiction graphic novel, your job is to write a persuasive essay that influences the reader to agree with your opinion.

3. **Step 3: Organization.** Here are some thoughts on how to possibly organize your essay:

   **A)** Introduction: name of creative nonfiction graphic novel, summary of its contents, and your stance on the author's use of the elements

   **B)** Body paragraph 1: first reason for your stance and examples

   **C)** Body paragraph 2: second reason for your stance and examples

   **D)** Body paragraph 3: third reason for your stance and examples

   **E)** Body paragraph 4: continue with list of reasons—however many you think are necessary (you may have five or six body paragraphs)

   **F)** Conclusion: summarize your points and find an engaging way to reflect on your entire essay (perhaps with a quotation, a new thought, a question, etc.)

Before we move to teaching graphic novels alongside media literacy skills and standards in Chapter 5, I would like to point out **Appendix O**, which provides a further list of references for teachers who wish to explore both the informational and creative nonfiction graphic novels currently available in their grade levels.

# CHAPTER 4 HIGHLIGHTS

Chapter 4 focused on teaching two types of graphic novel nonfiction in middle and high school ELA classrooms.

- There are two types of graphic novel nonfiction: informational nonfiction graphic novels and creative nonfiction graphic novels.

- The best reading strategy for informational nonfiction graphic novels is the Nonfiction Collaboration Stair-Step.

- In middle school ELA, the writing activity for informational nonfiction graphic novels centers on the informational writing standard.

- In high school ELA, the writing activity for informational nonfiction graphic novels centers on the expository or informational writing standards.

- The best reading strategy for creative nonfiction graphic novels is the Nonfiction Collaboration Journey.

- In middle school ELA, the writing activity for creative nonfiction graphic novels brings together the ELA standards for informational and creative writing.

- In high school ELA, the writing activity for creative nonfiction graphic novels centers on the pre-writing and persuasive writing standards.

- **Appendix O** offers a listing of both informational and creative nonfiction graphic novels.

# CHAPTER 5

## TEACHING MEDIA LITERACY WITH GRAPHIC NOVELS

"THE USE OF DIGITAL MEDIA AND POPULAR CULTURE TEXTS NOT ONLY STIMULATES
YOUNG PEOPLE'S ENGAGEMENT, MOTIVATION, AND INTEREST IN LEARNING, BUT ENABLES
THEM TO BUILD A RICHER, MORE NUANCED UNDERSTANDING OF HOW TEXTS OF ALL
KINDS WORK WITHIN A CULTURE."

*- Renee Hobbs, Reading the Media: Media Literacy in High School English -*

Since the early 1930s, media literacy has been emerging into the ELA curriculum (Buckingham, 2003; Leavis & Thompson, 1933). As a result, the English language *arts* no longer isolate print-text literacies as the dominant (or only!) literacy worth teaching, as the mere publication of a book like *Teaching Graphic Novels* illustrates. To teach the reality of literacy today, ELA teachers must adopt pedagogies of multi-literacies (The New London Group, 1996). Thus, in this chapter, we will continue our conversation about graphic novels by turning our attention to the natural, pedagogical connection between media literacy and graphic novels. To organize this discussion, the chapter will be divided into three sections:

1) Media Literacy and Graphic Novels
2) Teaching Media Literacy with Graphic Novels in Middle School ELA
3) Teaching Media Literacy with Graphic Novels in High School ELA

## MEDIA LITERACY AND GRAPHIC NOVELS

To date, most states have either adopted media literacy standards or strands into their ELA curriculum or, if not fully adopted, show evidence of media literacy. And although these latter states may not call them "media literacy standards or strands," there is ample evidence to suggest that these states are in fact teaching for media literacy. For a breakdown of how each state addresses media literacy, whether in title or in principle, please go to the following website, created and maintained by well-known media literacy scholar Frank Baker: http://www.frankwbaker.com/state_lit.htm.

Figure 5.1 presents the guiding source for most media literacy curricula, NCTE's position statement on teaching media literacy in ELA.

## Figure 5.1: NCTE's position on teaching media literacy in ELA

Media literacy education distinctively features the analytical attitude that teachers and learners, working together, adopt toward the media objects they study. The foundation of effective media analysis is the recognition that:

1. All media messages are constructed.
2. Each medium has different characteristics and strengths and a unique language of construction.
3. Media messages are produced for particular purposes.
4. All media messages contain embedded values and points of view.
5. People use their individual skills, beliefs, and experiences to construct their own meanings from media messages.
6. Media and media messages can influence beliefs, attitudes, values, behaviors, and the democratic process. (Source: www.ncte.org)

These six position statements can be broken into three steps for teaching media literacy in ELA. They are:

- **Media Construction:** focused on statements 1 and 2
- **Media Intention:** focused on statements 3 and 4
- **Media Analysis:** focused on statements 5 and 6

Before we discuss the specifics of teaching media literacy with graphic novels, let's take a brief, more intimate look at these three specific steps.

**Step 1: Media Construction.** All media—whether of image, sound, print, or screen—are constructed. And, for each media message, there are constructive characteristics. Chapter 1 of *Teaching Graphic Novels*, for instance, specifically details the construction of graphic novels in terms of panels, gutters, balloons, and critical-reading partnerships.

**Step 2: Media Intention.** Whenever a specific medium is created, it serves a purpose. The creator has an intended outcome or end goal. Creators, in other words, seek to convey a message. In conveying their message, creators use their knowledge of construction to influence the audience's perception(s).

When explaining intention, it is often helpful to ask students to think about Super Bowl commercials: "What are some of your favorite Super Bowl commercials?" "Why?" Since most

Super Bowl commercials are memorable because they generate laughter, students are able to piece together the elements, or the construction of the commercial, in order to understand intention.

When students are able to identify how construction reveals intention, they are next ready to conduct media literacy analysis.

**Step 3: Media Analysis.** The first time I truly understood the importance of being able to analyze media, I was reading Stephen Johnson's (2005) *Everything Bad Is Good for You*:

> Imagine an alternate world to ours save one techno-historical change: video games were invented and popularized *before* books. In this parallel universe, kids have been playing games for centuries—and then these page-bound texts come along and suddenly they're all the rage. What would the teachers, the parents, and the cultural authorities have to say about this frenzy of reading? (p. 19)

For decades, advocates of media literacy have had to respond to those voices who believe that the media cannot be read. Opposed to print-text literacies found in books, the argument often goes, readers of media are passively receiving media messages. People, as if empty receptacles, simply have media and media messages poured into their brains without even thinking about it—let alone reading it.

When we teach media literacy in ELA, we can see just how inaccurate this argument is.

As Johnson points out, we consider print-text literacies to be valuable, thought-provoking literacies simply because they are traditional literacies. If print-text literacies had come along after the video game, we may have heard authority figures saying things like, "Stop starring at that book, just looking at it! Play your videogame!"

To better understand media analysis, let's look at Hobbs' (2007) five questions for media analysis (Figure 5.2).[1]

## Figure 5.2: Hobbs' five questions for teaching media analysis

*1)* Who is sending the message and what is the author's purpose?
*2)* What techniques are used to attract and hold attention?
*3)* What lifestyles, values, and points of view are represented in this message?
*4)* How might different people interpret this message differently?
*5)* What is omitted from this message?

---

1   ALTHOUGH HOBBS' QUESTIONS CAN BE USED TO ANALYZE VARIOUS MEDIA, HER TEXT, READING THE MEDIA, FOCUSES ON SCREEN MEDIA.

When students ask the five media analysis questions, they are able to merge their understanding of construction and intention together to consider their own personal response to media or a media message.

With the three steps of media literacy in mind, we can now turn our attention to the connection between teaching graphic novels and teaching media literacy.

To begin, let me respond to the very first question I am asked when talking about teaching media literacy with graphic novels: "Why is the graphic novel considered media?"

Noted media literacy scholar, David Buckingham (2003), explains: "Media texts often combine several 'languages' or forms of communication—visual images (still or moving), audio (sound, music, or speech), and written language" (p. 4). Graphic novels combine print-text literacies with still image literacies. The use of these two types of literacies qualifies graphic novels as media texts. And although the graphic novel is not a fluid media, consistently moving across a screen environment like television or film, the graphic novel is an example of a static, still media. Françoise Mouly (Art Editor for *The New Yorker* and Editorial Director of Toon Books) recently explained the significance of still media to me by saying that "Kids can be the drivers." Since graphic novels are still, or static, kids can determine how fast or slow they will read. They can determine how many times they will read and even the different routes they will take to travel through the story over and over again.

The second question I am often asked is, "Since graphic novels are considered media texts, how can we better prepare students to read them?"

To answer this question, *Teaching Graphic Novels* will link the three steps of teaching media literacy to graphic novel terminology (see Figures 5.3-5.7). Figure 5.3 begins with a snapshot of the major terminology in both areas and uses a box symbol (✔) to indicate thematic, overlapping relationships. Figures 5.3-5.7 then further explain how to best teach these major, overlapping, and thematic relationships.

**Figure 5.3: Thematic, overlapping relationships between media literacy and graphic novels**

| MEDIA LITERACY TERMS | GRAPHIC NOVEL TERMS | | | |
|---|---|---|---|---|
| | Panels | Gutters | Word Balloons | Critical-reading Partnerships |
| Construction | ✔ | ✔ | ✔ | |
| Intention | ✔ | ✔ | ✔ | |
| Analysis | | | | ✔ |

As Figure 5.3 indicates, elements of media literacy (construction, intention, and analysis) can be found in graphic novels.

**Step 1: Media Literacy Construction and the Graphic Novel**

Graphic novels are primarily constructed with panels, gutters, and balloons[2] (see Figure 5.4).

**Figure 5.4: Step 1: Teaching media literacy construction and graphic novel terminology**

| STEP 1: MEDIA LITERACY CONSTRUCTION AND GRAPHIC NOVEL TERMINOLOGY | EXPLANATIONS |
|---|---|
| Panels | A graphic novel panel is the visual or implied boundary, and the contents within it, that tell a piece of the story. |
| Gutters | Graphic novel gutters are the space between a visual or implied panel. When moving through this space, from one panel to the next panel, readers come to some sort of understanding about the story being told. |
| Balloons | Typically found inside of a panel, graphic novel balloons commonly create visual boundaries. |

---

2    For a more technical discussion of graphic novel construction, please consult some of the following texts: Eisner's *Graphic Storytelling and Visual Narrative* (1996) and *Comics and Sequential Art* (1985); Scott McCloud's *Understanding Comics* (1993), *Reinventing Comics* (2000), and *Making Comics* (2006); and Jessica Abel and Matt Madden's *Drawing Words and Writing Pictures* (2008).

In the reading strategies for middle and high school ELA that follow, I suggest that teachers supplement Step 1 of teaching media literacy with graphic novels with Figures 1.4-1.5 and 1.8 (found in Chapter 1). These supplements offer students a chance to learn not only the major terms in regards to graphic novel construction, as noted above, but also the different types of panels, gutters, and balloons.

### Step 2: Media Literacy Intention and the Graphic Novel

The intention of one of my favorite graphic novels of all time, *Laika* by Nick Abadzis, is two-fold: first, to educate readers about the first living being in space and, second, to imagine the life and training that prepared Laika for her mission. How do I know this? When I read *Laika*, I am able to synthesize what I know about graphic novel construction to reveal intention(s).

Remember our conversation about Super Bowl commercials? When the commercial makes the reader laugh, he or she has followed the construction of the commercial and, indeed, understood the creator's intention: to evoke laughter.[3]

The same principle holds true for graphic novel construction and intention. When students understand graphic novel construction, they can better understand intention. For example, to encourage the reader to think about the story from one moment to the next moment, a graphic novel might specifically use a gutter construction, like the moment-to-moment gutter we saw in Abadzis' *Laika* (see Figure 5.5).

---

3   For more detail on reading other media, such as commercials, television, or film, please consult William Kist's (2004) *New Literacies in Action* or Renee Hobbs' (2007) *Reading the Media.*

**Figure 5.5: Abadzis' *Laika* demonstrates how the construction of graphic novel gutters—in this case, a moment-to-moment gutter—can reveal intention**

**Moment-to-moment:** From one panel to the next panel, readers witness little closure and instead simply see something from one instance to the next.

**Example: page 11 (top panels) of *Laika* by Nick Abadzis**

Figure 5.6 further explains how an awareness of graphic novel construction can reveal intention (and is intended to be copied for use with your students).

**Figure 5.6: Step 2: Teaching media literacy intention and graphic novel terminology**

| STEP 2: MEDIA LITERACY INTENTION AND GRAPHIC NOVEL TERMINOLOGY | EXPLANATIONS |
|---|---|
| Panels | Panels are the visual or implied boundaries, and the contents within them, that tell a piece of the story. The way the creator uses or displays these panels, then, reveals his or her intentions for communicating that story. In Chapter 1, we learned about the two different types of panels creators use: content panels and story panels.<br><br>Each of these panels reveals intention. If a creator uses a setting story panel, for instance, she is emphasizing where the story takes place. This is the intention of that specific panel. |
| Gutters | In Chapter 1, we also learned about graphic novel gutters and their relationship to the graphic novel panel. Gutters are the spaces between panels. Here, in the limbo of the gutter, the reader's imagination takes over and links panels together.<br><br>Six different types of gutters were discussed in Chapter 1: moment-to-moment, action-to-action, subject-to-subject, scene-to-scene, aspect-to-aspect, and non-sequitur. The type of gutter the creator chooses reveals her intention for that piece of the story.<br><br>For example, in Chapter 1, we saw Hope Larson's *Chiggers* use a series of moment-to-moment gutters in order to convey the passage of a brief amount of time. |
| Balloons | Balloons are also critical to graphic novel reading. Balloons not only allow creators to contextualize their story, but also to set tone. Five different balloons were discussed in Chapter 1: story balloon, thought balloon, dialogue balloon, sound effect balloon, and balloon-less words.<br><br>If a graphic novel creator decides to use a dialogue balloon, the intention is to give voice and personality to the characters in the story. |

The same supplemental handouts that ELA teachers used for step 1 (construction) of teaching media literacy with graphic novels are also used for step 2 (intention). They can be found in Chapter 1, Figures 1.4-1.5 and 1.8.

### Step 3: Media Analysis and the Graphic Novel

Step 3 of teaching media literacy with graphic novels is inspired by Hobbs' (2007) five media analysis questions. Figure 5.7 links these five questions to graphic novel critical-reading partnerships.

Figure 1.9, from Chapter 1, can be used as a supplemental handout for step 3 of teaching media literacy with graphic novels as well. (Figure 1.9 will also be referenced in the reading strategies.)

**Figure 5.7: Step 3: Teaching media literacy analysis alongside graphic novel critical-reading partnerships**

| STEP 3: MEDIA LITERACY ANALYSIS AND GRAPHIC NOVEL TERMINOLOGY | *FIVE MEDIA LITERACY ANALYSIS QUESTIONS* (Hobbs, 2007) <br><br> Once students understand construction (step 1) and intention (step 2), they can now analyze the graphic novel (step 3). Below, Hobbs' (2007) five media literacy analysis questions are listed and can be paired with each of the graphic novel's critical-reading partnerships. <br><br> **1.** Who is sending the message and what is the author's purpose? <br> **2.** What techniques are used to attract and hold attention? <br> **3.** What lifestyles, values, and points of view are represented in this message? <br> **4.** How might different people interpret this message differently? <br> **5.** What is omitted from this message? |
|---|---|
| **Compare and/or Contrast Partnership** | A partnership between images, words, or images and words that asks the reader to compare and/or contrast what he or she is reading. <br> **Example:** Apple image + "New York" = New York, the Big Apple (compare) or apple image + "orange" = comparing apples and oranges (contrast) |
| **Reference Partnership** | A partnership between words, images, or images and words that asks the reader to activate his or her own schema or background knowledge. <br> **Example:** Apple image + "temptation" = Adam and Eve in the Garden of Eden |
| **Story-Extension Partnership** | A partnership of words, images, or images and words that progresses the story and moves it forward. **Example:** Falling apple image + passing of time and motion = over time, the apple is falling. The story is moving forward. The reader is wondering what will happen and where the apple might land; specifically, in terms of elements of story, this partnership extends the story's plot. |
| **Potential Partnerships:** <br> **1.** _____ <br> **2.** _____ <br> **3.** _____ | What other partnerships can you find that exist between words, between images, and/or between images and words together? |

This third and final step of teaching media literacy with graphic novels is crucial because it asks students to work through all three steps (from construction—to intention—and, finally, to analysis). To answer the five media analysis questions, in other words, students will need to call upon their awareness and understanding of both graphic novel construction and intention.

## TEACHING MEDIA LITERACY WITH GRAPHIC NOVELS IN MIDDLE SCHOOL ELA

The very first time I taught media literacy with graphic novels in middle school, I was met with a welcome surprise. I had assumed that my students were going to struggle to read a graphic novel as a media text. My middle school students not only welcomed a graphic novel as a media text, but excelled at doing so.

But, of course, on day one, someone asked, "It's not really reading, you know?"

This was my "teachable moment."

My middle school students were not aware that when they READ a graphic novel as a media text they were in fact READING. I wondered what they thought it meant to *read* media texts.

Enter teaching media literacy with graphic novels in middle school ELA.

My middle school class and I began our unit on media literacy with graphic novels by asking ourselves, "What does it mean to read media texts that make use of both print-text and image literacies together?" Figure 5.8 presents some of their responses.

**Figure 5.8: Middle school ELA students define what it means to read media texts with both print-text and image literacies**

| READING MEDIA TEXTS WITH PRINT-TEXT AND IMAGE LITERACIES MEANS... |
| --- |
| "Getting messages from both." |
| "Pictures, words, and all that stuff. All the stuff that can mean something when we open the book." |
| "To understand when we see. To see it and get it." |
| "Seeing while reading." |
| "Not kid books. Longer books with pictures and better stories." |
| "Reading more than one thing. Not just words. Pictures that go with the words and make them better." |
| "I look at everything." |
| "To figure things out. When we don't know what's going on, we look at all the words and pictures and find a way to understand." |
| "When we learn from looking." |
| "When we understand words and pictures together." |
| "Like watching TV. What it shows and says goes together for the story." |
| "You read each little part, or box, like with camera shots." |
| "You read each piece of what's going on, and your mind puts it together." |

As impressed as I was with my middle school class on that day, I am even more impressed with them today. Their thoughts have stood the test of time. Over time, I have used them to help many more students and teachers understand what it means to read, in general, with both print-text and image literacies. Lesson Idea 5.A further explains this concept.

## LESSON IDEA 5.A: TEACHING MEDIA LITERACY WITH GRAPHIC NOVELS IN MIDDLE SCHOOL ELA

**The Graphic Novel:** Fiction graphic novel, nonfiction graphic novel, collection of short stories in graphic novel format; *Teaching Graphic Novels* recommends Aaron Renier's *Spiral-Bound* (Top Shelf Productions, 2005).

**The Standard:** Media literacy

**The Reading Strategies:** "And the Meaning Is....," "Graphic Novel Media and Me," and "Build It!"

**Steps for Teaching Media Literacy with Graphic Novels in Middle School ELA**

*1.* Since modern ELA students have grown up in a world full of diverse media literacies that make use of both print-text and image literacies, such as the graphic novel, it is worthwhile to ask them what they think it means to *read* with both. And even though some students may claim that they do not have such experiences, they probably do. (Students may say this because you are the first person to ask them to think about it!) The reading strategy "And the Meaning Is…" asks students to take the time to think about what it means to read with both print-text literacies and image literacies and to think about what steps they take, in their minds, to understand a story that uses both types of literacies. For each section of this initial reading strategy, it is recommended that students first free-write their thoughts and then engage in class discussion.

Note: Refer to **Appendix Q**, "And the Meaning Is…" middle school ELA reading strategy for teaching media literacy with graphic novels.

**2.** Once students have worked through the front-side of "And the Meaning Is…," build schema by introducing the graphic novel and discussing students' initial impressions (which they will write about on the back of the handout).

**3.** Next, move on to the second reading strategy for teaching media literacy with graphic novels in middle school ELA. Centered on the three steps of teaching media literacy with graphic novels, this reading strategy is called "Graphic Novel Media and Me: Reading and Responding to Print-text Literacies and Image Literacies."

**Note: Refer to Appendix P, "Graphic Novel Media and Me: Reading and Responding to Print-text Literacies and Image Literacies," and the accompanying Chapter 1 definition handouts in Appendix A. For the first and second steps in this strategy, you can also refer to Figures 1.4, 1.5, and 1.8 in Chapter 1; for the third step, use Figure 1.9.**

**4.** To begin using "Graphic Novel Media and Me," give students a reading assignment from the graphic novel. The length of this reading assignment is dependent upon the graphic novel of choice.

Note: Since media literacy with graphic novels is a relatively new concept in many ELA classrooms, it might also be useful to ask students to work through the second reading strategy ("Graphic Novel Media and Me") a few times, which can parallel how you divide the reading assignments as well. Students may need multiple copies of the reading strategy "Graphic Novel Media and Me."

**5.** After students work through "Graphic Novel Media and Me," they are now ready to think about the third reading strategy for teaching media literacy with graphic novels: "Build It!" (see **Appendix R**). The "Build It!" reading strategy asks students to reflect upon what they now know about graphic novels in terms of construction, intention, and analysis and, bringing this knowledge together, visualize a building.

The building students visualize will have three floors. These three floors will support their understanding of the three steps of media literacy and graphic novels:

- 1st floor: construction department
- 2nd floor: intention department
- 3rd floor: analysis department

As you can see in **Appendix R**, students will need to first name the building; the building name should be the author's last name, the title of the graphic novel, and the word "Building." For instance, if students are reading Aaron Renier's *Spiral-Bound*, students will name the building "Renier's Spiral-Bound Building."

Next, as the directions read, students will label each floor according to the steps of media literacy (blank spaces provided above the elevator image on each floor). The first floor will be labeled "1st Floor: Construction." The second floor will be labeled "2nd Floor: Intentions," and the third floor will be labeled "3rd Floor: Analysis."

On the bottom of the handout, students will also note a word bank that includes: *Construction, Intentions, Analysis, Panels, Gutters, Balloons,* and *Critical-reading Partnerships*. Besides labeling the three floors, students will need to place these terms in the appropriate nameplates that appear outside of each office (some words will be used more than once).

On the first floor, for example, students will pull out the term "Construction" and write it on the blank line below the elevator labeled "1st Floor: _____." Next, students will pull out the word "Panel" and place it on one of the office nameplates. Within the space for that particular office, students will then once again explain how the panels they referred to in "Graphic Novel Media and Me" were used. For each floor and office, students will follow this process. Students will probably need their completed "Media Literacy and Graphic Novel" reading strategies and supplemental handouts to complete "Build It!"

## Aaron Renier's *Spiral-Bound* (Top Shelf Productions, 2005)

### Summary
Cleverly written in a framed-genre format (in this case, a graphic novel posing as a notebook), *Spiral-Bound* presents a coming-of-age tale for readers of all ages. No matter how old or young you think you are, *Spiral-Bound* will have you not only identifying with the adorable cast of anthropomorphic characters, but also reflecting upon each individual character's plight. Readers of all ages will find themselves thinking about self-discovery, ambition, and the meaning of loyalty and friendship. In the end, a mystery will be solved, and the reader will be left feeling as though he or she has met one of the most brilliant, contemporary, visual and verbal storytellers of our own time.

### Creator: Aaron Renier (1977-present)
In the collected comic anthology edited by Ariel Schrag, entitled *Stuck in the Middle*, Aaron Renier reflects on his middle school years and sites Odyssey of the Mind (commonly referred to in schools as "O.M.") as an early outlet for his creative and artistic talents.

Growing up in Green Bay, Wisconsin, Renier states that he created numerous comics for school newspapers—even "when the school didn't have one." Later, Renier went to art school in Milwaukee, Wisconsin and then in New York City. He met the love of his life (his dog, Beluga), however, in Portland, Oregon. Today, Renier lives in Chicago, Illinois and is writing his second graphic novel, *Unsinkable Walker Bean*.

### Interesting Information
- In 2005, Renier received a nomination for Best Children's Album.
- Also, in 2005, he was the recipient of the Will Eisner Comic Industry Award for Talent Deserving Wider Recognition.
- To learn more about Renier and his work, go to: http://aaronrenier.com/.
- You can find a great interview with Renier about *Spiral-Bound* at: http://thedailycrosshatch.com/2007/04/23/interview-aaron-renier-pt-1-of-2/#more-348.

### From Aaron Renier
When interviewed by *The Daily Cross Hatch*, Renier states that, "In *Spiral-Bound*, a lot of my characters are based on my friends, and a lot of my friends are definitely cartoonists." (Source: Interviewed by Brian Heater and found at: http://thedailycrosshatch.com/2007/04/23/interview-aaron-renier-pt-1-of-2/#more-348)

# TEACHING MEDIA LITERACY WITH GRAPHIC NOVELS IN MIDDLE SCHOOL ELA: A WRITING ACTIVITY

NCTE's Standard 11 states that ELA "students participate as knowledgeable, reflective, creative, and critical members of a variety of literacy communities." When teaching media literacy with graphic novels, ELA teachers can engage their students as knowledgeable, reflective, creative, and critical members of two different literacy communities: the print-text literacy community and the image literacy community. Thus, a middle-school-level writing assignment might ask students to think about the critical link that exists between reading **and** writing with both types of literacies.

The writing activity, found in **Appendix U**, is recommended as a follow-up to the reading strategies for teaching media literacy with graphic novels in middle school ELA. It is called "I Write It!"

Note: To support your students writing with both print-text and image literacies, try to supply them with as many different art and pencil media as possible.

# TEACHING MEDIA LITERACY WITH GRAPHIC NOVELS IN HIGH SCHOOL ELA

During the summer of 2007, CNN reported that high school students accessed three million times the amount of information via the Internet than all the words in all the textbooks ever printed.

The message to today's high school ELA teacher: While the greatest communication revolution of all time is occurring (and has been occurring), we must teach it in our classrooms. We must teach modern students to be readers of both print-text and image literacies for, when they graduate, they will be expected to be competent readers of both. And, further, they will live, operate, and work in a multi-modal literacy world that places value on both.

Teaching media literacy with graphic novels in high school ELA is one way we can help prepare students to be competent readers of both print-text literacies and image literacies. And although the three steps for teaching media literacy in middle school and in high school ELA are thematically similar, the reading strategies are different. Lesson Idea 5.B further explains.

# LESSON IDEA 5.B: TEACHING MEDIA LITERACY WITH GRAPHIC NOVELS IN HIGH SCHOOL ELA

**The Graphic Novel:** Fiction graphic novel, nonfiction graphic novel, collection of short stories in graphic novel format; *Teaching Graphic Novels* suggests using Art Spiegelman's *Maus* (1986)
**The Standard or Emphasis:** Media literacy
**The Reading Strategies:** "Graphic Novel Media and Me: Reading and Responding to Print-Text Literacies and Image Literacies," and "If I Could Please Respond to This Graphic Novel..."

**Steps for Teaching Media Literacy with Graphic Novels in High School ELA**

**1.** The first reading strategy I suggest for teaching media literacy with graphic novels in high school ELA is a more intense version of "Graphic Novel Media and Me: Reading and Responding to Print-text Literacies and Image Literacies." Just like the middle school version of "Graphic Novel Media and Me," the high school version also focuses on the three steps of teaching media literacy with graphic novels.

**Note: Refer to Appendix S, "Graphic Novel Media and Me: Reading and Responding to Print-text Literacies and Image Literacies," and the accompanying Chapter 1 definition handouts in Appendix A. For the first and second steps in this strategy, you can also refer to Figures 1.4, 1.5, and 1.8 in Chapter 1; for the third step, use Figure 1.9.**

**2.** Before offering this reading strategy to students, however, it is a good idea to build schema about reading and responding to print-text literacies and image literacies together. You can start by giving students a blank sheet of paper.

- On the front-side of the paper, ask students to write down "one word that best describes" them. On the other side of the paper, ask them to draw "one illustration that best describes" them.

- After students have written a word and drawn an illustration, introduce the "Graphic Novel Media and Me" reading strategy (**Appendix S**). The first activity on this reading strategy asks students to discuss their word and illustration choices.

- After this class discussion, it is recommended that you and your students move through the "Graphic Novel Media and Me" reading strategy one step at a time: Step 1, Step 2, and then Step 3.

Since reading with graphic novels with a focus on media literacy is a relatively new concept in most high school ELA classrooms, I suggest you give students more than one reading assignment that asks them to work through "Graphic Novel Media and Me." My ELA students have typically needed to work through "Graphic Novel Media and Me" for the duration of reading the graphic novel.

Whenever you feel as though your students are able to successfully work through the reading strategy "Graphic Novel Media and Me," move onto the second reading strategy for teaching media literacy with graphic novels in high school ELA: "If I Could Please Respond to This Graphic Novel, I Would…" (**Appendix T**).

Since the second reading strategy calls on students to have a strong understanding of step 3 of teaching media literacy with graphic novels, it is usually assigned when students have read all (or a significant portion) of the graphic novel.

Focused even more directly on a student's individual response to the graphic novel, the "If I Could Please Respond to This Graphic Novel..." reading strategy asks students to take on a very active reading role with the graphic novel.

Note: "If I Could Please Respond to This Graphic Novel..." also includes a writing activity! Just like its middle school ELA counterpart, this writing activity also focuses on NCTE's standard that students should be able to "participate as knowledgeable, reflective, creative, and critical members of a variety of literacy communities" (p. 3). In the high school ELA writing activity, students are called on to be "knowledgeable, reflective, creative, and critical" participants of print-text and image literacies by writing a personal letter to the creator of the graphic novel.

## Art Spiegelman's *Maus* (Pantheon Books, 1986)

### Summary
Spiegelman's *Maus* is perhaps the most well-known graphic novel to teachers and has been taught in ELA and social studies courses alike for a number of years. But if we look at *Maus* anew, we can also envision it as a valuable text for teaching media literacy with graphic novels.

*Maus* details the experiences of Spiegelman's father, Vladek Spiegelman, as he survives the Holocaust and Hitler's dominance of Europe. The book is formatted as a frame story—a story within a story—and readers of *Maus* find themselves not only thinking about the historical terror of being a Jew in Hitler's Europe, but also about modern life and the lingering effects of such tragic historical situations. Note: *Maus* appears in many high school settings as required reading.

### Creator: Art Spiegelman (1948-present)
Art Spiegelman was the second son born to Vladek and Anja Spiegelman. And although he was born in Stockholm, Sweden, he grew up in Rego Park in Queens, New York.

As readers of *Maus* learn, the Spiegelmans' first son, Richieu, died tragically during the Holocaust. Due to the tragic death of Richieu and his parents' grief, Spiegelman reveals that he sometimes felt a sibling rivalry between himself and Richieu's photograph.

Acclaimed for a number of creative and comic works, Spiegelman's list of accolades includes a special Pulitzer Prize for *Maus II* (1991) in 1992, and, in 2005, recognition by *Time Magazine* as one of the "Top 100 Most Influential People." In terms of comics for use in secondary school settings, Spiegelman is most recognized for both *Maus I* (1986), *Maus II* (1991), and *In the Shadow of No Towers* (2004). In terms of early, younger readers, Spiegelman and his wife, Françoise Mouly, are known for their work on *The Little Lit Series* (2000, 2001, 2003, 2006), and on Toon Books, quality comics for readers four and up. Today, Spiegelman lives in downtown Manhattan with his wife, two children, and a cat named Houdini.

### Interesting Information
- The Toon Books website can be found at: www.toon-books.com.
- A wonderful resource for learning more about Spiegelman and his work can be found at: www.readyourselfraw.com/profiles/spiegelman/profile_spiegelman.htm.
- The creation of Toon Books was partly inspired by the experiences of Spiegelman's children as they learned to read.
- Spiegelman is also known for his work on the Garbage Pail Kids stickers and cards.
- One of his most famous works of art is *The New Yorker* cover published on September 24, 2001. It was re-created on the cover of *In the Shadow of No Towers*.

### From Art Spiegelman
When asked about drawing comics for younger readers and adults, Spiegelman once noted that he advised the *Little Lit* artists to think about "working with the most demanding audience because kids really look. They spend time with a book that adults do not. We were looking for sincerity." (Source: Interview with Indiebound's Christopher Monte Smith)

# CHAPTER 5 HIGHLIGHTS

Chapter 5 focused on teaching media literacy with graphic novels in middle and high school ELA classrooms.

- This chapter was divided into three sections: "Media Literacy and Graphic Novels," "Teaching Media Literacy with Graphic Novels in Middle School ELA," and "Teaching Media Literacy with Graphic Novels in High School ELA."

- For teaching media literacy with graphic novels in middle school ELA, the following reading strategies were recommended:

  o "And the Meaning Is..." (**Appendix Q**)

  o "Graphic Novel Media and Me: Reading and Responding to Print-text Literacies and Image Literacies" (**Appendix P**)

  o "Build It!" (**Appendix R**)

- The middle school writing activity for teaching media literacy with graphic novels in middle school ELA is called "I Write It!" (**Appendix U**).

- For teaching media literacy with graphic novels in high school ELA, the following reading and writing strategies were recommended:

  o "Graphic Novel Media and Me: Reading and Responding to Print-text Literacies and Image Literacies" (**Appendix S**)

  o "If I Could Please Respond to This Graphic Novel..." (**Appendix T**), a high-school-level writing activity

# SOME SUGGESTIONS FOR TEACHING GRAPHIC NOVELS TO ENGLISH LANGUAGE LEARNERS

One of the most important challenges for the future of teaching graphic novels lies in the graphic novel's relationship to language learning. When we learn another language, we often, if not always, use images to assist us. In fact, many literacy scholars would state that the use of image literacies in language learning is much more than an established pedagogical practice.

Under this hope for future collaboration between scholars of graphic novels and scholars of language learning, this chapter is written a bit differently than the earlier chapters. This chapter is written for teachers who have experience with English language learners and are interested in learning more about how graphic novels and comics may be helpful in language-learning contexts.

The U.S. Census Bureau has claimed that the minority population in the United States in 2042 will become the majority population.[4] To prepare and empower our students for this future transition, we must teach them to not only speak English, but also other diverse languages.

Thus, while *Teaching Graphic Novels* focuses on language-learning contexts in the United States, I personally hope to see more future scholarship that links graphic novels to many other language-learning settings as well. In fact, I would like to invite readers of *Teaching Graphic Novels* to post their successes and their adaptations of the lesson ideas found in this chapter on the *Teaching Graphic Novels* blog: http://teachinggraphicnovels.blogspot.com/. I look forward to hearing from and working with you, for the relationship between language learning and graphic novels has, until now, remained a relatively untilled field.

## TEACHING GRAPHIC NOVELS AND COMICS IN LANGUAGE-LEARNING CONTEXTS

Generally, language-learning scholars agree that there are four stages students pass through while developing fluency in a new language. Figure 6.1 (**Appendix V**) presents these four stages as they best relate to language learning with graphic novels and comics.

---

4    THE MAJORITY-MINORITY POPULATION INCREASE IS EVEN MORE INTENSE FOR FUTURE GENERATIONS. IN 2050, THE MINORITY STUDENT POPULATION IS EXPECTED TO INCREASE TO 62% OR MORE. SOURCE: WWW.AMERICA.GOV.

**Figure 6.1: Four stages of language learning, objectives that support the use of graphic novels and comics at each stage, and recommended graphic novels and comics**

| FOUR STAGES OF LANGUAGE LEARNING | IN THIS LANGUAGE-LEARNING STAGE, STUDENTS SHOULD BE ABLE TO: |
|---|---|
| **Stage 1: Pre-Production** | • Match words and images<br>• Use a picture dictionary<br>• Use visual cue cards that indicate positive/negative responses<br>• Sequence using pictures<br><br>**Some suggested comics for Stage 1:**<br>• All comics published by Toon Books<br>• Any picture book that places equal weight on print-text and image literacies |
| **Stage 2: Early Production** | • Continue work with the objectives from Stage 1<br>• Read texts that place equal emphasis on images and words<br>• Draw images and write basic dialogue<br><br>**Some suggested comics for Stage 2:**<br>• All comics published by Toon Books<br>• Steve Niles & Benjamin Roman's *The Cryptics*<br>• Ken Soo's *Jellaby* & *Jellaby: Monster in the City*<br>• Scott Christian Sava's *My Grandparents Are Secret Agents*<br>• Mark Alan Stamaty's *Alia's Mission: Saving the Books of Iraq* (Stamaty's text is probably best used as a bridge from Stage 2 to Stage 3) |
| **Stage 3: Speech Emergence** | • Continue work with the objectives from Stages 1 and 2<br>• Discuss and identify the elements of story<br>• Compose short stories using the elements of story<br><br>**Suggested early reader graphic novels for Stage 3:**<br>• Lewis Trondheim and Eric Cartier's *Kaput & Zosky*<br>• Scott Christian Sava and Diego Jourdan's *Ed's Terrestrials*<br>• Frank Cammuso's *Knights of the Lunch Table: The Dodgeball Chronicles*<br>• Jimmy Gownley's *Amelia Rules! Superheroes* |
| **Stage 4: Intermediate Fluency** | • Continue work with the objectives from Stages 1-3<br>• Participate in reader's theatre<br>• Write reader's theatre<br><br>**Suggested graphic novels for Stage 4:**<br>• Any graphic novel mentioned in *Teaching Graphic Novels*<br>• Jeff Smith's *Bone* series<br>• Barry Lyga's *Wolverine: Worst Day Ever*<br>• Brian Selznick's *The Invention of Hugo Cabaret* |

As Figure 6.1 points out, it is recommended that language learners begin reading comics and then move on to graphic novels.

Note: While the lesson ideas in this chapter recommend that language-learning teachers adopt comics and graphic novels, there are many children's picture books that place value on teaching students to read with both print-text and image literacies as well. Picture books that place an equal emphasis on storytelling with both words and images are the best picture books for preparing future graphic novel readers.

Further, please note that one of the most specific and well-respected publishers of teacher-friendly comics for early and emergent readers is Toon Books (www.toon-books.com).

## TEACHING COMICS TO EARLY LANGUAGE LEARNERS

When teachers use comics with early language learners, they can draw upon four particular objectives, also highlighted in Figure 6.1. These objectives state that students should be able to:

- Match words and images
- Use a picture dictionary
- Use visual cue cards to indicate positive/negative responses (i.e., respond to yes/no questions)
- Sequence using pictures

As the following lesson illustrates, one way to reach out to early language learners with comics is to create word walls.

# LESSON IDEA 6.A: TEACHING COMICS WITH EARLY LANGUAGE LEARNERS

**Early Reader Comics:** Any comic text published by Toon Books or any picture book that places equal emphasis on reading with both print-text and image literacies
**Emphasis:** Early language learning
**Activity Recommendation:** Word walls

**Steps for Teaching Early Language Learners with Comics**

1. Before introducing the comic text of choice, you will need to prepare the following:

   - Index cards

     o After reading the comic text of choice on your own, determine the significant vocabulary you would like to emphasize. On the front of the index cards, with a marker, write these words in the students' language of origin. On the back of the index cards, write these words in English. For frequently-used vocabulary words, you may want to create multiple index cards.

     o Each student needs their own set of vocabulary index cards.

     o You will also want to make individual index cards for each student with the word "Yes" on one side and the word "No" on the other side.

     o Note: If you have students with various languages of origin, it is recommended that you prepare index cards for each of them.

     o Finally, you will need to create a class set of vocabulary index cards, perhaps on even larger index cards than the individual sets. Instead of writing on the front and the back of the cards, simply write the vocabulary words on the front of the card. You will place Velcro on the back of the index card.

   - Copies of the comic text of choice

     o Each student needs a copy of the comic.

   - Laminated, enlarged copies of the comic

     o Enlarge and laminate each page of the comic.

     o These enlarged, laminated pages will be displayed in front of the class and used during the class activities.

   - Velcro

     o Place one side of the Velcro on the back of the class set of vocabulary index cards. Place the other side in the appropriate places on the enlarged, laminated pages from the comic.

   - Large, lined writing paper

     o Before you introduce the comic, you will introduce the new vocabulary on large, lined writing paper (both in English and in the students' languages of origin).

   - Markers

     o Markers will be used on the index cards and on the large, lined paper.

**2.** Once the above materials are prepared, follow these steps for teaching Stage 1 with a comic text.

- On the large, lined paper, write out and introduce students to the new vocabulary words. It is suggested that you discuss and pair each vocabulary word with the corresponding word in the students' languages of origin. Have students practice sounding out each word; also, to help with recall, ask students if they would like to make any notes alongside any of the new vocabulary words.

- It is now time to read through the comic text as a class.

  Note: It is recommended that you first engage students as a whole class by reading the comic text together on the enlarged, laminated pages, adhering to the appropriate vocabulary words where appropriate.

- Students can place their index cards on the appropriate pages of the text, without adhesive.

- Also, ask students yes/no questions about the story and the new vocabulary as you read along. Language-learning scholars claim that, during this stage, students are usually comfortable answering yes/no questions on visual cue cards.

- Since repetition is key in language learning, you and your students should read through the comic multiple times, asking yes/no questions and discussing each vocabulary choice more than once.

- Once students are able to read through the comic together as a class, applying the appropriate vocabulary, have them work independently (or with one or two friends). Either individually or in small groups, students should once again read the comic but, this time, work on applying their own vocabulary index cards to the appropriate pages.

- As a culminating activity, you can ask for volunteers (or small groups) to come to the front of the room and use the enlarged, laminated copies of the text and the class set of vocabulary words to lead the class through the comic.

## TEACHING EMERGENT READERS WITH COMICS

As students move from being early readers to being emergent readers of their new language, it is important to build upon their schema (prior knowledge). One way to reach out to students during this transitional state of development is to offer them a chance to demonstrate what they already know and then, with teacher-guidance, build upon that knowledge. A **K**now-**W**onder-**L**earn (KWL) chart (Ogle, 1986) asks students to build upon their existent knowledge by first considering what they *know* about a topic, then asking what they *wonder* about that topic, and finally, after reading a comic on that topic in their new language, discussing what they have *learned*.

As noted in Figure 6.1, students at this stage of language-learning development should be able to:
- Continue work with the objectives from Stage 1
- Read texts that place equal emphasis on images and words
- Draw images and write basic dialogue

Lesson Idea 6.B will outline how to use a KWL chart during this second stage of language-learning development.

# LESSON IDEA 6.B: TEACHING EMERGENT LANGUAGE LEARNERS WITH COMICS

**Emergent Reader Comics:** Any comic text published by Toon Books or any picture book that places equal emphasis on reading with both print-text and image literacies
**Emphasis:** Emergent language learners
**Activity Recommendation:** KWL chart

**Steps for Teaching Emergent Language Learners**

1. Before introducing the comic text, you will need the following:

   • A comic of your choice.

   • A topic from that comic that reaches out to your particular students' language-learning needs.

   • Large, lined paper or access to a chalkboard/dry-erase board. This paper or board area will be used to create the KWL chart.

   • Handouts of the KWL chart for students (below and **Appendix W**).

| KNOW | WONDER | LEARN |
|------|--------|-------|
|      |        |       |

   • Writing utensils
   • Copies of the emergent reader comic for each student

2. First, pass out the KWL handout. You will also want to have a large KWL chart prepared (either on large, lined paper or on the board). The whole class should be able to view this KWL chart.

3. On the top of the handout, ask students to fill out the topic for the lesson and the name of the comic text (space provided in **Appendix W** as well).

4. Before reading the comic, ask students to think about the topic, particularly about what they ALREADY KNOW about the topic: "Before we read, what do you know about _____?"

- Record their responses under the "Know" category of the KWL chart.
- Once you and your students have worked through the "Know" category, ask students what they WONDER about that topic: "What do you wonder about _____?"
- Record their responses under the "Wonder" category of the KWL chart.

5. It is now time to read through the comic with your students, perhaps a few times.

6. After you have read and discussed the comic with students, ask them to think about what they LEARNED: "What did you learn from reading this comic?"

Record their responses under the "Learn" category of the KWL chart.

7. When the KWL chart is complete, ask students to meet with friends and discuss what they knew, what they wondered, and what they learned. Encourage students to draw images to represent the things they knew, wondered, and learned. Follow up their individual discussions with a whole-class discussion.

8. Because students are now familiar with a KWL chart, it is suggested that you follow up with a similarly themed comic and second KWL chart or, if ready for a new comic and a new topic, a newly themed comic and KWL chart.

# SUPPORTING EMERGENT READERS AND WRITERS WITH COMICS AND GRAPHIC NOVELS

During this third stage of development, students are emerging as both readers and writers of their new language. Thus, at this stage, language learning needs to focus on bridging the reading-writing connection. To help students emerge as both readers and writers of their new language during this third stage, I recommend that teachers begin to use early reader graphic novels.

The objectives for this third stage of language learning stress the importance of bridging the reading-writing connection with higher-level stories:
- Continue work with the objectives from Stages 1 and 2
- Discuss and identify the elements of story
- Compose short stories using the elements of story

As language learners transition to early reader graphic novels they will become more and more familiar with the equitable use of print-text literacies and image literacies to develop the elements of story. Lesson Idea 6.C further explains.

# LESSON IDEA 6.C: TEACHING EMERGENT LANGUAGE LEARNERS WITH EARLY READER GRAPHIC NOVELS

**Emergent Reader and Early Reader Graphic Novels:** If your students are ready, it is suggested that you introduce early reader graphic novels at this time (suggestions found in Figure 6.1).
**Emphasis:** Emergent language learners
**Activity Recommendation:** Elements of story and story mapping

**Steps for Teaching Emergent Language Learners**

*1.* Before introducing the early reader graphic novel, you will need the following:

- An early reader graphic novel of your choice

- Two copies of **Appendix X** for each student

- Overhead of **Appendix X**

- Large, lined paper or access to a chalkboard/dry-erase board

- Writing utensils

- Art supplies for developing (writing and drawing) students' own story maps

*2.* To begin, introduce the early reader graphic novel of your choice.

*3.* Ask students to complete a picture walk with you through the text. Make sure that students have copies of **Appendix X** and that you are displaying **Appendix X** for the whole class to see (on an overhead). Discuss the elements of story from the handout as you and your students complete the picture walk. Encourage students to take notes on the handout.

*4.* After the class has discussed the elements of story during a picture walk, ask students to read through the story again, and complete the two sets of directions on the handout. In between each set of directions and student work, engage in a class discussion and make more notes on the handout.

*5.* To continue emergence with reading and writing in their new language, it is strongly encouraged that the class engage in discussions and in asking questions about their own and each other's stories.

# SUPPORTING EMERGENT-FLUENT READERS AND WRITERS WITH GRAPHIC NOVELS

As students move toward fluency in their new language, teachers should continue to nurture the reading-writing connection. Along with nurturing this connection, teachers may also want to consider moving forward in their text selection from early reader graphic novels to graphic novels.

Please note the difference between early reader graphic novels and graphic novels rests in story complexity and maturity level. So, even though high school students may be ready to read graphic novels, middle school teachers may want to continue reading early reader graphic novels with their students (suggestions can be found in Figure 6.1).

For both middle and high school students, however, the objectives for this fourth stage of language learning remain the same. These objectives state that students should be able to:
- Continue work with the objectives from Stages 1-3
- Participate in reader's theatre
- Write reader's theatre

Lesson Idea 6.D will explain how teachers can use reader's theatre as a reading and writing activity with soon-to-be-fluent language learners.

# LESSON IDEA 6.D: TEACHING SOON-TO-BE-FLUENT LANGUAGE LEARNERS WITH EARLY READER GRAPHIC NOVELS OR GRAPHIC NOVELS

**Emergent Reader Comics:** Suggestions found in Figure 6.1
**Emphasis:** Soon-to-be-fluent language learners
**Activity Recommendation:** Reader's theatre reading and writing activity

**Steps for Teaching Soon-to-be-fluent Language Learners**

1. Before introducing the early reader graphic novel or graphic novel, you will need the following:

   - Early reader graphic novel or graphic novel
   - A copy of **Appendix Y** for each student
   - Overhead of **Appendix Y**
   - Writing utensils

2. Begin by reading either the early reader graphic novel or graphic novel of your choice.

3. After reading and discussing the story, explain reader's theatre to your students (explanation found in **Appendix Y**).
   Note: The reader's theatre handout (**Appendix Y**) speaks directly to teachers and students. Thus, you will want to read through these directions before handing them out to students. Also, you will want to have the first reader's theatre script ready.

## A FINAL THOUGHT ON TEACHING GRAPHIC NOVELS IN LANGUAGE-LEARNING CONTEXTS

As students emerge as fluent readers of their new language with comics and graphic novels, they can work with all the lesson ideas in *Teaching Graphic Novels*.

For instance, even though a simplified version of the elements of story is recommended for the third stage of language development, your students may be ready to work with the more complex listing of the elements of story found in earlier chapters.

Feel free to substitute any of the language-learning ideas found in this chapter with those from earlier chapters. You are the best judge of your students' abilities.

## APPENDIX A: BASIC GRAPHIC NOVEL VOCABULARY FOUND IN CHAPTER 1, INTENDED FOR YOUR CLASSROOM TEACHING USE

**Figure 1.2: Basic definitions for the graphic novel panel and gutter**

*PANEL:* A visual or implied boundary, and the contents within it, that tell a piece of the story.

*GUTTER:* The space between the panels. In this space, the reader moves from one panel to the next and comes to a conclusion about what is happening.

**Figure 1.3: Three types of content panels**

| THREE TYPES OF CONTENT PANELS |
| --- |
| Content panels rely on formatting or style to convey their message to the reader, whether that message be expressed with words, images, or with images and words together. |
| **1. WORD PANEL:** The contents within this type of panel ONLY use words to tell a piece of the story. |
| **2. IMAGE PANEL:** The contents within this type of panel ONLY use images to tell a piece of the story. |
| **3. WORD AND IMAGE PANELS:** The contents within this type of panel use BOTH words and images to tell a piece of the story. |

**Figure 1.4: Eleven different types of story panels found in graphic novels**

## ELEVEN TYPES OF STORY PANELS

Based in the elements of story familiar to ELA teachers when teaching traditional literature, story panels develop or detail the story/text.

**1. PLOT PANEL:** These panels develop the graphic novel's plot, or the main set of events that unfold in the story.

**2. CHARACTER PANEL:** These panels develop individual or multiple characters, often referred to in ELA as *characterization*.

**3. SETTING PANEL:** These panels develop setting, the place(s) where the graphic novel takes place.

**4. CONFLICT PANEL:** These panels develop the source of conflict in the graphic novel, the tension that motivates the story.

**5. RISING ACTION PANEL:** These panels develop the set of events that stem from the conflict, give rise to that conflict, and lead to the climax in the graphic novel.

**6. CLIMAX PANEL:** These panels develop the point of greatest intensity in the story.

**7. RESOLUTION PANEL:** These panels develop the final outcome that solves the primary conflict(s) in the graphic novel.

**8. SYMBOLS PANEL:** These panels usually contain images and/or words that stand for something larger than themselves.

**9. THEME PANEL:** These panels develop the main idea(s) in the graphic novel.

**10. FORESHADOWING PANEL:** These panels develop the story by hinting at or alluding to what is to come later.

**11. COMBINATION STORY PANELS:** These panels use two or more of the above types of panels.

**Figure 1.5: Six different types of gutters (McCloud, 1993)**

Note: Examples taken from *Laika* (2007) by Nick Abadzis (First-Second Books).

*Laika* is the story of the world's first space-traveler, a dog named Laika, who was sent into orbit on Sunday, November 3, 1957 by the Soviet Space Program.

*GUTTER:* The space between the panels

**Moment-to-moment Gutter:** From one panel to the next panel, readers witness little closure and instead simply see something from one instance to the next.
**Example:** page 11 (top panels)

**Action-to-action Gutter:** Between these panels, readers see a single subject going through specific transitions.
**Example:** page 14 (top panels)

**Subject-to-subject Gutter:** While sticking with a single idea, these panels move the reader from one subject to the next subject, often progressing the storyline. McCloud reminds us to "note the degree of reader involvement necessary to render these transitions meaningful" (71).
**Example:** page 162 (middle panels)

**Scene-to-scene Gutter:** In reading these panels, readers often need to exercise deductive reasoning, for these panels move the reader across "significant distances of time and space" (McCloud, 1993).
**Example:** page 195 (bottom two panels)

**Aspect-to-aspect Gutter:** Because these gutters ask readers to think about the feelings or emotions being conveyed from one panel to the next panel, they are comparable to tone or mood.
**Example:** page 169 (bottom panels)

**Non-sequitur Gutter:** Sometimes it might appear that there is no logical relationship between panels. However, graphic novelists use the non-sequitur gutter to make a point: sometimes depicting symbolism, sometimes conveying confusion, and sometimes foreshadowing something to come later. There can actually be many reasons for a graphic novelist to use this type of gutter. But the point is: when the reader comes to a non-sequitur gutter, he should assume that what at first seems illogical does in fact have some sort of greater significance. What is that significance?
**Example:** page 88 (bottom panel)

Even though some gutters may be very easily identifiable as one type of gutter (like the non-sequitur example), other gutters may not be so clearly indicative of only one type. The key here is to know that, when you are reading graphic novel gutters, you may sometimes see more than one possibility. For instance, let's look at another example from Abadzis' *Laika* on page 175.

### Figure 1.6 Two gutter possibilities

In this example, the gutter can be read as moving from aspect-to-aspect or from moment-to-moment. If you read the gutter as moving from aspect-to-aspect, you are paying particular attention to the facial expressions and the sense of an emotional countdown. If you read the gutter as moving from moment-to-moment, you are paying particular attention to the sense of time, a sense of moving inevitably forward, toward ignition. In short, depending on how you read the gutter, you can sometimes come up with different types of gutter possibilities.

**Figure 1.7: Different types of graphic novel balloons**

**GRAPHIC NOVEL BALLOONS:** Typically found inside of a panel, graphic novel balloons commonly create visual boundaries.

**Word Balloon:** Word balloons enclose print-text words within a visual boundary that divides the artwork from the printed-text.
**Example:** Copyright and dedication pages of Hope Larson's *Chiggers* (2008).

Reprinted with the permission of Atheneum Books for Young Readers, an imprint of Simon & Schuster Children's Publishing Division from CHIGGERS by Hope Larson. Copyright © 2008 Hope Larson.

**Story Balloon:** Story balloons focus on progressing the storyline.
**Example:** Page 23, first panel, of Gene Luen Yang's *American Born Chinese* (2006)

**Thought Balloon:** Thought balloons focus on a character's or characters' thoughts/ideas.
**Example:** Page 177, second top panel, of Gene Luen Yang's *American Born Chinese* (2006)

**Dialogue Balloon:** These balloons focus on conversation between characters (or one character simply speaking aloud to him or herself).
**Example:** Page 96, panel on bottom left, of Emmanuel Guibert's *Alan's War: The Memories of G.I. Alan Cope* (2008, First Second Books)

**Possible label for this balloon-less balloon:**

**Sound Effect Balloon:** These balloons use words or images to convey a sense of sound in the story. **Example:** Page 4, second panel, of James Sturm, Andrew Arnold, and Alexis Frederick-Frost's *Adventures in Cartooning* (2009, First Second Books)

**Balloon-less Balloons:** Sometimes graphic novelists choose not to use the visual boundary that defines the balloon feature. The words or images appear alone, as if floating inside of the panel. Since there are a number of different reasons why graphic novelists choose this feature, first identify ballon-less balloons and, second, use story contextualization to understand why the graphic novelist might have chosen this balloon-less style. Come up with your own balloon labels for balloon-less balloons. **Example:** Page 182, bottom panel, of Emmanuel Guibert's *Alan's War* (2008, First Second Books)

**Figure 1.8: Common types of critical-reading partnerships found in graphic novels**

| COMMON TYPES OF CRITICAL-READING PARTNERSHIPS FOUND IN GRAPHIC NOVELS | |
|---|---|
| **PARTNERSHIP NAME** | **DESCRIPTION** |
| **Critical-reading Partnership of Comparison and/or Contrast:** A partnership between images, words, or images and words that asks the reader to compare and/or contrast what he or she is reading. | **Example:** Apple image + "New York" = New York, the Big Apple (compare) OR apple image + "orange" = comparing apples and oranges (contrast) |
| **Critical-reading Partnership of Reference:** A partnership between words, images, or images and words that asks the reader to activate his or her own schema or background knowledge. | **Example:** Apple image + "temptation" = Adam and Eve in the Garden of Eden |
| **Story-extension Partnership:** A partnership of words, images, or images and words that progresses the story and moves it forward. | **Example:** Falling apple image + passing of time and motion = Time is passing and the apple is falling. The story is moving forward. The reader is wondering what will happen and where the apple might land; specifically, in terms of elements of story, this partnership extends the story's plot. |
| **New Critical-reading Partnership** | |

SOURCE: ABEL & MADDEN, 2008

# APPENDIX B: THREE STORY-MAPPING HANDOUTS FOR TEACHING READING COMPREHENSION WITH GRAPHIC NOVELS IN MIDDLE SCHOOL ELA

**Figure 2.4: Handout #1—Comprehending Graphic Novels in Middle School ELA**

Name: _____

## COMPREHENDING GRAPHIC NOVELS IN MIDDLE SCHOOL ELA

There are three windows to look through when reading a graphic novel.

**1.** **The Words Window:** As you read through the words window, you will focus on all of the words in the graphic novel. For this window, it would be a good idea to recall the different types of word balloons.

**2.** **The Images Window:** As you read through the images window, you will focus on all of the images in the graphic novel. When selecting images for the images window, it would be a good idea to recall the different types of panels and gutters that occur between them. In short, if you understand what is happening in the panels and in their gutters, you will make wise decisions about the images window.

**3.** **The Words and Images Window:** As you read through the words and images window, you will consider how the images and the words in the graphic novel work together to tell the story. This consideration should hopefully remind you of the critical-reading partnerships possible between words and images in graphic novels. Note: Putting together a combination of the responses you had for the words window and the images window could also work here.

**Directions:** On this first handout, and the accompanying other two handouts, you will find a story map. Your goal is to read the assigned section of the graphic novel, look through the window assigned to each handout, and fill out the story map accordingly.

# COMPREHENDING GRAPHIC NOVELS THROUGH THE WORDS WINDOW

*** For this window, please use words to fill in your map. ***

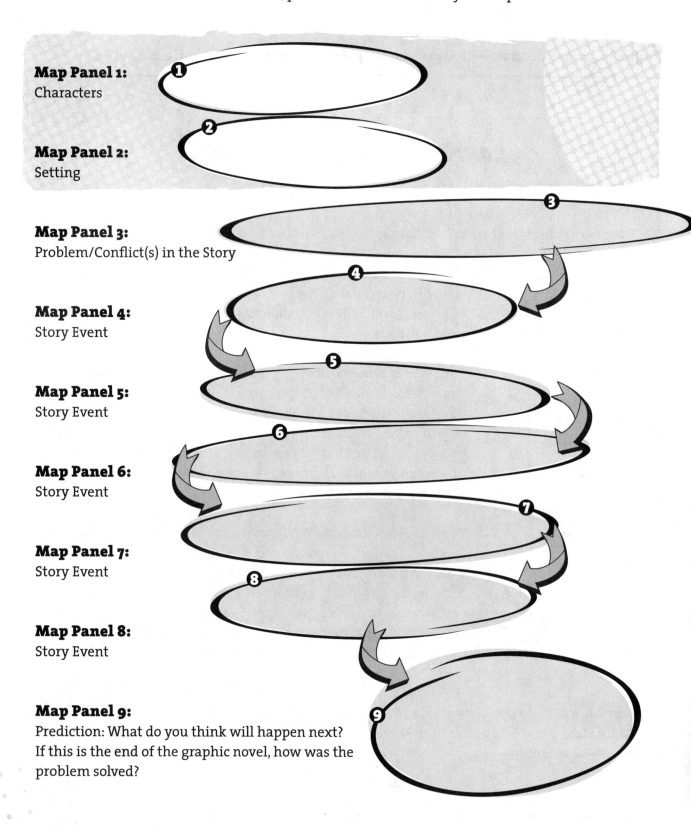

**Map Panel 1:**
Characters

**Map Panel 2:**
Setting

**Map Panel 3:**
Problem/Conflict(s) in the Story

**Map Panel 4:**
Story Event

**Map Panel 5:**
Story Event

**Map Panel 6:**
Story Event

**Map Panel 7:**
Story Event

**Map Panel 8:**
Story Event

**Map Panel 9:**
Prediction: What do you think will happen next?
If this is the end of the graphic novel, how was the
problem solved?

**Figure 2.5: Handout #2—Comprehending Graphic Novels through the Images Window (Middle School)**

Name: _____

# COMPREHENDING GRAPHIC NOVELS THROUGH THE IMAGES WINDOW

*** For this reading window, please use images to fill in your map. ***

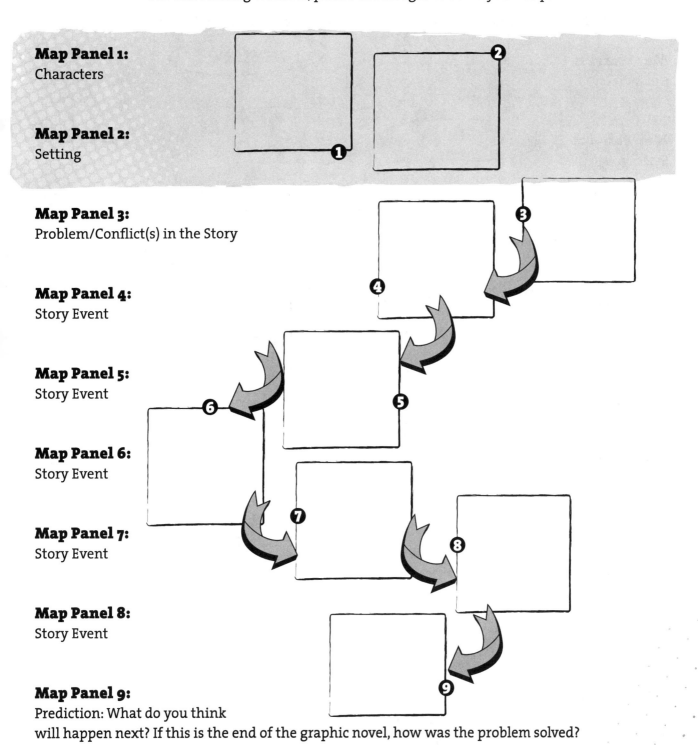

**Map Panel 1:**
Characters

**Map Panel 2:**
Setting

**Map Panel 3:**
Problem/Conflict(s) in the Story

**Map Panel 4:**
Story Event

**Map Panel 5:**
Story Event

**Map Panel 6:**
Story Event

**Map Panel 7:**
Story Event

**Map Panel 8:**
Story Event

**Map Panel 9:**
Prediction: What do you think
will happen next? If this is the end of the graphic novel, how was the problem solved?

**Figure 2.6: Handout #3—Comprehending Graphic Novels through the Words and Images Window (Middle School)**

Name: _____

# COMPREHENDING GRAPHIC NOVELS THROUGH THE WORDS AND IMAGES WINDOW

*** For this reading window, please use images and words to fill in your map. ***

**Map Panel 1:**
Characters

**Map Panel 2:**
Setting

**Map Panel 3:**
Problem/Conflict(s) in the Story

**Map Panel 4:**
Story Event

**Map Panel 5:**
Story Event

**Map Panel 6:**
Story Event

**Map Panel 7:**
Story Event

**Map Panel 8:**
Story Event

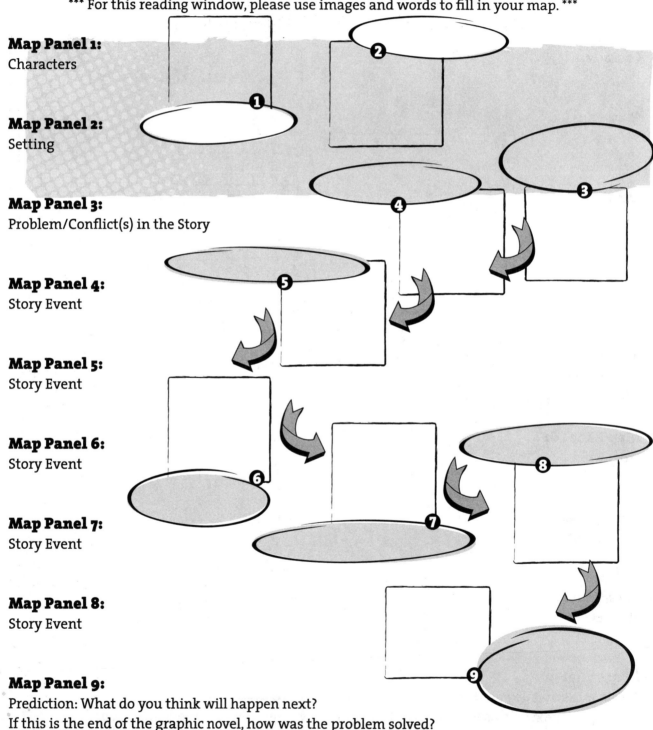

**Map Panel 9:**
Prediction: What do you think will happen next?
If this is the end of the graphic novel, how was the problem solved?

# APPENDIX C: THREE STORY-MAPPING HANDOUTS FOR TEACHING READING COMPREHENSION WITH GRAPHIC NOVELS IN HIGH SCHOOL ELA

**Figure 2.10: Handout #1—Comprehending Graphic Novels in High School ELA**

Name: _____

## COMPREHENDING GRAPHIC NOVELS IN HIGH SCHOOL ELA

There are three windows to look through when reading a graphic novel.

**1.** **The Words Window:** As you read through the words window, you will focus on all of the words in the graphic novel. For this window, it would be a good idea to recall the different types of word balloons.

**2.** **The Images Window:** As you read through the images window, you will focus on all of the images in the graphic novel. When selecting images for the images window, it would be a good idea to recall the different types of panels and gutters that occur between them. In short, if you understand what is happening in the panels and in their gutters, you will make wise decisions about the images window.

**3.** **The Words and Images Window:** As you read through the words and images window, you will consider how the images and the words in the graphic novel work together to tell the story. This consideration should hopefully remind you of the critical-reading partnerships possible between words and images in graphic novels.

Note: Putting together a combination of the responses you had for the words window and the images window could also work here.

**Directions:** On this first handout, and the accompanying other two handouts, you will find two story maps. Your goal is to read the assigned section of the graphic novel, look through the window assigned to each handout, and fill out the story maps accordingly.

# COMPREHENDING GRAPHIC NOVELS THROUGH THE WORDS WINDOW

*** For this window, please use words to fill in your map. ***

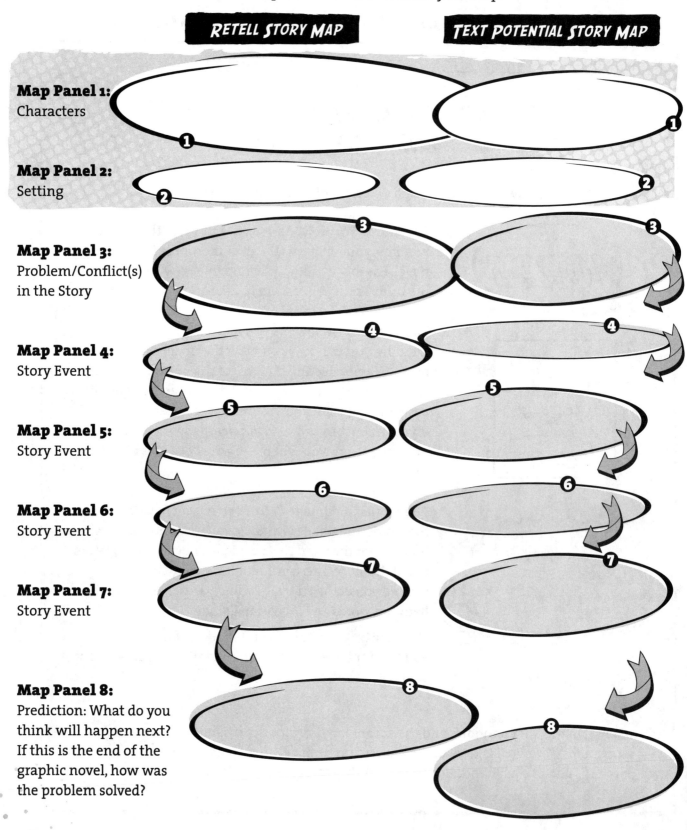

RETELL STORY MAP

TEXT POTENTIAL STORY MAP

**Map Panel 1:**
Characters

**Map Panel 2:**
Setting

**Map Panel 3:**
Problem/Conflict(s)
in the Story

**Map Panel 4:**
Story Event

**Map Panel 5:**
Story Event

**Map Panel 6:**
Story Event

**Map Panel 7:**
Story Event

**Map Panel 8:**
Prediction: What do you
think will happen next?
If this is the end of the
graphic novel, how was
the problem solved?

Name: _____

# COMPREHENDING GRAPHIC NOVELS THROUGH THE IMAGES WINDOW

*** For this reading window, please use your own drawings/images to fill in your maps ***

**RETELL STORY MAP**          **TEXT POTENTIAL STORY MAP**

**Map Panel 1:**
Characters

**Map Panel 2:**
Setting

**Map Panel 3:**
Problem/Conflict(s) in the Story

**Map Panel 4:**
Story Event

CONTINUED ➡

# COMPREHENDING GRAPHIC NOVELS THROUGH THE IMAGES WINDOW (CONT'D.)

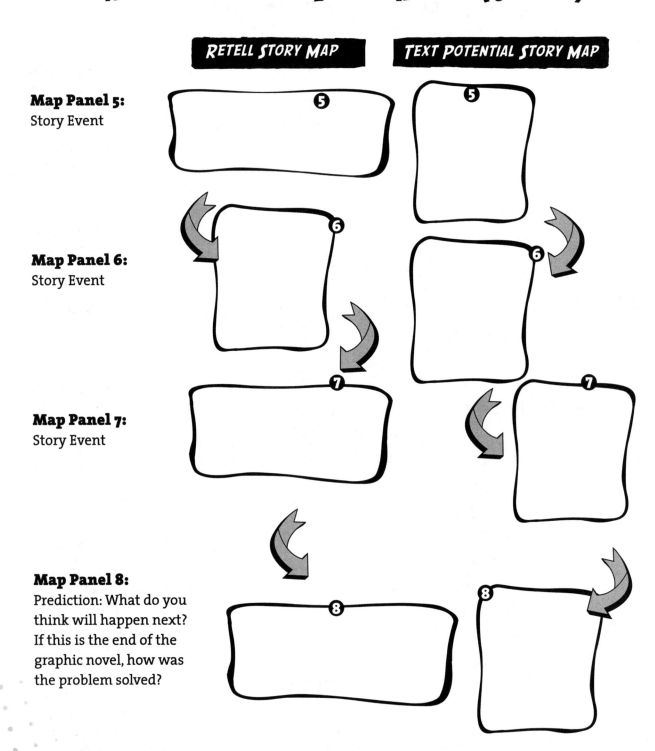

**RETELL STORY MAP**

**TEXT POTENTIAL STORY MAP**

**Map Panel 5:**
Story Event

**Map Panel 6:**
Story Event

**Map Panel 7:**
Story Event

**Map Panel 8:**
Prediction: What do you think will happen next? If this is the end of the graphic novel, how was the problem solved?

**Figure 2.12: Handout #3—Comprehending Graphic Novels through the Words and Images Window (High School)**

Name: _____

## COMPREHENDING GRAPHIC NOVELS THROUGH THE WORDS AND IMAGES WINDOW

*** For this reading window, please use images and words to fill in your maps. ***

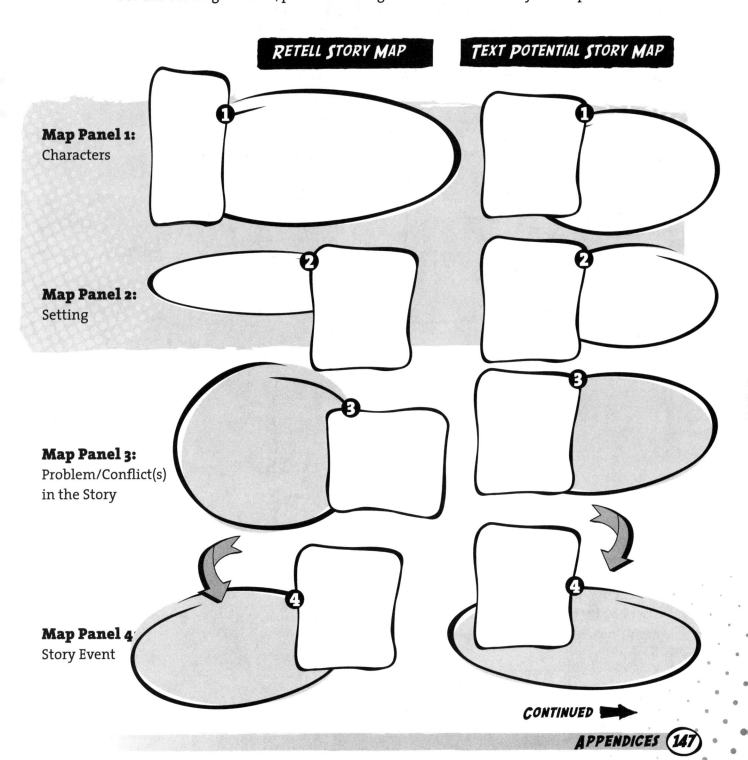

RETELL STORY MAP

TEXT POTENTIAL STORY MAP

**Map Panel 1:**
Characters

**Map Panel 2:**
Setting

**Map Panel 3:**
Problem/Conflict(s)
in the Story

**Map Panel 4:**
Story Event

CONTINUED ➤

# COMPREHENDING GRAPHIC NOVELS THROUGH THE WORDS AND IMAGES WINDOW (CONT'D.)

*** For this reading window, please use images and words to fill in your maps. ***

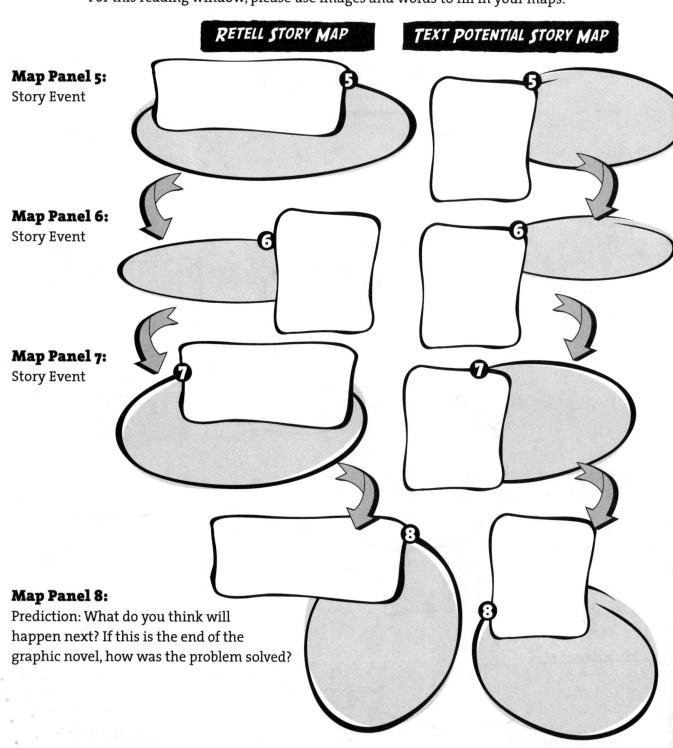

**Map Panel 5:**
Story Event

**Map Panel 6:**
Story Event

**Map Panel 7:**
Story Event

**Map Panel 8:**
Prediction: What do you think will happen next? If this is the end of the graphic novel, how was the problem solved?

# APPENDIX D: THE LITERATE EYE READING STRATEGY FOR MIDDLE SCHOOL ELA STUDENTS

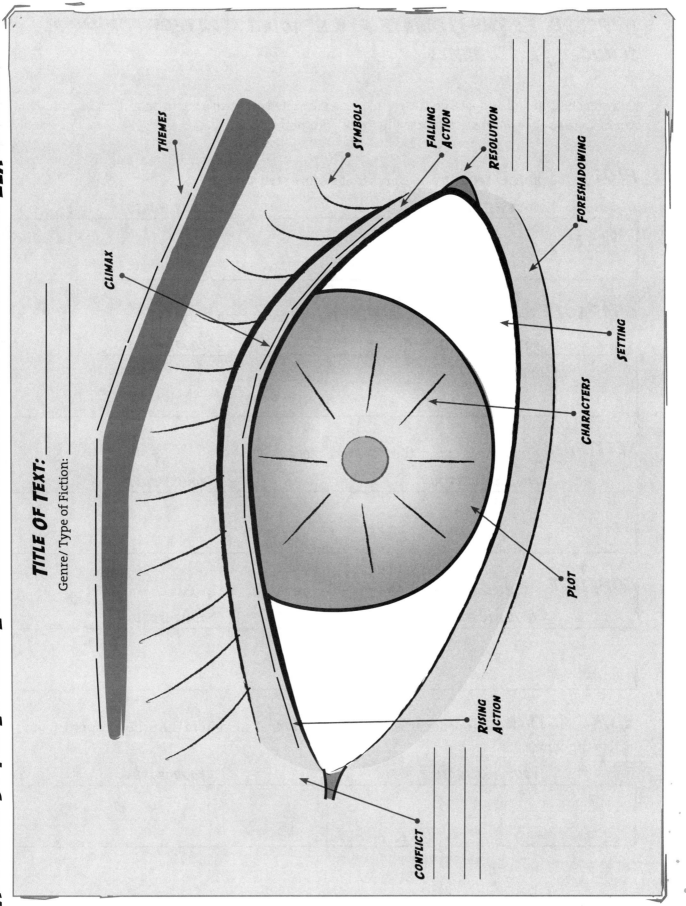

TITLE OF TEXT: _____

Genre/Type of Fiction: _____

THEMES

SYMBOLS

FALLING ACTION

RESOLUTION

FORESHADOWING

CLIMAX

SETTING

CHARACTERS

PLOT

RISING ACTION

CONFLICT

# APPENDIX E: THE LITERATE EYE READING STRATEGY FOR MIDDLE SCHOOL ELA STUDENTS

Below each term, in the space on the right, please rewrite this term and its definition in your own words. In the space on the left, please illustrate your definition.

## PLOT — the primary sequence of events that setup or tell a story

| YOUR ILLUSTRATION | YOUR WORDS |
|---|---|
|  |  |

## CHARACTER — a person, persona, or identity within a fiction story

| YOUR ILLUSTRATION | YOUR WORDS |
|---|---|
|  |  |

## SETTING — where the events of the story take place

| YOUR ILLUSTRATION | YOUR WORDS |
|---|---|
|  |  |

## CONFLICT — the tension, disagreement, or discord that occurs in a story

| YOUR ILLUSTRATION | YOUR WORDS |
|---|---|
|  |  |

## RISING ACTION — the action or events in the story that stem from the primary conflict and lead to the climax

| YOUR ILLUSTRATION | YOUR WORDS |
|---|---|
|  |  |

**CLIMAX** — the point of greatest intensity in a story, a culminating point, usually led up to by rising action and followed by a resolution

| YOUR ILLUSTRATION | YOUR WORDS |
| --- | --- |
|  |  |

**RESOLUTION** — the final outcome to solve or address the conflict

| YOUR ILLUSTRATION | YOUR WORDS |
| --- | --- |
|  |  |

**SYMBOLS** — an iconic representation that stands for something larger than itself

| YOUR ILLUSTRATION | YOUR WORDS |
| --- | --- |
|  |  |

**THEME** — a main idea or emphasized aspect of a story

| YOUR ILLUSTRATION | YOUR WORDS |
| --- | --- |
|  |  |

**FORESHADOWING** — a moment in the story when the reader feels like something to happen later in the story is alluded to or referenced

| YOUR ILLUSTRATION | YOUR WORDS |
| --- | --- |
|  |  |

# APPENDIX F: REFERENCE LIST OF GRAPHIC NOVEL ADAPTATIONS OF TRADITIONAL PRINT-TEXT FICTION

Austen, J. (1818). *Northanger Abbey*. (Adapted by Molly Kiely, Trina Robbins, & Anne Timmons). Mount Horeb, WI: Eureka.

Balzac, H. (1900). *The Thing at Ghent*. (Adapted by Mark Dancey). Mount Horeb, WI: Eureka.

Bardet, D., & Nhaoua. (2009). *Arabian Nights*. San Diego, CA: IDW.

Baum, F.L. (1900). *The wizard of Oz*. (Adapted by Michael Cavallaro, 2005). New York: Puffin.

Bierce, A. (2008). *Graphic Classics Volume # 6, 2ⁿᵈ Edition*. (Adapted by Mort Castle, Rod Lott, Antonella Caputo, et. al). Mount Horeb, WI: Eureka.

Burrows, A., Caputo, A., Rainey, R. et. al. (2008). *Graphic classics Volume #16: Oscar Wilde*. Mount Horeb, WI: Eureka.

Castle, M., Slack, M., Gane, S., et al. (2004). *Graphic classics Volume #9: Robert Louis Stevenson*. Mount Horeb, WI: Eureka.

Cervantes, M. (2009). *Don Quixote*. San Diego, CA: IDW.

Colfer, E., & Donkin, A. (2007). *Artemis Fowl: The graphic novel*. (Art by Giovanno Rigano; Color by Paolo Lamanna). New York: Hyperion.

Crane, S. (1895). *The red badge of courage*. (Adapted by Wayne Vansant, 2005). New York: Puffin.

Defoe, D. (2009). *Robinson Crusoe*. (Adapted by Jean-Christophe Vergne). San Diego, CA: IDW.

Dickens, C. (2009). *Oliver Twist*. (Adapted by David Cerquiera & Philippe Chanoinat). San Diego, CA: IDW.

Doyle, Arthur Conan. (2002). *Graphic Classics # 2: Arthur Conan Doyle*. (Adapted by Rick Geary, Nestor Redondo, & Donald Marquez). Mount Horeb, WI: Eureka.

Fitzgerald, F. Scott. (1921). *The curious case of Benjamin Button*. (Adapted by Nunzio DeFillippis, Christina Weir; Illustrated by Kevin Cornell, 2008). Philadelphia, PA: Quirk Books.

Gownley, J. (2006). *Amelia rules! Superheroes*. Harrisburg, PA: Renaissance Press.*

Kafka, F. (1915). *The metamorphosis*. (Adapted by Peter Kuper; Translated by Kerstin Hasenpusch). New York: Random House.

Kipling, R. (2009). *The jungle book*. (Adapted by Jean-Blaise Mitildji & Tieko). San Diego, CA: IDW.

London, J. (2006). *Graphic Classics Volume # 5: Jack London, 2ⁿᵈ Edition*. (Adapted byRod Lott, Trina Robbins, Antonella Caputo, et. al). Mount Horeb, WI: Eureka.

McPherson, J, & Gout, L. (2009). *Daniel X: Alien hunter*. (Art by Klaus Lyndeled, Jon Girin, & Joseph McLamb). New York: Little, Brown & Co.

Melville, H. (1851). *Moby Dick*. (Adapted by Pascal Alixe & Roy Thomas). New York: Marvel.*

Petrucha, S., & Murase, S. (2005). *Nancy Drew: The demon of River Heights*. New York:Simon & Schuster.*

Poe, Edgar Allan. (2006). *Graphic Classics Volume # 1: Edgar Allan Poe*. Mount Horeb, WI: Eureka.

Poe, Edgar Allan. (2008). *Nevermore: A graphic adaptation of Edgar Allan Poe's short stories*. New York: Sterling.**

Shakespeare, W. (1606). *Macbeth*. (Adapted by Arthur Byron Cover; Illustrated by Tony Leonard Tamai, 2005). New York: Puffin.

Shakespeare, W. (1610). *The tempest*. (Adapted by David Messer, 2005). New York:  Random House.

Shelley, M. (1818). *Frankenstein*. (Adapted by Gary Reed; Illustrated by Frazer Irving, 2005). New York: Puffin.

Stroker, B. (2003). *Graphic Classics Volume # 7*. (Adapted by John Pierard, Gary Alanquilan, & Lesley Reppeteaux). Mount Horeb, WI: Eureka.

Telgemeier, R. (2006). *The baby-sitters club: Kristy's great idea*. New York: Scholastic.*

Thomas, R. (2007). *Treasure Island*. New York: Marvel.*

Thomas, R. (2007). *The Odyssey*. New York: Marvel.*

Thomas, R. (2008). *The Iliad*. New York: Marvel.*

Thomas, R. (2009). *The Three Musketeers*. New York: Marvel.*

Tolstoy, L. (2009). *War and Peace*. (Adapted by Frederic Bremaud & Thomas Campi). San Diego, CA: IDW.

Twain, M. (2007). *Graphic Classics Volume  #8: Mark Twain*. (Edited by Tom Pomplun). Mount Horeb, WI: Eureka.

Verne, J., & Millien, C. (2009). *Around the world in 80 days*. San Diego, CA: IDW.

Wilde, O. (1890). *Picture of Dorian Gray*. (Adapted by Roy Thomas). New York: Marvel.*

* Some graphic novel adaptations see the original print-text versions as foundations for building new stories with the same characters, plots, and themes.
** In this collection, a number of artists offer graphic novel adaptations of Poe's work.

# APPENDIX G: THE LITERATE EYE READING STRATEGY FOR HIGH SCHOOL ELA STUDENTS

(For student use, copy this same page as a front and back.)

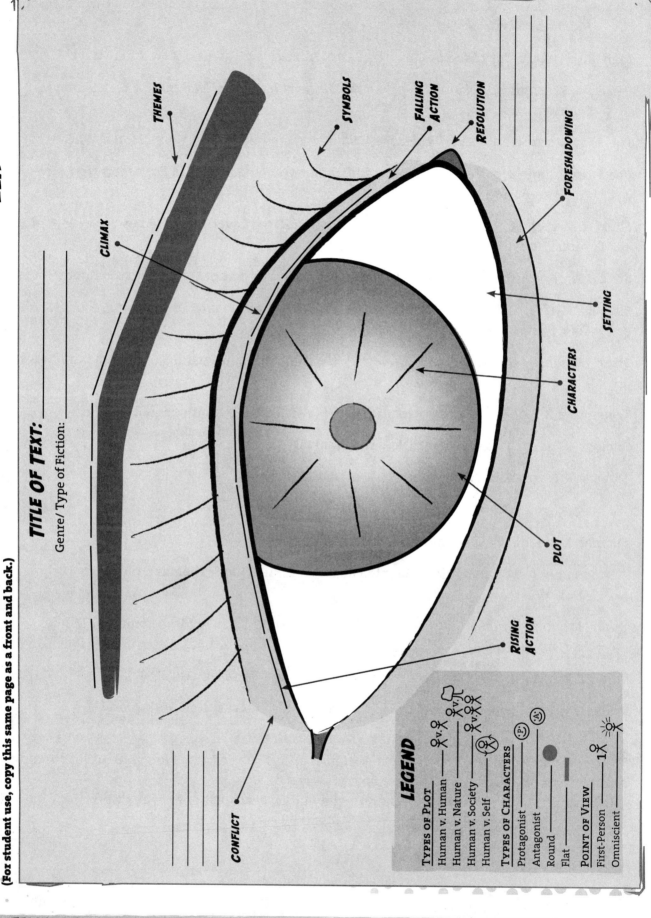

**TITLE OF TEXT:** _____

Genre/ Type of Fiction: _____

THEMES

CLIMAX

SYMBOLS

FALLING ACTION

RESOLUTION

FORESHADOWING

SETTING

CHARACTERS

PLOT

RISING ACTION

CONFLICT

**LEGEND**

**TYPES OF PLOT**
Human v. Human
Human v. Nature
Human v. Society
Human v. Self

**TYPES OF CHARACTERS**
Protagonist
Antagonist
Round
Flat

**POINT OF VIEW**
First-Person
Omniscient

# APPENDIX H: SUPPLEMENT TO THE LITERATE EYE READING STRATEGY FOR HIGH SCHOOL ELA STUDENTS

## Elements of Story

Directions: Please discuss the elements of fiction, and rewrite the definitions in your own words. Below each term, in the space on the right, please rewrite this term and its definition in your own words. In the space on the left, please illustrate your definition.

**PLOT** — the primary sequence of events that setup or tell a story

- Types of plot

    **1.** Human vs. human—the sequence of events sets up a conflict between two or more characters

    **2.** Human vs. nature—the primary conflict in this sequence of events is between a character (or characters) and the natural environment

    **3.** Human vs. society—one or more of the characters experiences a sequence of events that places him (or them) at odds with the larger community

    **4.** Human vs. self—in this sequence of events, a character struggles with him- or herself

| YOUR ILLUSTRATION | YOUR WORDS |
|---|---|
|  |  |

**CHARACTERS** — a person, persona, or identity within a fiction story

- Types of characters

    **1.** Protagonist—typically the main character, the protagonist is usually the character highlighted in the story, the character whom the plot revolves around

    **2.** Antagonist—the source of conflict for the protagonist

    **3.** Round—full, well-developed character

    **4.** Flat—dull, poorly developed character

| YOUR ILLUSTRATION | YOUR WORDS |
|---|---|
|  |  |

# POINT OF VIEW (POV) — the perspective from which the story is told

- Types of POV

    1. First-person—the narrator speaks from an "I" perspective
    2. Omniscient—either the writer is all-knowing about all of the characters and the plot that involves them, or the writer chooses one character to be the main source of information to the reader, thus making him or her all knowing
    3. Objective—the writer is a detached observer who tells what happens without disclosing what he/she thinks or feels
    4. Third-person—the narrator is an outside voice who tells how the characters feel but does not participate in the action of the story

| YOUR ILLUSTRATION | YOUR WORDS |
|---|---|
|  |  |

# SETTING — where the events of the story take place

| YOUR ILLUSTRATION | YOUR WORDS |
|---|---|
|  |  |

# CONFLICT — the tension, disagreement, or discord that occurs in a story

| YOUR ILLUSTRATION | YOUR WORDS |
|---|---|
|  |  |

# RISING ACTION — the action or events in the story that stem from the primary conflict and lead to the climax

| YOUR ILLUSTRATION | YOUR WORDS |
|---|---|
|  |  |

**CLIMAX** — the point of greatest intensity in a story, a culminating point, usually led up to by rising action and followed by a resolution

| YOUR ILLUSTRATION | YOUR WORDS |
| --- | --- |
| | |

**RESOLUTION** — the final outcome to solve or address the conflict

| YOUR ILLUSTRATION | YOUR WORDS |
| --- | --- |
| | |

**SYMBOL** — an iconic representation that stands for something larger than itself

| YOUR ILLUSTRATION | YOUR WORDS |
| --- | --- |
| | |

**THEME** — a main idea or emphasized aspect of a story

| YOUR ILLUSTRATION | YOUR WORDS |
| --- | --- |
| | |

**FORESHADOWING** — a moment in the story when the reader feels like something to happen later in the story is alluded to or referenced

| YOUR ILLUSTRATION | YOUR WORDS |
| --- | --- |
| | |

# Critical-reading Lenses for High School Readers of Graphic Novel Fiction

Directions: Please discuss the critical-reading lenses listed below. Under each lens, please explain the term and its meaning in your own words (you may either write or draw).

1. **Reader Response Lens:** Through this lens, you will pay particular attention to your own reaction to the text. What do you think about when you are reading? Why? Try to connect your thoughts to the elements of fiction. Why does a certain element make you think _____?

2. **Marxist Lens:** Similar to the Feminist lens, the Marxist lens asks you to think about the political and historical context the author is writing from. Specifically, Marxism seeks to foster questions about how texts are socially constructed. Who has power? Who does not? Why? Which social classes are represented? Which are not? Why? Essentially, you are to read through this lens with a mind for thinking about how society is constructed in the text and what the author is trying to say about society—during that time and place in history. When filling out the Literate Eye with a Marxist lens, you might ask yourself: "How do the elements of style reflect social construction for the characters?"

**3.** **Feminist Lens:** Just like the Marxist lens, the Feminist lens is also political and social in nature. The major emphasis for the Feminist lens, however, rests on power. The questions that guide the Feminist lens are: Who has power? Who does not? What is being said about gender? What is considered masculine? Feminine? Who has a voice? Who does not? Overall, what is being said about males and about females in this text? How do the elements of style illustrate this point?

**4.** **Cultural Lens:** When you look through the cultural lens, you will want to think about how different types of people and their histories and/or backgrounds are represented. Who is visible? Who is not? Does a certain group hold any sort of power? How so? Who makes up the majority? The minority? In the end, you are reading with an eye toward different cultural backgrounds and experiences, paying particular attention to issues of diversity in the text, and how the elements of style highlight or shun such issues.

# NONFICTION COLLABORATION STAIR-STEP

NAME: _____

READING ASSIGNMENT: _____
MIDDLE SCHOOL ELA

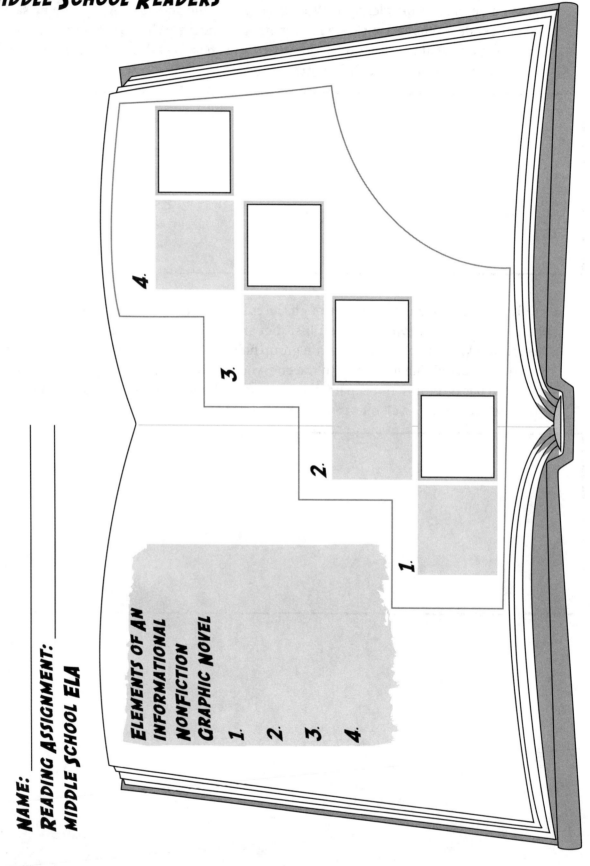

ELEMENTS OF AN
INFORMATIONAL
NONFICTION
GRAPHIC NOVEL

1.

2.

3.

4.

**A.** **Step 1: Identification.** For this reading strategy, you will first identify the elements of an informational nonfiction graphic novel. You will find a box for listing these elements on the front of your handout. They are: format, discoveries, and main idea.

- **Format:** Format relates to organization or sequencing of information. For example, are there chapter titles, subtitles, headings, subheadings, bold-faced words, lists, charts, figures, pictures, anecdotes, quotations, and so on?

- **Discoveries:** Discoveries relate to all of the interesting and/or fun facts, curious information, significant details, or new knowledge gained from reading the informational nonfiction graphic novel.

- **Main Idea:** The main idea is the key piece (or pieces) of information the creator is trying to convey.

**B.** **Step 2: Organization.** After identifying the elements of nonfiction in the box on the front side of the Nonfiction Collaboration Stair-Step, you can now start to organize these elements on the stairs.

Note: Above each stair, identify an element of the informational nonfiction graphic novel, in order.

**C.** **Step 3: Analyze.** Just like a graphic novel, this reading strategy asks you to next think in terms of words and images.

- Each stair is divided into two. On each stair, you are to put both the words and the images that help explain that element of nonfiction. On the left, you will write the words. On the right, you will draw the images.

- In short, you are to ask yourself: "What are the words that remind me of this element of nonfiction and, further, what are the images that remind me of this element of nonfiction?"

# APPENDIX J: NONFICTION COLLABORATION STAIR-STEP SUPPLEMENT (MIDDLE SCHOOL OR HIGH SCHOOL)

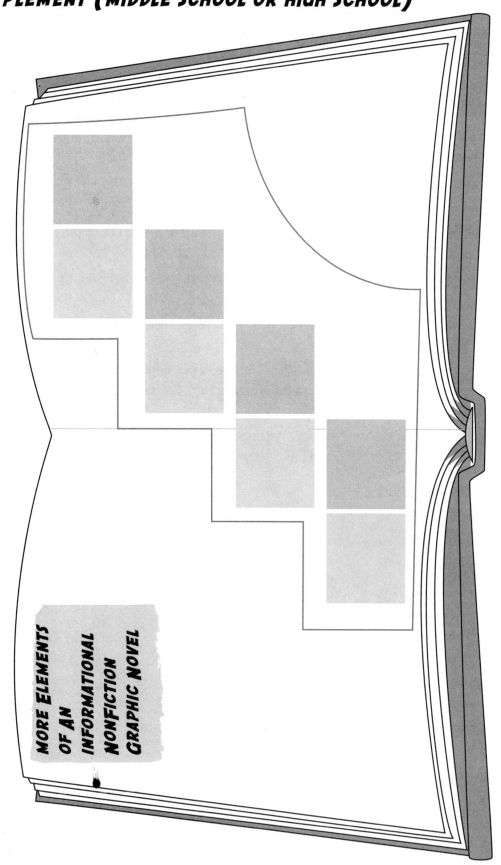

MORE ELEMENTS OF AN INFORMATIONAL NONFICTION GRAPHIC NOVEL

# APPENDIX K: NONFICTION COLLABORATION JOURNEY FOR MIDDLE SCHOOL READERS

## NONFICTION COLLABORATION JOURNEY

NAME: _____

READING ASSIGNMENT: _____

MIDDLE SCHOOL ELA

### ELEMENTS OF A CREATIVE NONFICTION GRAPHIC NOVEL

1.

2.

3.

4.

1.

2.

3.

4.

**A.** **Step 1: Identification.** You will first identify the elements of a creative nonfiction graphic novel. A box for listing these is on the front of your handout. They are:

- **Element of Historical Fact:** Historical fact is the information in the graphic novel that is accurate and factual. The element of historical fact can be broken down into the following identifying categories:

*1)* Factual event: historically accurate and known event

*2)* Factual people: historically real person/people

*3)* Factual time: historically accurate time period or moment in time

*4)* Factual place: historically accurate place or location

*5)* Factual artifact: historically accurate, existent document or artifact

- **Element of Author Storytelling:** The author's storytelling is the creative technique(s) the author uses to help shape the story he or she wishes to tell about the nonfiction event, people, place, and/or time. Author storytelling can be broken down into the following identifying categories:

*1)* Creator's voice: The author's own voice/tone used to influence the story

*2)* Creator's style: How the words or images influence the story being told

*3)* Creator's device: A situation, person, place, event, or artifact the author creates for his or her own storytelling purposes

**B.** **Step 2: Application/Organization.** After identifying the elements of a creative nonfiction graphic novel and listing them in the box, you can now start to organize these elements. On each arrow, write the name of the identified element (the more specific—what type/category of historical element or author storytelling element—the better!).

**C.** **Step 3: Analyze.** Just like a graphic novel, this reading strategy then asks you to think in terms of words and images. Above and below each arrow, you will find a rectangle.

- The rectangles above the arrow should be filled out with words that represent that element and category of the graphic novel. **Try asking yourself: "Which words in this creative nonfiction graphic novel remind me of this element and category?"**
- The rectangle below the arrow should be filled out with illustrations that represent that element and category of the creative nonfiction graphic novel. **Try asking yourself: "Which images in this graphic novel remind me of this element and category?"**

### A Writing Activity

Choosing a character from the graphic novel, retell the story through that character's perspective. You will need to base your ideas in historical truth and in creative storytelling; in other words, you will need to demonstrate an understanding of how to tell a story using both creative storytelling techniques and factual information. For this writing assignment, you will be working with both of the elements of a creative nonfiction graphic novel . This time, however, you will not be reading the text but instead writing the text.

# APPENDIX L: NONFICTION COLLABORATION JOURNEY SUPPLEMENT (MIDDLE SCHOOL OR HIGH SCHOOL)

## NONFICTION COLLABORATION JOURNEY

NAME: _____

READING ASSIGNMENT: _____

### ELEMENTS OF A NONFICTION GRAPHIC NOVEL

# APPENDIX M: NONFICTION COLLABORATION STAIR-STEP FOR HIGH SCHOOL READERS

You will complete three steps in order to fill out the Nonfiction Collaboration Stair-Step:

**1.** You will identify and pull out the elements of nonfiction from the informational nonfiction graphic novel and write each of these elements in the identification box labeled "elements."

**2.** Next, you will need to place the elements on the stairs, appropriately, in order of their appearance. Lines are provided above each stair.

**3.** Finally, just like a graphic novel, this reading strategy asks you to next think in terms of words and images. Each stair is divided into two. On each stair, you are to put both the words and the images that help explain that element of nonfiction. On the left, you will write the words. On the right, you will draw the images.

NAME: _____

READING ASSIGNMENT: _____

HIGH SCHOOL ELA

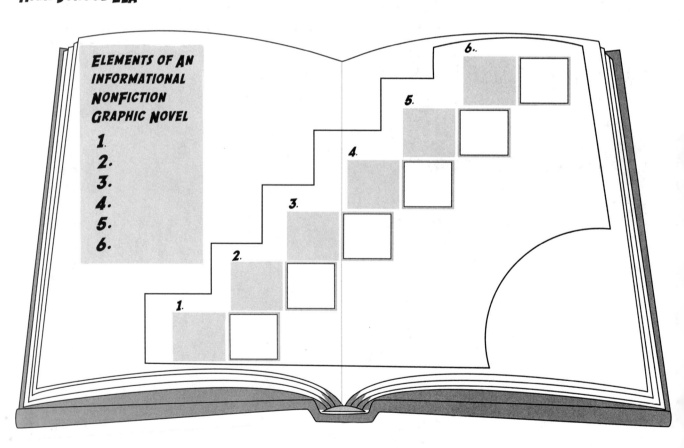

Directions: Working in small groups, please use the resources around the room to initially come up with definitions for each of the informational nonfiction graphic novel elements. When you are done doing this, we will discuss these definitions as a class.

- **FORMAT:**

- **DISCOVERIES:**

- **STYLE:**

- **TONE:**

- **MAIN IDEA:**

- **VALIDITY:**

For this writing assignment, you will write a research-based, informational or expository essay. Your topic will be the same topic found in our informational nonfiction graphic novel (topic: _____). When you write your essay, you will need to consider three sources of information. They are:

**1.** The topic of the informational nonfiction graphic novel
**2.** Your own experiences/feelings about this topic
**3.** Research you find on this topic

With these three topics in mind, your essay will then be organized as follows:

**A)** Introduction to topic: Develop an engaging highlight of everything your essay will discuss
**B)** Information about the informational nonfiction graphic novel
**C)** Information about your own experiences/feelings on this topic
**D)** Information you have researched on this topic
**E)** Conclusion: Find a way to bring all three areas of information together and close your thoughts for the reader, who has now learned about the graphic novel, you, and the research you found.*

*Note: Your essay does NOT have to follow this format. This is only an example.

# APPENDIX N: NONFICTION COLLABORATION JOURNEY FOR HIGH SCHOOL READERS

## NONFICTION COLLABORATION JOURNEY

NAME: _____

READING ASSIGNMENT: _____

HIGH SCHOOL ELA

### ELEMENTS OF A CREATIVE NONFICTION GRAPHIC NOVEL

1.

2.

3.

4.

1.

2.

3.

4.

**Step 1: Identification.** For this reading strategy, you will first need to identify the elements of a creative nonfiction graphic novel. You will find a box for listing these elements on the front of your handout. There are two main elements found in a creative nonfiction graphic novel:

- **The Element of Historical Fact:** Historical fact is the information in the graphic novel that is accurate and factual. The elements of historical fact fall into the following categories:

  **1)** Factual event: historically accurate and known event

  **2)** Factual people: historically real person/people

  **3)** Factual time: historically accurate time period or moment in time

  **4)** Factual place: historically accurate place or location

  **5)** Factual artifact: historically accurate, existent document or artifact

- **The Element of Author Storytelling:** The author's storytelling is the creative technique(s) the author uses to help shape the story he or she wishes to tell about the nonfiction event, people, place, and/or time. The elements of author storytelling fall into the following categories:

  **1)** Creator's voice: The author's own voice/tone is used to influence the story

  **2)** Creator's style: How the words or images influence the story being told

  **3)** Creator's device: A situation, person, place, event, or artifact the author creates for his or her own storytelling purposes.

**Step 2: Application/Organization.** After identifying the elements of a creative nonfiction graphic novel and listing them on the front of the handout (in the elements box), you can now start to organize those elements. On each arrow, and in order of their appearance, write the name of the identified elements (the more specific the category—historical fact element or author element—the better!).

**Step 3: Analyze.** Just like a graphic novel, this reading strategy then asks you to think in terms of words and images. Above and below each arrow you will find a rectangle:

- The rectangles above the arrow should be filled out with words that represent that element and category of the creative nonfiction graphic novel.

- The rectangles below the arrow should be filled out with your own drawings/images that you feel best represent that element and category.

- In order to help fill out each of the rectangles, try asking yourself: "What are the words in this creative nonfiction graphic novel that remind me of this element and category, and, further, what are the images that remind me of this element and category?"

**Step 4: Reflection.** After you have identified, organized, and analyzed the elements and categories of a creative nonfiction graphic novel, you will next need to reflect on your reasons for choosing each element and category. In short, you will need to write explanations for your choices in paragraph form.

- Try asking yourself: "Given the definitions for each element and category, what made me select this element and category? Why did I choose these words or these images to represent this element and category?"

- Please write these paragraph reflections on your own paper and staple your paper to your Nonfiction Collaboration Journey handout when you turn it in.

**Pre-writing and Persuasive Writing for Creative Nonfiction Graphic Novels in High School**

*1.* **Step 1: Research.** First, you need to engage in some research on our nonfiction topic. After you research the topic and consult your own reflection paragraphs, decide whether or not you agree with the author's interpretation of the events, places, people, and/or times. Decide whether you think the author did one of three things:

 *A)* Used his or her storytelling to stray too far away from the truth

 *B)* Used an appropriate balance of fact and storytelling

 *C)* Used too much fact and not enough storytelling

*2.* **Step 2: Persuasive Writing.** Once you have performed your research and know how you personally feel about the author's use of the elements of a creative nonfiction graphic novel, your job is to write a persuasive essay that influences the reader to agree with your opinion.

*3.* **Step 3: Organization.** Here are some thoughts on how to possibly organize your essay:

 *A)* Introduction: name of creative nonfiction graphic novel, summary of its contents, and your stance on the author's use of the elements

 *B)* Body paragraph 1: first reason for your stance and examples

 *C)* Body paragraph 2: second reason for your stance and examples

 *D)* Body paragraph 3: third reason for your stance and examples

 *E)* Body paragraphs: continue with list of reasons—however many you think are necessary

 *F)* Conclusion: summarize your points and find an engaging way to reflect on your entire essay (perhaps with a quotation, a new thought, a question, etc.)

# APPENDIX O: NONFICTION GRAPHIC NOVEL REFERENCE LIST FOR MIDDLE SCHOOL AND HIGH SCHOOL ELA

## Informational Nonfiction Graphic Novels for Middle School

Adamson, H. (2006). *The Challenger explosion*. Mankato, MN: Capstone.

Adamson, T.K. (2007). *The first moon landing*. Mankato, MN: Capstone.

Anderson, J. (2007). *Amelia Earhart: Legendary aviator*. Mankato, MN: Capstone.

Braun, E. (2006). *Booker T. Washington: Great American educator*. Mankato, MN: Capstone.

Braun, E. (2006). *Cesar Chavez: Fighting for farmworkers*. Mankato, MN: Capstone.

Braun, E. (2006). *The story of Jamestown*. Mankato, MN: Capstone.

Burgan, M. (2005). *The curse of King Tut's tomb*. Mankato, MN: Capstone.

Burgan, M. (2006). *The battle of Gettysburg*. Mankato, MN: Capstone.

Burgan, M. (2006). *The Boston massacre*. Mankato, MN: Capstone.

Burgan, M. (2006). *Nat Turner's slave rebellion*. Mankato, MN: Capstone.

Burgan, M. (2007). *The creation of the U.S. Constitution*. Mankato, MN: Capstone.

Butzer, C.M. (2008). *Gettysburg: The Graphic Novel*. New York, NY: Bowen Press.

Doeden, M. (2005). *The battle of the Alamo*. Mankato, MN: Capstone.

Doeden, M. (2005). *The Boston tea party*. Mankato, MN: Capstone.

Doeden, M. (2005). *The sinking of the Titanic*. Mankato, MN: Capstone.

Doeden, M. (2006). *George Washington: Leading a new nation*. Mankato, MN: Capstone.

Doeden, M. (2006). *John Sutter and the California gold rush*. Mankato, MN: Capstone.

Doeden, M. (2006). *The Hindenburg disaster*. Mankato, MN: Capstone.

Doeden, M. (2006). *Thomas Jefferson: Great American*. Mankato, MN: Capstone.

Doeden, M. (2006). *Winter at Valley Forge*. Mankato, MN: Capstone.

Doeden, M. (2007). *Samuel Adams: Patriot and statesman*. Mankato, MN: Capstone.

Enger, L. (2006). *Wilma Rudolph: Olympic track star*. Mankato, MN: Capstone.

Englar, M. (2007). *The pilgrims and the first Thanksgiving*. Mankato, MN: Capstone.

Fandel, J. (2007). *Alexander Graham Bell and the telephone*. Mankato, MN: Capstone.

Fandel, J. (2007). *Martin Luther King, Jr.: Great civil rights leader*. Mankato, MN: Capstone.

Geary, R. (2005). *The murder of Abraham Lincoln*. New York, NY: ComicsLit.

Glaser, J. (2006). *Buffalo soldiers and the American west*. Mankato, MN: Capstone.

Glaser, J. (2006). *Jackie Robinson: Baseball's great pioneer*. Mankato, MN: Capstone.

Glaser, J. (2006). *John Brown's raid on Harpers Ferry*. Mankato, MN: Capstone.

Glaser, J. (2006). *Molly Pitcher: Young American patriot*. Mankato, MN: Capstone.

Glaser, J. (2006). *Patrick Henry: Liberty or death*. Mankato, MN: Capstone.

Gunderson, J. (2006). *The triangle shirtwaist factory fire*. Mankato, MN: Capstone.

Gunderson, J. (2006). *Young riders of the Pony Express*. Mankato, MN: Capstone.

Gunderson, J. (2007). *The Lewis and Clark expedition*. Mankato, MN: Capstone.

Gunderson, J. (2007). *Sacagawea: Journey into the west*. Mankato, MN: Capstone.

Hoena, B.A. (2006). *Matthew Henson: Arctic adventurer*. Mankato, MN: Capstone.

Hoena, B.A. (2006). *Shackleton and the Lost Antarctic expedition*. Mankato, MN: Capstone.

Jacobson, R. (2006). *Eleanor Roosevelt: First lady of the world*. Mankato, MN: Capstone.

Jacobson, R. (2006). *The story of the star-spangled banner*. Mankato, MN: Capstone.

Jacobson, R. (2007). *William Penn: Founder of Pennsylvania*. Mankato, MN: Capstone.

Krohn, K.E. (2006). *Jane Goodall: Animal scientist*. Mankato, MN: Capstone.

Krohn, K.E. (2007). *Jonas Salk and the polio vaccine*. Mankato, MN: Capstone.

Krohn, K.E. (2007). *Madam C.J. Walker and new cosmetics*. Mankato, MN: Capstone.

Lassieur, A. (2006). *Clara Barton: Angel of the battlefield*. Mankato, MN: Capstone.

Lassieur, A. (2006). *Lords of the sea: The Vikings explore the north Atlantic*. Mankato, MN: Capstone.

Lassieur, A. (2006). *The voyage of the Mayflower*. Mankato, MN: Capstone.

Lemke, D.B. (2006). *The Apollo 13 mission*. Mankato, MN: Capstone.

Lemke, D.B. (2006). *The brave escape of Ellen and William Craft*. Mankato, MN: Capstone.

Lemke, D.B. (2006). *Steve Jobs, Steve Wozniak, and the personal computer*. Mankato, MN: Capstone.

Martin, M. (2005). *Harriet Tubman and the underground railroad*. Mankato, MN: Capstone.

Martin, M. (2005). *The Salem witch trials*. Mankato, MN: Capstone.

Miller, C.C. (2006). *Elizabeth Cady Stanton: Women's rights*. Mankato, MN: Capstone.

Miller, C.C. (2007). *Marie Curie and radioactivity*. Mankato, MN: Capstone.

Miller, C.C. (2007). *Mother Jones: Labor leader*. Mankato, MN: Capstone.

Miller, C.C. (2007). *Rosa Parks and the Montgomery bus boycott*. Mankato, MN: Capstone.

Niz, E.S. (2007). *Philo Farnsworth and the television*. Mankato, MN: Capstone.

Niz, X. (2006). *The story of the Statue of Liberty*. Mankato, MN: Capstone.

Niz, X. (2007). *The mystery of the Roanoke colony*. Mankato, MN: Capstone.

Niz, X. (2007). *Paul Revere's ride*. Mankato, MN: Capstone.

O'Hearn, M. (2007). *Henry Ford and the model T*. Mankato, MN: Capstone.

O'Hearn, M. (2007). *Jake Burton Carpenter and the snowboard*. Mankato, MN: Capstone.

Olson, K.M. (2005). *The Assassination of Abraham Lincoln*. Mankato, MN: Capstone.

Olson, K.M. (2006). *Betsy Ross and the American flag*. Mankato, MN: Capstone.

Olson, K.M. (2006). *The great Chicago fire of 1871*. Mankato, MN: Capstone.

Olson, K.M. (2007). *Johann Gutenberg and the printing press*. Mankato, MN: Capstone.

Olson, N. (2006). *George Washington Carver: Ingenious inventor*. Mankato, MN: Capstone.

Olson, N. (2007). *The Building of the Transcontinental railroad*. Mankato, MN: Capstone.

Olson, N. (2007). *Levi Strauss and blue jeans*. Mankato, MN: Capstone.

Olson, N. (2007). *Nathan Hale: Revolutionary spy*. Mankato, MN: Capstone.

Ottaviani, J., Cannon, Z., & Cannon, K. (2009). *T-Minus: The race to the moon*. Bel Air, CA: Aladdin.

Ottaviani, J., Badger, M., Barr, D., & Bieri, S. (2001). *Two fisted science: Stories about scientists*. Ann Arbor, MI: G.T. Labs.

Robbins, T. (2007). *Elizabeth Blackwell: America's first woman doctor*. Mankato, MN: Capstone.

Robbins, T. (2007). *Hedy Lamarr and a secret communication system*. Mankato, MN: Capstone.

Rosinsky, N. (2009). *Write your own graphic novel*. Mankato, MN: Capstone.

Smalley, R. (2005). *The adventures of Marco Polo*. Mankato, MN: Capstone.

Smalley, R. (2006). *Dolley Madison saves history*. Mankato, MN: Capstone.

Sutcliffe, J. (2006). *The Attack on Pearl Harbor*. Mankato, MN: Capstone.

Welvaert, S. (2006). *The Donner party*. Mankato, MN: Capstone.

Welvaert, S. (2006). *Helen Keller: Courageous advocate*. Mankato, MN: Capstone.

Welvaert. S. (2007). *Thomas Edison and the lightbulb*. Mankato, MN: Capstone.

## Creative Nonfiction Graphic Novels for Middle School

Abadzis, N. (2007). *Laika*. New York, NY: First Second Books.

The American Red Cross. (2002). *9-11: Emergency relief*. Gainesville, FL: Alternative Comics.

Crowley, M., & Goldman, D. (2009). *08: A graphic diary of the campaign trail*. New York, NY: Three Rivers Press.

## Informational Nonfiction Graphic Novels for High School

Buhle, P. (Ed.). *The beats: A graphic history*. New York, NY: Hill and Wang.

Crowley, M., & Goldman, D. (2009). *08: A graphic diary of the campaign trail*. New York, NY: Three Rivers Press.

Geary, R. (2008). *J. Edgar Hoover: A graphic biography*. New York, NY: Hill and Wang.

Gonick, L. (1978). *Cartoon history of the universe: Volumes 1—6*. New York, NY: Collins.

Gonick, L. (1987). *Cartoon history of the universe: Is everything sacred*. New York, NY: Collins.

Gonick, L. (1988). *The cartoon guide to U.S. history: 1865—now*. New York, NY: Collins.

Gonick, L. (1991). *The cartoon guide to the computer*. New York, NY: Collins.

Gonick, L. (1991). *The cartoon guide to genetics*. New York, NY: Collins.

Gonick, L. (1991). *The cartoon guide to physics*. New York, NY: Collins.

Gonick, L. (1991). *The cartoon history of the universe: Volumes 1—7*. New York, NY: Collins.

Gonick, L. (1993). *The cartoon guide to statistics*. New York, NY: Collins.

Gonick, L. (1996). *The cartoon guide to the environment*. New York, NY: Collins.

Gonick, L. (2005). *The cartoon chemistry*. New York, NY: Collins.

Gonick, L. (2006). *The cartoon history of the modern world part 1: From Columbus to the U.S. Constitution*. New York, NY: Collins.

Gonick, L. (2009). *The cartoon history of the modern world, part 2: Bastille to Baghdad*. New York, NY: Collins.

Helfer, A., & DuBurke, R., Staton, J. (2006). *Malcolm X: A graphic biography*. New York, NY: Hill and Wang.

Helfer, A., & Buccellato, S. (2007). *Ronald Reagan: A graphic biography*. New York, NY: Hill and Wang.

Jacobson, S., & Colón, E. (2006). *The 9/11 report: A graphic adaptation*. New York, NY: Hill and Wang.

Jacobson, S., & Colón, E. (2008). *After 9/11: America's War on Terror*. New York, NY: Hill and Wang.

McCloud, S. (1994). *Understanding comics*. New York, NY: HarperCollins.

McCloud, S. (2000). *Reinventing comics*. New York, NY: HarperCollins.

McCloud, S. (2006). *Making comics*. New York, NY: HarperCollins.

Ottaviani, J. (2003). *Dignifying science: Stories of women scientists*. Ann Arbor, MI: G.T. Labs.

Ottaviani, J., Et. Al. (2004). *Suspended in language: Neil Bohr's life, discoveries and the Century he shaped*. Ann Arbor, MI: G.T. Labs.

Ottaviani, J., Et. Al. (2005). *Bone sharps, cowboys, and thunder lizards: A tale of Edward Drinker Cope, Othniel Charles Marsh, and the Gilded Age of Paleontology*. Ann Arbor, MI: G.T. Labs.

Rodriquez, S., & Buhle, P. (2008). *Che: A graphic biography*. New York, NY: Verso.

Rudahl, S., Buhle, P. (2007). *Dangerous woman: The graphic biography of Emma Goldman*. New York, NY: New Press.

Sacco, J., & Hitchens, C. (2002). *Safe area gorazde: The war in Eastern Bosnia 1992 – 1995*. Seattle, WA: Fantagraphics.

Sacco, J. (2005). *War's end: Profiles from Bosnia 1995—1996*. Quebec, Canada: Drawn and Quarterly.

## Creative Nonfiction Graphic Novels for High School

Bechdel, A. (2006). *Fun home*. New York, NY: Houghton Mifflin.

Brown, C. (2002). *I never liked you*. Quebec, Canada: Drawn & Quarterly.

Cruse, H. (1995). *Stuck rubber baby*. New York, NY: Paradox.

David, B. (2006). *Epileptic*. New York, NY: Pantheon.

Delisle, G. (2006). *Shenzhen: A travelogue from China*. Quebec, Canada: Drawn & Quarterly.

Delisle, G. (2007). *Pyongyang: A journey in North Korea*. Quebec, Canada: Drawn & Quarterly.

Delisle, G. (2008). *The Burma chronicles*. Quebec, Canada: Drawn & Quarterly.

Fies, B. (2009). *Whatever Happened to the World of Tomorrow?* New York, NY: Abrams.

Guibert, E. (2008). *Alan's war: The memories of G.I. Alan Cope*. New York, NY: First Second Books.

Fleming, A.M. (2007). *The magical life of long tack sam*. New York, NY: Riverhead.

McGruder, A., Hudlin, R., Baker, K. (2005). *Birth of a nation*. New York, NY: Three Rivers Press.

Ottaviani, J. (2001). *Fallout*. Ann Arbor, MI: G.T. Labs.

Kubert, J. (1998). *Fax from Sarajevo*. New York, NY: Marvel.

Pekar, H. (2003). *American splendor*. New York: Ballantine Books.

Pekar, H., Buhle, P., & Dumm, G. (2008). *Students for a democratic society*. New York, NY: Hill and Wang.

Satrapi, M. (2003). *Persepolis: The story of a childhood*. New York, NY: Pantheon.

Satrapi, M. (2005). *Persepolis: The story of a return*. New York, NY: Pantheon.

Spiegelman, A. (1986). *Maus*. New York: Pantheon.

Spiegelman, A. (1991). *Maus II*. New York: Pantheon.

Spiegelman, A. (2004). *In the shadow of no towers*. New York, NY: Pantheon.

Tatsumi, Y. (2009). *A drifting life*. New York, NY: Hill and Wang.

Thompson, C. (2004). *Blankets*. Marietta, GA: Top Shelf.

Winick, J. (2000). *Pedro and me*. New York, NY: Henry Holt.

# APPENDIX P: "GRAPHIC NOVEL MEDIA AND ME: READING AND RESPONDING TO PRINT-TEXT LITERACIES AND IMAGE LITERACIES" MIDDLE SCHOOL ELA READING STRATEGY FOR TEACHING MEDIA LITERACY WITH GRAPHIC NOVELS

### Step 1: Media Literacy Construction and the Graphic Novel

Take a minute and think about what it means to build or construct something. What do you do when you build or construct something? Make a list in the space provided:

After thinking about what it means to build or construct something, review and discuss the following table, which centers on the connection between media literacy construction and graphic novels.

Your teacher will give you supplemental handouts to support your work. These handouts build upon the terms used in graphic novel construction by explaining the different types of panels, gutters, and balloons listed in the table.

**Directions:** After you review the terminology and your supplemental handouts, find examples and types of graphic novel construction. Take your notes in the table.

| STEP 1: MEDIA LITERACY CONSTRUCTION AND GRAPHIC NOVEL TERMINOLOGY | EXPLANATIONS |
|---|---|
| **PANELS** | A graphic novel panel is a constructive characteristic that uses visual or implied boundaries, and the contents within those boundaries, to tell a piece of the story.<br><br>Find an example in the graphic novel:<br>Page # _____<br>Type: _____<br>Description: |
| **GUTTERS** | Graphic novel gutters are the spaces between a visual or implied panel. When moving through this space, from one panel to the next panel, readers come to some sort of understanding about the story being told.<br><br>Find an example in the graphic novel:<br><br>Page # _____<br>Type: _____<br>Description: |
| **BALLOONS** | Different types of graphic novel balloons use words, or print-text literacies, to progress the story.<br><br>Find an example in the graphic novel:<br><br>Page # _____<br>Type: _____<br>Description: |

Now that you have thought about graphic novel construction, talk to a friend about why you think the creator constructed the graphic novel the way he or she did. Take notes here:

## Step 2: Media Literacy Intention and the Graphic Novel

Meet with a friend and discuss what happens when you set a goal. Try asking yourselves the following questions. .

*1.* What are some of your goals? These could be goals for school, personal goals you have for yourself (with sports, music, videogames), and so on.

*2.* How do you intend to reach these goals? What steps might you take?

*3.* Graphic novel creators also have intentions or goals. Specifically, their intention is to tell you a story using print-text literacies and image literacies.

Think about the graphic novel you are now reading and then review your responses to graphic novel construction (step 1).

Again, write down the page number and description for the different types of panels, gutters, and balloons you found. But, this time, ask yourself *how* and *why* the graphic novel is constructed that way.

| STEP 2: MEDIA LITERACY INTENTION & GRAPHIC NOVEL TERMINOLOGY | EXPLANATIONS |
|---|---|
| **PANELS** | As we already know, panels are the visual or implied boundaries, and the contents within them, that tell a piece of the story. The way the creator uses or displays these panels reveals her intentions for communicating that story. In Chapter 1, we learned about the two different types of panels creators use: content panels and story panels.

Each of these panels reveals intention. If a creator uses a setting story panel, for instance, she is emphasizing where the story takes place. This is the intention of that specific panel.

**Can you find any examples in the graphic novel?**

Page # _____
Type: _____

How did the creator use this panel?

Why do you think the creator chose to use the panel this way? |

| STEP 2: MEDIA LITERACY INTENTION & GRAPHIC NOVEL TERMINOLOGY | EXPLANATIONS |
|---|---|
| **PANELS (CONT'D.)** | Page # _____<br>Type: _____<br><br>How did the creator use the panel?<br><br><br>Why do you think the creator chose to use the panel this way?<br><br><br><br>Page # _____<br>Type: _____<br>Description:<br><br><br><br><br><br>How did the creator use the panel?<br><br><br><br>Why do you think the creator choose to use the panel this way? |

| STEP 2: MEDIA LITERACY INTENTION & GRAPHIC NOVEL TERMINOLOGY | EXPLANATIONS |
|---|---|
| **GUTTERS** | Gutters are the spaces between panels. Here, in the limbo of the gutter, the reader's imagination takes over and links panels together.<br><br>The six different types of gutters we previously discussed are: moment-to-moment, action-to-action, subject-to-subject, scene-to-scene, aspect-to-aspect, and non-sequitur. The type of gutter the creator of a graphic novel chooses reveals her intention for that piece of the story.<br><br>**Can you find any examples in the graphic novel?**<br><br>Page # _____<br>Type: _____<br><br>How did the creator use the gutter?<br><br><br><br>Why do you think the creator chose to use the gutter this way? |

| STEP 2: MEDIA LITERACY INTENTION & GRAPHIC NOVEL TERMINOLOGY | EXPLANATIONS |
|---|---|
| **GUTTERS (CONT'D.)** | Page # _____<br>Type: _____<br><br>How did the creator use this gutter?<br><br><br><br><br><br><br>Why do you think the creator chose to use the gutter this way?<br><br><br><br><br><br><br><br><br>Page # _____<br>Type: _____<br><br>How did the creator use this gutter?<br><br><br><br><br><br><br>Why do you think the creator chose to use the gutter this way? |

| STEP 2: MEDIA LITERACY INTENTION & GRAPHIC NOVEL TERMINOLOGY | EXPLANATIONS |
|---|---|
| **BALLOONS** | Balloons are also critical to graphic novel reading. Balloons not only allow creators to contextualize their story, but also to set tone. The five different balloons we discussed are: story balloon, thought balloon, dialogue balloon, sound effect balloon, and balloon-less words.<br><br>If a graphic novel creator decides to use a dialogue balloon, the intention is to give voice and personality to the characters in the story.<br><br>**Can you find any examples in the graphic novel?**<br><br>Page # _____<br>Type: _____<br><br>How did the creator use this balloon?<br><br><br><br><br><br>Why do you think the creator chose to use the balloon this way? |

| STEP 2: MEDIA LITERACY INTENTION & GRAPHIC NOVEL TERMINOLOGY | EXPLANATIONS |
|---|---|
| **BALLOONS (CONT'D.)** | Page # _____<br>Type: _____<br><br>How did the creator use this balloon?<br><br><br><br>Why do you think the creator chose to use the balloon this way?<br><br><br><br><br><br>Page # _____<br>Type: _____<br>Description:<br><br><br><br>How did the creator use the balloon?<br><br><br><br>Why do you think the creator choose to use the balloon this way? |

## Step 3: Media Literacy Analysis and the Graphic Novel

For step 3, your teacher will provide you with another supplemental handout.

**Directions:** As a class, read through the different types of critical-reading partnerships and, in the far left column, find the best examples from your graphic novel reading assignments (pages: _____).

After working together as a class, meet in small groups to discuss answers to the five media analysis questions.

Note: Step 3 is focused on your own analysis of the graphic novel.

| STEP 3: MEDIA LITERACY ANALYSIS AND GRAPHIC NOVEL TERMINOLOGY | FIVE QUESTIONS FOR MEDIA LITERACY ANALYSIS |
| --- | --- |
| **Compare and/or Contrast Partnership:**<br><br>A partnership between images, words, or images and words that asks the reader to compare and/or contrast what he or she is reading.<br><br>**Example:** Apple image + "New York" = New York, the Big Apple (compare) or apple image + "orange" = comparing apples and oranges (contrast)<br><br>As a class, identify an example from the graphic novel you are reading:<br><br>Page #:<br><br>Description: This is a compare and/or contrast partnership because... | *1.* Who is sending the message and what is the author's purpose?<br><br>*2.* What techniques are used to attract and hold attention?<br><br>*3.* What lifestyles, values, and points of view are represented in this message?<br><br>*4.* How might people interpret this message differently?<br><br>*5.* What is omitted from this message? |

| STEP 3: MEDIA LITERACY ANALYSIS AND GRAPHIC NOVEL TERMINOLOGY | FIVE QUESTIONS FOR MEDIA LITERACY ANALYSIS |
| --- | --- |
| **Reference Partnership:** A partnership between words, images, or images and words that asks the reader to activate his or her own schema or background knowledge.<br><br>**Example:** Apple image + "temptation" = Adam and Eve in the Garden of Eden<br><br>As a class, identify an example from the graphic novel you are reading:<br><br>Page #:<br><br>Description: This is a reference partnership because…. | *1.* Who is sending the message and what is the author's purpose?<br><br>*2.* What techniques are used to attract and hold attention?<br><br>*3.* What lifestyles, values, and points of view are represented in this message?<br><br>*4.* How might people interpret this message differently?<br><br>*5.* What is omitted from this message? |

| STEP 3: MEDIA LITERACY ANALYSIS AND GRAPHIC NOVEL TERMINOLOGY | FIVE QUESTIONS FOR MEDIA LITERACY ANALYSIS |
|---|---|
| **Story-Extension Partnership:** A partnership of words, images, or images and words that progresses the story and moves it forward. | *1.* Who is sending the message and what is the author's purpose? |
| **Example:** Falling apple image + passing of time and motion = over time, the apple is falling. The story is moving forward. The reader is wondering what will happen and where the apple might land; specifically, in terms of elements of story, this partnership extends the story's plot. | *2.* What techniques are used to attract and hold attention? |
| As a class, identify an example from the graphic novel you are reading: | *3.* What lifestyles, values, and points of view are represented in this message? |
| Page #: | |
| Description: This is a story-extension partnership because... | *4.* How might people interpret this message differently? |
| | *5.* What is omitted from this message? |

| STEP 3: MEDIA LITERACY ANALYSIS AND GRAPHIC NOVEL TERMINOLOGY | FIVE QUESTIONS FOR MEDIA LITERACY ANALYSIS |
|---|---|
| **Potential Partnerships:** What other partnerships can you find that exist between words, between images, and/or between images and words together?<br><br>*1.* _____<br><br>Page #:<br><br>This is a _____ partnership because...<br><br><br><br>*2.* _____<br><br>Page #:<br><br>This is a _____ partnership because...<br><br><br><br>*3.* _____<br><br>Page #:<br><br>This is a _____ partnership because... | *1.* Who is sending the message and what is the author's purpose?<br><br><br><br>*2.* What techniques are used to attract and hold attention?<br><br><br><br>*3.* What lifestyles, values, and points of view are represented in this message?<br><br><br><br>*4.* How might people interpret this message differently?<br><br><br><br>*5.* What is omitted from this message? |

# APPENDIX Q: "AND THE MEANING IS..." MIDDLE SCHOOL ELA READING STRATEGY FOR TEACHING MEDIA LITERACY WITH GRAPHIC NOVELS

## READING STRATEGY: AND THE MEANING IS. . .

**Part I:** In the blank spaces below, brainstorm what you think it means to read with both print-text literacies (words) and image literacies (pictures) together.

**Part II:** What steps do you take, in your mind, to understand a story that uses both print-text literacies and image literacies? Discuss your thoughts in the space below.

**Part III:** Can you think of any other reading experiences that use print-text literacies and image literacies together? List them below.

1.

2.

3.

4.

5.

Now that you have thought about reading both print-text literacies and image literacies together, please look at the graphic novel we will be reading. On the back of this handout, write your first impressions of this graphic novel.

# APPENDIX R: "BUILD IT!" READING STRATEGY FOR MIDDLE SCHOOL ELA

"Build It!" asks you to reflect upon what you now know about graphic novels in terms of construction, intention, and analysis and, bringing this knowledge together, visualize a building.

The building you visualize will have three floors. These three floors will support your understanding of the three steps of media literacy and graphic novels:
- 1st floor: construction department
- 2nd floor: intention department
- 3rd floor: analysis department

You will need to first name the building; the building name should be the author's last name, the title of the graphic novel, and the word "Building." For instance, if you are reading Aaron Renier's *Spiral-Bound*, you will name the building "Renier's Spiral-Bound Building."

Next, label each floor according to the steps of media literacy (blank spaces provided above the elevator image on each floor). The first floor will be labeled "1st Floor: Construction." The second floor will be labeled "2nd Floor: Intentions," and the third floor will be labeled "3rd Floor: Analysis."

On the bottom of this handout, note a word bank that includes: *Construction, Intentions, Analysis, Panels, Gutters, Balloons,* and *Critical-reading Partnerships*. Besides labeling the three floors, you will need to place these terms in the appropriate nameplates that appear outside of each office (some words will be used more than once).

On the first floor, for example, pull out the term "Construction" and write it on the blank line below the elevator labeled "1st Floor: _____." Next, pull out the word "Panel" and place it on one of the office nameplates. Within the space for that particular office, once again explain how the panels you referred to in "Graphic Novel Media and Me" were used. For each floor and office, follow this process. You will probably need your completed reading strategy handouts (and supplemental material) to complete "Build It!"

# Appendix R: "Build It!" Reading Strategy for Middle School ELA (Cont'd.)

BUILDING NAME _____

3RD FLOOR

OFFICE

OFFICE

OFFICE

2ND FLOOR

OFFICE

OFFICE

OFFICE

1ST FLOOR

OFFICE

OFFICE

OFFICE

## WORD BANK

INTENTIONS
PANELS
CRITICAL-READING PARTNERSHIPS
GUTTERS

BALLOONS
ANALYSIS
CONSTRUCTION

## THE THREE STEPS OF MEDIA LITERACY

### STEP 1: CONSTRUCTION

### STEP 2: INTENTIONS

### STEP 3: ANALYSIS

# APPENDIX S: "GRAPHIC NOVEL MEDIA AND ME: READING AND RESPONDING TO PRINT AND IMAGE LITERACIES" READING STRATEGY IN HIGH SCHOOL ELA

## Graphic Novel Media and Me:
### Reading and Responding to Print-Text Literacies and Image Literacies

### Step 1: Construction

Take a minute and think about your self-descriptive word and illustration choices. Each of your choices demonstrates an awareness of construction. Your choices, in other words, helped you to convey an idea. Explain those choices below.

## WORD CHOICE:

## ILLUSTRATION CHOICE:

**\*\*\* Stop and discuss your ideas with a friend, and then with the class. \*\*\***

After thinking about your own construction choices, review the terminology used to construct graphic novels: panels, gutters, and word balloons.

To support your understanding of graphic novel construction, your teacher will also give you some supplemental handouts. These handouts will further discuss graphic novel construction by talking about the different types of panels, gutters, and word balloons.

After you are familiar with all of the terminology regarding graphic novel construction, read the following section of the graphic novel (Pages: _____ ) and work through the table found on the next page.

| STEP 1: MEDIA LITERACY CONSTRUCTION AND GRAPHIC NOVEL TERMINOLOGY | EXPLANATIONS |
|---|---|
| **PANELS** | A graphic novel panel is a constructive characteristic that uses visual or implied boundaries, and the contents within those boundaries, to tell a piece of the story.<br><br>Find an example in the graphic novel:<br>Page # _____<br>Type: _____<br>Description: |
| **GUTTERS** | Graphic novel gutters are the spaces between a visual or implied panel. When moving through this space, from one panel to the next panel, readers come to some sort of understanding about the story being told.<br><br>Find an example in the graphic novel:<br><br>Page # _____<br>Type: _____<br>Description: |
| **BALLOONS** | Different types of graphic novel balloons use words, or print-text literacies, to progress the story.<br><br>Find an example in the graphic novel:<br><br>Page # _____<br>Type: _____<br>Description: |

Review your answers and talk to a friend about the following question: What might the creator have intended with each construction choice? Take notes here:

Panel example, page _____:

Gutter example, page _____:

Balloon example, page _____:

## Step 2: Intention

In the spaces below and with a friend, discuss what happens when you set a goal.

**1.** Identify and list some of your goals. These could be goals for school, personal goals you have for yourself (with sports, music, videogames, and so on), goals for your future, goals for your friendships, etc.

- 
- 
- 
- 

**2.** How do you intend to reach these goals? What steps might you take?

- 
- 
- 
- 

**3.** Graphic novel creators also have intentions or goals. Their intention, or goal, is to tell you a story using words and images.

**Each panel, gutter, and word balloon has its own intention, its own purpose, goal, or plan for telling a piece of the story.**

Drawing upon what you now know about graphic novel construction, review the next table (focused on step 2 of media literacy and graphic novels) and think about intention.

You will need to reference your work on graphic novel construction (step 1) in order to answer these questions.

| STEP 2: MEDIA LITERACY INTENTION AND GRAPHIC NOVEL TERMINOLOGY | EXPLANATIONS |
|---|---|
| **PANELS** | As we already know, panels are the visual or implied boundaries, and the contents within them, that tell a piece of the story. The way the creator uses or displays these panels reveals her intentions for communicating that story. We learned about the two different types of panels creators use: content panels and story panels.<br><br>Each of these panels reveals intention. If a creator uses a setting story panel, for instance, she is emphasizing where the story takes place. This is the intention of that specific panel.<br><br>Can you find any examples in the graphic novel?<br><br>Page # _____<br>Type: _____<br><br>How did the creator use this panel?<br><br><br><br><br><br>Why do you think the creator chose to use the panel this way? |

| STEP 2: MEDIA LITERACY INTENTION AND GRAPHIC NOVEL TERMINOLOGY | EXPLANATIONS |
|---|---|
| **PANELS (CONT'D.)** | Page # _____<br>Type: _____<br><br>How did the creator use the panel?<br><br><br>Why do you think the creator chose to use the panel this way?<br><br><br><br>Page # _____<br>Type: _____<br>Description:<br><br><br><br>How did the creator use the panel?<br><br><br>Why do you think the creator choose to use the panel this way? |

| STEP 2: MEDIA LITERACY INTENTION AND GRAPHIC NOVEL TERMINOLOGY | EXPLANATIONS |
|---|---|
| **GUTTERS** | Gutters are the spaces between panels. Here, in the limbo of the gutter, the reader's imagination takes over and links panels together.<br><br>The six different types of gutters we previously discussed are: moment-to-moment, action-to-action, subject-to-subject, scene-to-scene, aspect-to-aspect, and non-sequitur. The type of gutter the creator of a graphic novel chooses reveals her intention for that piece of the story.<br><br>Can you find any examples in the graphic novel?<br><br>Page # _____<br>Type: _____<br><br>How did the creator use the gutter?<br><br><br><br><br><br><br>Why do you think the creator chose to use the gutter this way? |

| STEP 2: MEDIA LITERACY INTENTION AND GRAPHIC NOVEL TERMINOLOGY | EXPLANATIONS |
|---|---|
| **GUTTERS (CONT'D.)** | Page # _____<br>Type: _____<br><br>How did the creator use this gutter?<br><br><br><br>Why do you think the creator chose to use the gutter this way?<br><br><br><br><br><br>Page # _____<br>Type: _____<br>Description:<br><br><br><br>How did the creator use the gutter?<br><br><br><br>Why do you think the creator choose to use the gutter this way? |

| STEP 2: MEDIA LITERACY INTENTION AND GRAPHIC NOVEL TERMINOLOGY | EXPLANATIONS |
| --- | --- |
| **BALLOONS** | Balloons are also critical to graphic novel reading. Balloons not only allow creators to contextualize their story, but also to set tone. The five different balloons we discussed are: story balloon, thought balloon, dialogue balloon, sound effect balloon, and balloon-less words.<br><br>If a graphic novel creator decides to use a dialogue balloon, the intention is to give voice and personality to the characters in the story.<br><br>Can you find any examples in the graphic novel?<br><br>Page # _____<br>Type: _____<br><br>How did the creator use this balloon?<br><br><br><br><br><br><br><br>Why do you think the creator chose to use the balloon this way? |

| STEP 2: MEDIA LITERACY INTENTION AND GRAPHIC NOVEL TERMINOLOGY | EXPLANATIONS |
|---|---|
| **BALLOONS (CONT'D.)** | Page # _____<br>Type: _____<br><br>How did the creator use this balloon?<br><br><br><br><br>Why do you think the creator chose to use the balloon this way?<br><br><br><br><br><br>Page # _____<br>Type: _____<br><br>How did the creator use this balloon?<br><br><br><br><br>Why do you think the creator chose to use the balloon this way? |

## Step 3: Analysis

**Directions:** Building upon your knowledge of graphic novel construction and graphic novel intention, you are now ready to think about graphic novel analysis.

As a class, read through the different types of graphic novel critical-reading partnerships found in the table below. In the far left column identify the best examples of each from your graphic novel reading assignment (pages: _____).

Once you have found examples, work independently on the media literacy analysis questions. These questions ask you to think about your own individual response(s) to each critical-reading partnership.

| STEP 3: MEDIA LITERACY ANALYSIS AND GRAPHIC NOVEL TERMINOLOGY | FIVE QUESTIONS FOR MEDIA LITERACY ANALYSIS |
|---|---|
| **Compare and/or Contrast Partnership:** A partnership between images, words, or images and words that asks the reader to compare and/or contrast what he or she is reading. | **1.** Who is sending the message and what is the author's purpose? |
| **Example:** Apple image + "New York" = New York, the Big Apple (compare) or apple image + "orange" = comparing apples and oranges (contrast) | **2.** What techniques are used to attract and hold attention? |
| As a class, identify an example from the graphic novel you are reading: | **3.** What lifestyles, values, and points of view are represented in this message? |
| Page #: | |
| Description: This is a compare and/or contrast partnership because... | **4.** How might people interpret this message differently? |
| | **5.** What is omitted from this message? |

| STEP 3: MEDIA LITERACY ANALYSIS AND GRAPHIC NOVEL TERMINOLOGY | FIVE QUESTIONS FOR MEDIA LITERACY ANALYSIS |
|---|---|
| **Reference Partnership:** A partnership between words, images, or images and words that asks the reader to activate his or her own schema or background knowledge.<br><br>**Example:** Apple image + "temptation" = Adam and Eve in the Garden of Eden<br><br>As a class, identify an example from the graphic novel you are reading:<br><br>Page #:<br><br>Description: This is a reference partnership because…. | *1.* Who is sending the message and what is the author's purpose?<br><br><br>*2.* What techniques are used to attract and hold attention?<br><br><br>*3.* What lifestyles, values, and points of view are represented in this message?<br><br><br>*4.* How might people interpret this message differently?<br><br><br>*5.* What is omitted from this message? |

| STEP 3: MEDIA LITERACY ANALYSIS AND GRAPHIC NOVEL TERMINOLOGY | FIVE QUESTIONS FOR MEDIA LITERACY ANALYSIS |
|---|---|
| **Story-Extension Partnership:** A partnership of words, images, or images and words that progresses the story and moves it forward.<br><br>**Example:** Falling apple image + passing of time and motion = Over time, the apple is falling. The story is moving forward. The reader is wondering what will happen and where the apple might land; specifically, in terms of elements of story, this partnership extends the story's plot.<br><br>As a class, identify an example from the graphic novel you are reading:<br><br>Page #:<br><br>Description: This is a story-extension partnership because... | *1.* Who is sending the message and what is the author's purpose?<br><br><br>*2.* What techniques are used to attract and hold attention?<br><br><br>*3.* What lifestyles, values, and points of view are represented in this message?<br><br><br>*4.* How might people interpret this message differently?<br><br><br>*5.* What is omitted from this message? |

| STEP 3: MEDIA LITERACY ANALYSIS AND GRAPHIC NOVEL TERMINOLOGY | FIVE QUESTIONS FOR MEDIA LITERACY ANALYSIS |
|---|---|
| **Potential Partnerships:** What other partnerships can you find that exist between words, between images, and/ or between images and words together?<br><br>**1.** _____<br><br>Page #:<br><br>This is a _____ partnership because…<br><br>**2.** _____<br><br>Page #:<br><br>This is a _____ partnership because…<br><br>**3.** _____<br><br>Page #:<br><br>This is a _____ partnership because… | **1.** Who is sending the message and what is the author's purpose?<br><br>**2.** What techniques are used to attract and hold attention?<br><br>**3.** What lifestyles, values, and points of view are represented in this message?<br><br>**4.** How might people interpret this message differently?<br><br>**5.** What is omitted from this message? |

# APPENDIX T: "IF I COULD PLEASE RESPOND TO THIS GRAPHIC NOVEL…" READING STRATEGY AND WRITING ACTIVITY FOR HIGH SCHOOL LEVEL ELA

### "If I Could Please Respond to This Graphic Novel…" Reading Strategy and Writing Activity for High School ELA

**Directions:** To complete this reading strategy you will need to review your responses from "Graphic Novel Media and Me: Reading and Responding to Print-text Literacies and Image Literacies."

Just like your "Graphic Novel Media and Me" reading strategy, this reading strategy and writing activity is also divided into the three steps for integrating media literacy with graphic novels: construction, intention, and analysis.

### Step 1: Construction

For step 1, think about graphic novel construction and consult your "Graphic Novel Media and Me" handouts. Thinking about each term, finish the statement in bold.

## 1. "IF I COULD PLEASE RESPOND TO THE CONSTRUCTION OF THIS GRAPHIC NOVEL, I WOULD SAY THAT THE…"

### PANELS (FINISH STATEMENT IN THIS SPACE)…

Definition for graphic novel **panel** construction (in my own words):

Panels I am specifically **responding** to:

My response to these graphic novel panels and their construction is:

# GUTTERS *(FINISH STATEMENT IN THIS SPACE)...*

Definition for graphic novel gutter construction (in my own words):

Gutters I am specifically responding to:

My response to these graphic novel gutters and their construction is:

# BALLOONS *(FINISH STATEMENT IN THIS SPACE)...*

Definition for graphic novel balloon construction (in my own words):

Balloons I am specifically responding to:

My response to these graphic novel balloons and their construction is:

## Step 2: Intention

For step 2, think about graphic novel intention and once again consult your "Graphic Novel Media and Me" handouts.

## "IF I COULD PLEASE RESPOND TO THE INTENTION(S) OF THIS GRAPHIC NOVEL, I WOULD SAY THAT THE…."

### PANELS (FINISH STATEMENT IN THIS SPACE)…

Definition for graphic novel panel intention (in my own words):

Panels I am specifically responding to:

My response to these graphic novel panels and their intention is:

**GUTTERS** *(FINISH STATEMENT IN THIS SPACE)...*

Definition for graphic novel gutter intention (in my own words):

Gutters I am specifically responding to:

My response to these graphic novel gutters and their construction is:

**BALLOONS** *(FINISH STATEMENT IN THIS SPACE)...*

Definition(s) for graphic novel balloon intention (in my own words):

Balloons I am specifically responding to:

My response to these graphic novel balloons and their intention(s) is:

## Step 3: Analysis

For step 3, think about your responses to the five media analysis questions from your "Graphic Novel Media and Me" reading strategy. After referring back to your thoughts, make a list of the top three or four things you would like to ask/say to the graphic novel creator.

**1.**

**2.**

**3.**

**4.**

Finally, turn these thoughts and/or questions into a written letter addressed to the graphic novel creator. You can organize your letter in one of two ways.

**Letter Option #1 (by paragraphs):**
1. Introduction and main idea (thesis)
2. Discussion of graphic novel panels
3. Discussion of graphic novel gutters
4. Discussion of graphic novel word balloons
5. Closing thoughts

**Letter Option #2 (by paragraphs):**
1. Introduction and main idea (thesis)
2. Discussion of graphic novel construction
3. Discussion of graphic novel intention
4. Discussion of graphic novel analysis
5. Closing thoughts

Dear _____,

My class just read your graphic novel, _____. I am writing to you because I would like to share some of my thoughts about this graphic novel.

# APPENDIX U: "I WRITE IT!" WRITING ACTIVITY FOR TEACHING MIDDLE SCHOOL ELA MEDIA LITERACY WITH GRAPHIC NOVELS

## "I Write It!"

**Directions:** On the last page, you will find a blank graphic novel panel format, just like those you might have seen in the graphic novel. Please use this format to write a new ending to the graphic novel using both words and images. In the spaces below, answer the following questions about your new ending's construction, intention, and analysis.

Since you will be asked to explain your story in regards to what you now know about media literacy and graphic novels (construction, intention, and analysis), you might want to reference your completed reading strategies—"Graphic Novel Media and Me" and "Build It!"—and take writing notes in the margins.

### WHAT DID YOU USE TO CONSTRUCT THIS NEW ENDING IN TERMS OF WORDS AND IMAGES?

Words:

Images:

### WHAT DID YOU INTEND FOR THE READER OF THIS NEW ENDING TO LEARN OR THINK?

Words:

Images:

## IF YOU COULD ANALYZE YOUR OWN ENDING, WHAT MIGHT YOU SAY IN RESPONSE TO THE FIVE QUESTIONS OF MEDIA LITERACY ANALYSIS?

**1.** Who is sending the message and what is the author's purpose?

**2.** What techniques are used to attract and hold attention?

**3.** What lifestyles, values, and points of view are represented in this message?

**4.** How might different people interpret this message differently?

**5.** What is omitted from this message?

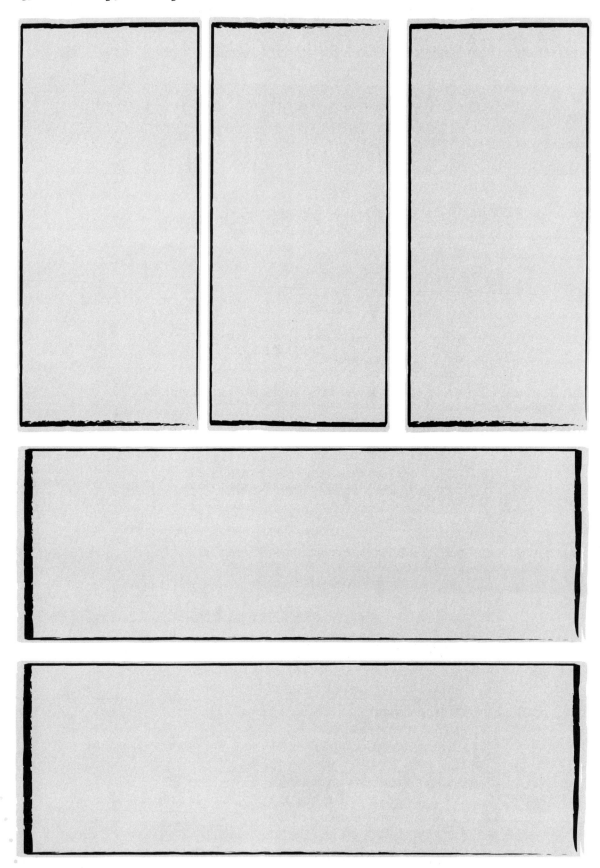

# APPENDIX V: FOUR STAGES OF LANGUAGE LEARNING, OBJECTIVES THAT SUPPORT THE USE OF GRAPHIC NOVELS AND COMICS AT EACH STAGE, AND RECOMMENDED GRAPHIC NOVELS AND COMICS

| FOUR STAGES OF LANGUAGE LEARNING | IN THIS LANGUAGE-LEARNING STAGE, STUDENTS SHOULD BE ABLE TO: |
|---|---|
| **STAGE 1: PRE-PRODUCTION** | • Match words and images<br>• Use a picture dictionary<br>• Use visual cue cards that indicate positive/negative responses<br>• Sequence using pictures<br><br>**Some suggested comics for Stage 1:**<br>• All comics produced by Toon Books<br>• Any picture book that places equal weight on print-text and image literacies |
| **STAGE 2: EARLY PRODUCTION** | • Continue work with the objectives from Stage 1<br>• Read texts that place equal emphasis on images and words<br>• Draw images and write dialogue<br><br>**Some suggested comics for Stage 2:**<br>• All comics published by Toon Books<br>• Steve Niles & Benjamin Roman's *The Cryptics*<br>• Ken Soo's *Jellaby* & *Jellaby Monster in the City*<br>• Scott Christian Sava's *My Grandparents Are Secret Agents*<br>• Mark Alan Stamaty's *Alia's Mission: Saving the Books of Iraq* (Stamaty's text is probably best used as a bridge from Stage 2 to Stage 3) |
| **STAGE 3: SPEECH EMERGENCE** | • Continue work with the objectives from Stages 1 and 2<br>• Discuss and identify the elements of story<br>• Compose short stories using the elements of story<br><br>**Suggested early reader graphic novels for Stage 3:**<br>• Lewis Trondheim and Eric Cartier's *Kaput & Zosky*<br>• Scott Christian Sava and Diego Jourdan's *Ed's Terrestrials*<br>• Frank Cammuso's *Knights of the Lunch Table: The Dodgeball Chronicles*<br>• Jimmy Gownley's *Amelia Rules! Superheroes* |
| **STAGE 4: INTERMEDIATE FLUENCY** | • Continue work with the objectives from Stages 1-3<br>• Participate in reader's theatre<br>• Write reader's theatre<br><br>**Suggested graphic novels for Stage 4:**<br>• Any graphic novel mentioned in *Teaching Graphic Novels*<br>• Jeff Smith's *Bone* series<br>• Barry Lyga's *Wolverine: Worst Day Ever*<br>• Brian Selznick's *The Invention of Hugo Cabaret* |

# APPENDIX W: KWL CHART FOR EMERGENT LANGUAGE LEARNERS

Topic: _____

Text: _____

| KNOW | WONDER | LEARN |
|------|--------|-------|
|      |        |       |

# APPENDIX X: ELEMENTS OF STORY AND STORY MAP ACTIVITY FOR TEACHING LANGUAGE-LEARNING STUDENTS ABOUT THE READING-WRITING CONNECTION (THIRD STAGE OF LANGUAGE-LEARNING DEVELOPMENT)

## The Elements of Story

Name: _____

Directions: As you complete a picture walk of this early reader graphic novel, please review the following vocabulary with your teacher. Space is provided for taking notes and listing examples from the story.

## 1. PLOT—THE EVENTS IN THE STORY; WHAT HAPPENS

- Please list words in English and in your native language that will help you remember **plot**:

- Examples:

## 2. CHARACTERS—PEOPLE IN THE STORY

- Please list words in English and in your native language that will help you remember **characters**:

- Examples:

## 3. SETTING-WHERE THE STORY TAKES PLACE

- Please list words in English and in your native language that will help you remember **setting**:

- Examples:

## 4. CONFLICT-THE PROBLEM IN THE STORY

- Please list words in English and in your native language that will help you remember **conflict**:

- Examples:

## 5. RISING ACTION-THE EVENTS IN THE STORY THAT INTENSIFY THE PROBLEM

- Please list words in English and in your native language that will help you remember **rising action**:

- Examples:

## 6. CLIMAX-THE CONFLICT AND RISING ACTION LEAD TO THE CLIMAX, THE FINAL AND GREATEST POINT OF TENSION

- Please list words in English and in your native language that will help you remember **climax**:

- Examples:

## 7. RESOLUTION-HOW THE CONFLICT/PROBLEM IS SOLVED

- Please list words in English and in your native language that will help you remember **resolution**:

- Examples:

**Direction 1:** Try reading the text on your own and filling in the blank story map below with the elements of story (feel free to consult your notes).

**Direction 2:** Below is another story map, but this story map is blank. Write your own story using a story map.

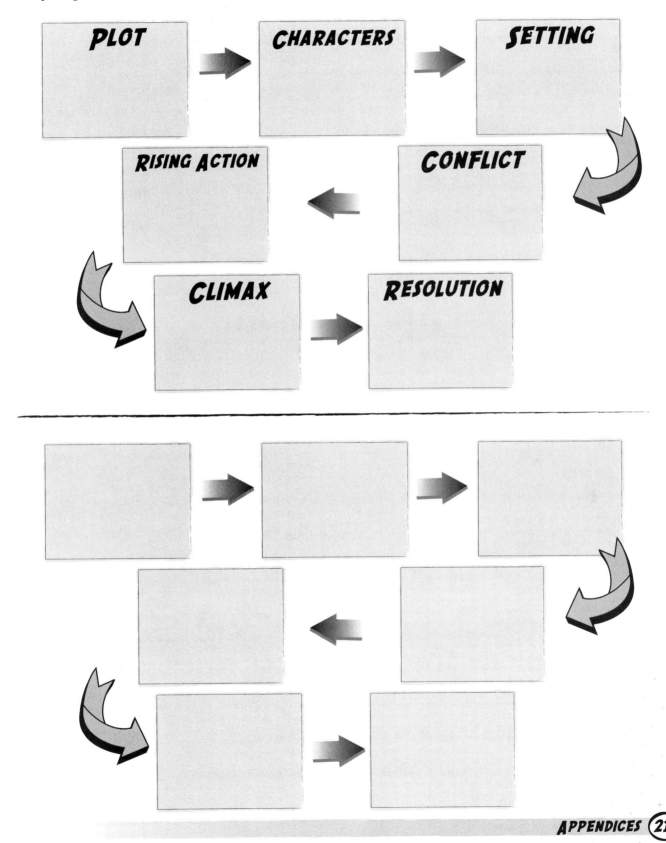

PLOT → CHARACTERS → SETTING

RISING ACTION ← CONFLICT

CLIMAX → RESOLUTION

# APPENDIX Y: READER'S THEATRE HANDOUT

## Reader's Theatre

Name: _____

## WHAT IS READER'S THEATRE?

Reader's theatre is a script written for students to read aloud in front of the class. When you read a reader's theatre, you get a chance to show off how well you know your new language!

So let's practice! Your teacher has a reader's theatre for the graphic novel you just read. Together, with your teacher and your class, read through this reader's theatre a few times.

Once you and your friends feel comfortable, your teacher will ask you to get into small groups. In these groups, everyone should take a reading role. When everyone has a role, practice reading the reader's theatre again.

After practicing with your group, let your teacher know when you are ready to read the reader's theatre in front of the class. Each group will take a turn reading in front of the class.

## WRITING A READER'S THEATRE

**1.** Now that you are an excellent reader of reader's theatre, let's try writing a reader's theatre!

**2.** You will write your reader's theatre about the following graphic novel:

_____.

**3.** Before you write your reader's theatre, read this graphic novel together as a class, perhaps a few times.

**4.** Next, divide into small groups and make a list of questions you have about the story. As a class, listen to and answer each other's questions. If you need to, take notes here:



**5.** Now you are ready to write your reader's theatre. On the back of this handout, in your small groups, write a reader's theatre for this graphic novel.

**6.** When you are done writing, proofread your script.

**7.** After proofreading, practice your reader's theatre as a small group.

**8.** When you are ready, perform your reader's theatre for the class.

# Graphic Novel Reference List for Middle School ELA Fiction

Azzarello, B., & Bermejo, L. (2006). *Lex Luthor: Man of steel*. New York, NY: DC Comics.

Baker, K. (2004). *Plastic man on the lam!* New York, NY: DC Comics.

Baron, M., Dodson, T., & Nowlan, K. (1998). *Star wars: Dark force rising*. Milwaukie, OR: Dark Horse.

Bendis, B., Reed, B., & the Luna Brothers. (2007). *Spider-woman: Origin*. New York, NY: Marvel.

Busiek, K., & Immonen, S. (2004). *Superman: Secret identity*. New York: DC Comics.

The Clone Wars. (2004). Milwaukie, OR: Dark Horse.

Colfer, E., & Donkin, A. (2007). *Artemis Fowl: The graphic novel*. New York, NY: Hyperion.

Guibert. E., & Sfar, J. (2000). *Sardine in outer space*. New York, NY: First Second Books.

*Flight: Volume 1*. (2005). Berkeley, CA: Image Comics.

Fontes, J., Fontes, R., & Witt, D. (2007). *Twisted journeys #1: Captured by pirates*. Minneapolis, MN: Graphic Universe.

Holm, J., & Castaldi, E. (2007). *Middle school is worse than meatloaf*. New York, NY: Simon & Schuster.

Kibuishi, K. (2008). *Amulet: The stonekeeper*. New York, NY: Scholastic.

Kibuishi, K. (2006). *Daisy Kutter: The last train*. Irving, TX: Viper.

Larson, H. (2008). *Chiggers*. New York, NY: Simon & Schuster.

Mechner, J., Sina, A.B., Pham, L., & Puvilland, A. (2008). *Prince of Persia: The graphic novel*. New York, NY: First Second Books.

Medley, L. (2006). *Castle waiting*. Seattle, WA: Fantagraphic.

Millar, M., Johnson, D., Plunkett, K., et. Al. (2004). *Superman: Red son*. New York: DC Comics.

Moore, A., ONeill, K., Dimagmaliw, B., & Oakley, B. (2000). *The league of extraordinary gentlemen*. La Jolla, CA: America's Best Comics.

NCTE/IRA. (1996). *Standards for the English Language Arts*. Urbana, IL: NCTE.

Niles, S., & Roman, B. (2008). *The Cryptics*. San Diego, CA: IDW.

Rasinski, T., & Padak, N. (2008). *From phonics to fluency*. New York, NY: Pearson.

Patterson, J. & Gout, L. (2008). *Daniel X: Alien hunter*. New York, NY: Little, Brown.

Peeters, F. (2008). *Blue pills: A positive love story*. New York, NY: Houghton Mifflin.

Petersen, D. (2007). *Mouse guard: Fall 1152*. Fort Lee, NJ: ASP Comics.

Schrag, A. (Ed.). (2007). *Stuck in the middle: Seventeen comics from an UNPLEASANT age*. New York, NY: Penguin.

Smith, J. (2005). *Bone: Out from Boneville*. New York, NY: Scholastic.

Soo, K. (2008). *Jellaby*. New York, NY: Hyperion.

Sturm, J., Arnold, A., & Frederick-Frost, A. (2009). *Adventures in cartooning*. New York: First Second.

Tan, S. (2006). *The arrival*. New York, NY: Scholastic.

Tezuka, O. *Buddha: Volume one*. New York, NY: Vertical.

Trondheim, L. (2006). *A.L.I.E.E.E.N*. New York, NY: First Second Books.

Trondheim, L., & Cartier, E. (2002). *Kaput & Zosky*. New York, NY: First Second Books.

Trondheim, L., & Parme, F. (2004). *Tiny tyrant*. New York, NY: First Second Books.

Yang, G. (2006). *American born Chinese*. New York, NY: First Second Books.

## Graphic Novel Reference List for High School ELA Fiction

Appollo, & Trondheim, L. (2008). *Bourbon island 1730*. New York, NY: First Second Books.

Busiek, K., & Anderson, B. (2005). *Astro city: Local heroes*. La Jolla, CA: Wildstorm.

Cruse, H. (1995). *Stuck rubber baby*. New York, NY: Paradox Fiction.

Gaiman, N., Kubert, A., & Isanove, R. (2006). *Marvel 1602*. New York, NY: Marvel.

Gipi. (2005). *Garage band*. New York, NY: First Second Books.

Gipi. (2004). *Notes for a war story*. New York, NY: First Second Books.

Guibert, E. (2008). *Alan's war: The memories of G.I. Alan Cope*. New York, NY: First Second Books.

Klein, G. (2006). *The lost colony: Book No.1, the Snodgrass conspiracy*. New York, NY: First Second Books.

Meltzer, B. (2005). *Identity crisis*. New York, NY: DC Comics.

Miller, F. (1996). *Batman: The Dark Knight Returns*. New York, NY: DC Comics.

Moore, A., & Gibbons, D. (1986). *Watchmen*. New York, NY: DC Comics.

Moore, A., & Lloyd, D. (1988). *V for vendetta*. New York, NY: DC Comics.

Morrison, G., & Quitely, F. (2007). *All star Superman: Volume 1*. New York, NY: DC Comics.

Sfar, J., & Guibert, E. (2007). *The professor's daughter*. New York, NY: First Second Books.

Simmonds, P. (2007). *Tamara Drewe*. New York, NY: Houghton Mifflin.

Stassen. (2006). *Deogratias: A tale of Rwanda*. (Trans. by Alexis Siegel). New York, NY: First Second Books.

Sturm, J., Arnold, A., & Frederick-Frost, A. (2009). *Adventures in cartooning*. New York: First Second.

Van den Bogaert, H.M., & O'Connor, G. (2006). *Journey into Mohawk country*. New York, NY: First Second Books.

Vaughan, B.K. (2006). *Pride of Baghdad*. New York, NY: Vertigo.

Vaughan, B.K. (2005). *The runaways*. New York, NY: Marvel.

Waid, M., Yu, L.F., & Alanguilan, G. (2004). *Superman: Birthright*. New York, NY: DC Comics.

# Cross-index of Middle School Graphic Novels and Themes

## THEME

| TITLE AND AUTHOR | Act of Reading | Action-Adventure | Bravery | Coming of Age | Community | Culture | Diversity & Tolerance | Domestic Relations | Fairy Tales, Fables, & Folklore | Family | Fate, Destiny, and/or Chance | Foreign Relations | Friendship | Gender | Good & Evil | Heroes & Villains | Historical Context | Humanitarianism | Humor | Identity | Leadership | Loyalty & Trust | Myth & Legend | Narration | Plot Twists & Turns | Point of View | Relationships | School Life | Science Fiction | Space | Tradition | World Travel |
|---|---|---|---|---|---|---|---|---|---|---|---|---|---|---|---|---|---|---|---|---|---|---|---|---|---|---|---|---|---|---|---|---|
| A.L.I.E.E.E.N., Trondheim, L. | ✓ | | | ✓ | | | | | | | | | | | | | | | ✓ | | | | | | | | | | ✓ | ✓ | | |
| American Born Chinese, Yang, G. | | | | ✓ | | ✓ | | | ✓ | | | | | | | | | | ✓ | ✓ | | | | | | | | ✓ | | | ✓ | |
| Amulet: The Stonekeeper, Kibuishi, K. | | ✓ | ✓ | | | | | | | ✓ | | | | | ✓ | | | | | | | | | | | | | | ✓ | | | |
| Artemis Fowl: The Graphic Novel, Colfer, E. & Donkin, A. | | ✓ | | ✓ | | | | | ✓ | | | | | | | ✓ | | | ✓ | | | | | ✓ | ✓ | | | | ✓ | | | |
| Bone: Out from Boneville, Smith, J. | | ✓ | | | | | | | | ✓ | | | ✓ | | ✓ | | | | | | | ✓ | | | | | ✓ | | | | | |
| Buddha: Volume One, Tezuka, O. | | | | | | | | | | | | | | | ✓ | | ✓ | | | | ✓ | ✓ | | | | | | | | | | |
| Castle Waiting, Medley, L. | | | | | ✓ | | ✓ | | ✓ | | | | ✓ | ✓ | | | ✓ | | | | | ✓ | | | | | | | | | | |
| Chiggers, Larson, H. | | | | | | | | | | | | | ✓ | ✓ | | | | | ✓ | ✓ | | | | | | | | | | | | |
| Daisy Kutter: The Last Train, Kibuishi, K. | | ✓ | | | | | | | | | | | | | ✓ | | | | | | | | | | | | | | ✓ | | | |
| Daniel X: Alien Hunter, Patterson, J. & Gout, L. | | ✓ | ✓ | | | | | | | ✓ | | | ✓ | | | ✓ | | | ✓ | | ✓ | | | | | | ✓ | ✓ | ✓ | | | ✓ |
| Jellaby, Soo, K. | | ✓ | | | | | | | | | | | ✓ | | | | | | ✓ | | | | | | | | | | | ✓ | | |
| Kaput & Zosky, Trondheim, L. | | ✓ | | | | | | | | | | | | | ✓ | | | | ✓ | | | | | | | | | | | | | |
| Lex Luthor: Man of Steel, Azzarello, B. & Bermejo, L. | ✓ | ✓ | | | | ✓ | | ✓ | | | ✓ | | | | | ✓ | | ✓ | | ✓ | | ✓ | | ✓ | ✓ | ✓ | | | ✓ | ✓ | ✓ | ✓ |

# Cross-index of Middle School Graphic Novels and Themes (cont'd.)

## THEME

| TITLE AND AUTHOR | Act of Reading | Action-Adventure | Bravery | Coming of Age | Community | Culture | Diversity & Tolerance | Domestic Relations | Fairy Tales, Fables, & Folklore | Family | Fate, Destiny, and/or Chance | Foreign Relations | Friendship | Gender | Good & Evil | Heroes & Villains | Historical Context | Humanitarianism | Humor | Identity | Leadership | Loyalty & Trust | Myth & Legend | Narration | Plot Twists & Turns | Point of View | Relationships | School Life | Science Fiction | Space | Tradition | World Travel |
|---|---|---|---|---|---|---|---|---|---|---|---|---|---|---|---|---|---|---|---|---|---|---|---|---|---|---|---|---|---|---|---|---|
| Middle School is Worse Than Meatloaf, Holm, J. & Castaldi, E. | | | | ✓ | ✓ | | ✓ | | | | | | ✓ | ✓ | | | | | ✓ | ✓ | | | | | | | ✓ | ✓ | | | | |
| Mouse Guard: Fall 1152, Petersen, D. | | ✓ | ✓ | | | | | | | ✓ | | | ✓ | | | | ✓ | | | | ✓ | | | | | | | | | | | |
| Plastic Man on the Lam!, Baker, K. | | ✓ | ✓ | | | | | | | | | | | | ✓ | ✓ | | | | | | | | | | | | | | | | |
| Prince of Persia: The Graphic Novel, Mechner, J., Sina, A.B, Pham, L., & Puvilland, A. | | | | ✓ | | | | | | ✓ | | | | | | | ✓ | | | | ✓ | | ✓ | | | | | | | | ✓ | |
| Sardine in Outer Space, Guibert. E. & Sfar, J. | | | | | | | | | | ✓ | | | ✓ | | | | | | ✓ | | | | | | | | | | ✓ | ✓ | | |
| Spider-Woman: Origin, Bendis, B., Reed, B., & the Luna Brothers | | | | ✓ | | | | | | | | | | ✓ | ✓ | ✓ | | | | | | | | | | | | | | | ✓ | |
| Star Wars: Dark Force Rising, Baron, M., Dodson, T., & Nowlan, K. | | ✓ | ✓ | ✓ | | | | | | | ✓ | | | | ✓ | | | | | | | | | | ✓ | | | | ✓ | | ✓ | |
| Stuck in the Middle: Seventeen Comics from an UNPLEASANT Age, Schrag, A. | | | | ✓ | | | ✓ | | | | | | ✓ | | | | | | ✓ | | | | | | | | | ✓ | | | | |
| Superman: Red Son, Millar, M., Johnson, D., Plunkett, K., et al | | | | | | | | | | | ✓ | | | | ✓ | | ✓ | | | | | | | | ✓ | ✓ | | | ✓ | | | |

# Cross-index of Middle School Graphic Novels and Themes (cont'd.)

| TITLE AND AUTHOR | Act of Reading | Action-Adventure | Bravery | Coming of Age | Community | Culture | Diversity & Tolerance | Domestic Relations | Fairy Tales, Fables, & Folklore | Family | Fate, Destiny, and/or Chance | Foreign Relations | Friendship | Gender | Good & Evil | Heroes & Villains | Historical Context | Humanitarianism | Humor | Identity | Leadership | Loyalty & Trust | Myth & Legend | Narration | Plot Twists & Turns | Point of View | Relationships | School Life | Science Fiction | Space | Tradition | World Travel |
|---|---|---|---|---|---|---|---|---|---|---|---|---|---|---|---|---|---|---|---|---|---|---|---|---|---|---|---|---|---|---|---|---|
| *Superman: Secret Identity*, Busiek, K. & Immonen, S. | | | | ✓ | | | | | | | | | | | | ✓ | | | | ✓ | | | ✓ | ✓ | ✓ | | | | ✓ | | ✓ | |
| *The Arrival*, Tan, S. | | | ✓ | | | | | | | ✓ | | | ✓ | | | | ✓ | | | | | | | | | | | | | | | |
| *The Clone Wars*, Black, R., Blackman, H., & Fillbach Brothers | | ✓ | | | | | | | | | | | | | ✓ | ✓ | | | | | | ✓ | | | ✓ | | | | ✓ | ✓ | ✓ | |
| *The Cryptics*, Niles, S. & Roman, B. | | | | | | | | | ✓ | | | | ✓ | | | | | | ✓ | | | | | | | | | ✓ | | | | |
| *The League of Extraordinary Gentlemen*, Moore, A., O'Neill, K., Dimagmaliw, B., & Oakley, B. | | ✓ | | | | | | | | | | | | | ✓ | ✓ | ✓ | | | | ✓ | | | | | | | | ✓ | | | |
| *Tiny Tyrant*, Trondheim, L. & Parme, F. | | | | ✓ | | | | | | | | | | | | | | | ✓ | | ✓ | ✓ | | | | | | | | | | |
| *Twisted Journeys #1: Captured by Pirates*, Fontes, J., Fontes, R., & Witt, D. | ✓✓ | ✓ | | | | | | | | | ✓ | | | | | | | | | | | | | ✓✓ | ✓✓ | | | | | | | |

**Cross-index of High School Graphic Novels and Themes**

| TITLE AND AUTHOR | Act of Reading | Action-Adventure | Bravery | Coming of Age | Community | Culture | Diversity & Tolerance | Domestic Relations | Fairy Tales, Fables, & Folklore | Family | Fate, Destiny, and/or Chance | Foreign Relations | Friendship | Gender | Good & Evil | Heroes & Villains | Historical Context | Humanitarianism | Humor | Identity | Leadership | Loyalty & Trust | Myth & Legend | Narration | Plot Twists & Turns | Point of View | Relationships | School Life | Science Fiction | Space | Tradition | World Travel |
|---|---|---|---|---|---|---|---|---|---|---|---|---|---|---|---|---|---|---|---|---|---|---|---|---|---|---|---|---|---|---|---|---|
| *All Star Superman: Volume 1*, Morrison, G. & Quitely, F. | | ✓ | | | | | | | | | | | | | ✓ | ✓ | | | | ✓ | ✓ | | | | | | ✓ | | | | | |
| *Astro City: Local Heroes*, Busiek, K. & Anderson, B. | | ✓ | | | | | | | | | | | | | ✓ | ✓ | | | | | | ✓ | | | | | | | ✓ | | | |
| *Batman: The Dark Knight Returns*, Miller, F. | | ✓ | | | | | | | | | | | | | ✓ | ✓ | | ✓ | ✓ | | ✓ | | | | | | | | | | | |
| *Bourbon Island 1730*, Appollo & Trondheim, L. | | ✓ | | | | | | | | | | | | | ✓ | ✓ | ✓ | | | | ✓ | ✓ | | | | | | | | | | |
| *Deogratias: A Tale of Rwanda*, Stassen, J.P. | | | ✓ | ✓ | | ✓ | | | | ✓ | | | ✓ | | | | ✓ | | | ✓ | | | | | | | | | | | | |
| *Garage Band*, Gipi | | | | ✓ | | | | | | ✓ | | | ✓ | | | | | | | | ✓ | ✓ | | | | | ✓ | | | | | |
| *Identity Crisis*, Meltzer, B. | | ✓ | | | | | | | | | | | | | | | | | | | ✓ | ✓ | | | | | | | | | | |
| *Journey into Mohawk Country*, Van den Bogaert, H.M. & O'Connor, G. | | | | | | | | | | ✓ | | | ✓ | | ✓ | ✓ | ✓ | ✓ | | | ✓ | ✓ | | | | | | | | | ✓ | |
| *Marvel 1602*, Gaiman, N., Kubert, A., & Isanove, R. | | ✓ | | | | | | | | ✓ | | | ✓ | | | | ✓ | | | | ✓ | ✓ | | | | | | | | | | |
| *Notes for a War Story*, Gipi | | ✓ | | ✓ | | | | | | ✓ | | | | | | | ✓ | | | | ✓ | ✓ | | | | | | | | | | |
| *Pride of Baghdad*, Vaughan, B.K. | | ✓ | ✓ | | ✓ | ✓ | | | | | | | | | | | ✓ | | | | | | | | | | | | | | | |

# Cross-index of High School Graphic Novels and Themes (cont'd.)

| TITLE AND AUTHOR | Act of Reading | Action-Adventure | Bravery | Coming of Age | Community | Culture | Diversity & Tolerance | Domestic Relations | Fairy Tales, Fables, & Folklore | Family | Fate, Destiny, and/or Chance | Foreign Relations | Friendship | Gender | Good & Evil | Heroes & Villains | Historical Context | Humanitarianism | Humor | Identity | Leadership | Loyalty & Trust | Myth & Legend | Narration | Plot Twists & Turns | Point of View | Relationships | School Life | Science Fiction | Space | Tradition | World Travel |
|---|---|---|---|---|---|---|---|---|---|---|---|---|---|---|---|---|---|---|---|---|---|---|---|---|---|---|---|---|---|---|---|---|
| Stuck Rubber Baby, Cruse, H. | | | | ✓ | | | | | | ✓ | | | ✓ | | | | ✓ | | | | | ✓ | | | | | | | | | | |
| Superman: Birthright, Waid, M., Yu, L.F., & Alanguilan, G. | | ✓ | | ✓ | | | | | | ✓ | | | ✓ | | ✓ | ✓ | | | | | ✓ | | | | | | | | | | | ✓ |
| Tamara Drewe, Simmonds, P. | ✓ | | | | ✓ | | | | | ✓ | | | | | | | | | | ✓ | | | | | | | ✓ | | | | | |
| The Lost Colony: Book No.1: The Snodgrass Conspiracy, Klein, G. | | | | | | ✓ | | | | | | | | | | | ✓ | | | | ✓ | | | | | | ✓ | | | | | |
| The Professor's Daughter, Sfar, J. & Guibert, E. | | | | | | | | | | | ✓ | | | | | | ✓ | | | | | ✓ | | | | ✓ | ✓ | | | | | |
| The Runaways, Vaughan, B.K. | | | ✓ | | ✓ | | | | | | | | ✓ | ✓ | ✓ | ✓ | ✓ | | | | ✓ | ✓ | | | | | | | | | | |
| V for Vendetta, Moore, A. & Lloyd, D. | | ✓ | | | | | | | | | | | | | ✓ | ✓ | ✓ | | | ✓ | ✓ | | | | | | | | | | | |
| Watchmen, Moore, A. & Gibbons, D. | | ✓ | | | | | | | | | | | | | ✓ | ✓ | | | | ✓ | ✓ | ✓ | | | | | | | | | | |

# REFERENCES

Abadzis, N. (2007). *Laika*. New York, NY: First Second Books.

Abel, J., & Madden, M. (2008). *Drawing words and writing pictures*. New York, NY: F First Second Books.

Afflerbach, P., Pearson, P. David, & Paris, Scott, G. (2008). Clarifying differences between reading skills and reading strategies. *The Reading Teacher*. 61.5, 364 - 73.

Appollo, & Trondheim, L. (2008). *Bourbon Island 1730*. New York, NY: First Second Books.

Bercaw, Edna C. (2000). *Halmoni's day*. Darby, PA: Diane.

Buckingham, D. (2003). *Media education: Literacy, learning and contemporary culture*. Malden, MA: Polity.

Butzer, C.M. (2009). *Gettysburg: The graphic novel*. New York, NY: HarperCollins.

Cammuso, F. (2008). *Knights of the lunch table*. New York, NY: Scholastic.

Carter, J.B. (2007). *Building literacy connections with graphic novels*. Urbana, IL: NCTE.

Clark, R. (1983). Reconsidering research on learning from media. *Review of Educational Research*, 53.4, 445-459.

Curtis, Jamie Lee. (2006). *Is there really a human race?* New York, NY: Random House.

Dorros, A. (1997). *Abuela*. New York, NY: Puffin.

Dr. Seuss. (1954). *Horton hears a who*. New York: Random House.

Dr. Seuss. (1957). *The cat in the hat*. New York, NY: Random House.

Dunbar, P. (2008). *Penguin*. London: Walker Books Limited.

Eisner, W. (1978). *A Contract with God*. New York, NY: Norton.

Fehlman, R.H. (1992). Making meanings visible: Critically reading TV. *The English Journal*, 81.7, 19-24.

Fierstein, H. (2005). *The sissy duckling*. New York, NY: Simon & Schuster.

Gardner, H. (1983). *Frames of mind: The theory of multiple intelligences*. New York: Basic Books.

Gee, J.P. (2003). *What Videogames Have to Teach Us About Learning and Literacy*. New York: Palgrave.

Gownley, J. (2006). *Amelia's rules: Superheroes*. Harrisburg, PA: Renaissance Press.

Grabois, A. (2007). *Graphic novels*. Retrieved August 20. 2007, from http://www.beneaththecover. com/2007/08/20/graphic-novels/

Guibert, E. (2008). *Alan's war*. New York, NY: First Second Books.

Hajdu, D. (2008). *The ten-cent plague: The great comic-book scare and how it Changed America*. New York: FSG.

Harste, J., Woodward, V., & Burke, C. (1984). *Language stories and literacy lessons*. New York: Heinemann.

Hart, A., & Benson, A. (1996). Researching media education in English classrooms in the UK. *Journal of Educational Media*, 22.1, 7-22.

Hinton, S.E. (1967). *The Outsiders*. New York, NY: Penguin.

Hobbs, R. (1998). The Simpsons meet Mark Twain: Analyzing popular media in the classroom. *The English Journal*, 87.1, 49-51.

Hobbs, R. (2007). *Reading the media: Media literacy in high school English*. New York: Teachers College Press.

Hoffman, D.D. (1998). *Visual Intelligence*. New York, NY: Norton.

Hull, G., & Schultz, K. (2002). *School's out: Bridging out-of-school literacies with classroom practice*. New York: Teachers College Press.

Jacboson, S., Colón, E. *The 9/11 Report: A graphic adaptation*. New York, NY: Hill and Wang.

Johnson, S. (2005). *Everything bad is good for you*. New York, NY: Riverhead.

Kress, G. (2003). *Literacy in the new media age*. New York: Routledge.

Langer, J. (1989). Thinking and doing literature: An eight-year study. *English Journal*, 87(2). 16-23.

Larson, H. (2008). *Chiggers*. New York, NY: Simon & Schuster.

Leavis, F.R., & Thompson, D. (1933). *Culture and Environment: The Training of Critical Awareness*. Portsmouth, NH: Greenwood.

Lyga, B. (2009). *Wolverine: Worst day ever*. New York, NY: Marvel.

Masterman, L. (1985). *Teaching the media*. New York: Routledge.

Maloney, H.B. (1960). Stepsisters of print: The public arts in the high school English Class. The English Journal, 49.8, 570-79.

Mayer, Marianna, & Mayer, Mercer. *Beauty and the Beast*. San Francisco, CA: Chronicle.

McCloud, S. (2006). Making comics: Storytelling secrets of comics, manga and graphic *Novels*. New York: HarperCollins.

McCloud, S. (2000). *Reinventing comics: How imagination and technology are revolutionizing an art form*. New York: HarperCollins.

McCloud, S. (1993). *Understanding comics: The invisible art*. New York: HarperCollins

McLuhan, M. (1964). *Understanding media: The extensions of man*. New York: McGraw-Hill.

Meiners, C.J. (2003). *Share and take turns*. Minneapolis, MN: Free Spirit.

Nafisi, A. (2003). *Reading Lolita in Tehran*. New York: RandomHouse.

The Newsom Report. (1963). *Half our future*. London: HMSO.

The New London Group. (1996). A pedagogy of multi-literacies: Designing social Futures. *Harvard Educational Review*, 66.1, 60-92.

Newman, L. (1989). *Heather has two mommies*. New York, NY: Alyson.

Niles, S., & Roman, B. (2008). *The cryptics*. San Diego, CA: IDW.

Ogle, D. (1986). KWL: A teaching model that develops active reading of expository text. *The Reading Teacher*, 32, 564-570.

Potok, C. (1967). *The chosen*. New York: Simon & Schuster.

Renier, A. (2005). *Spiral-Bound*. Marietta, GA: Top Shelf.

Richards, I.A. (1929). *Practical criticism: A study of literary judgment*. New York: Harvest.

Rosenblatt, L. (1938). *The reader, the text, the poem: The transactional theory of the literary work*. Carbondale, IL: Southern Illinois University.

Sava, S.C., & Jourdan, D. (2008). *Ed's Terrestrials*. San Diego, CA: IDW.

Sava, S.C., & Saavedra, J.M. (2009). *My grandparents are secret agents*. San Diego, CA: IDW.

Say, A. (2008). *Grandfather's journey*. Mooloolaba, QLD: Sandpiper.

Schwarz, G. (2002). Graphic novels for multiple literacies. *Journal of Adolescent & Adult Literacy*, 46.3, 262-65.

Selznick, B. (2007). *The invention of Hugo Cabaret*. New York, NY: Scholastic.

Sims, L. (2008). *Stories for little girls*. Eveleth, MN: Usborne.

Smith, D.V. (1952). *The English language arts*. Urbana: NCTE.

Smith, J. (2005). *Bone*. New York, NY: Scholastic.

Soo, K. (2008). *Jellaby*. New York, NY: Hyperion.

Soo, K. (2009). *Jellaby: Monster in the city*. New York, NY: Hyperion.

Spiegelman, A. (1986). *Maus I*. New York, NY: Pantheon.

Spiegelman, A. (1991). *Maus II*. New York, NY: Pantheon.

Stamaty, Mark Alan. (2004). *Alia's Mission*. New York, NY: Knopf.

Sturm, J., Arnold, A., & Frederick-Frost, A. (2009). *Adventures in cartooning*. New York: First Second.

Tarpley, Natasha A. (2003). *I love my hair*. New York, NY: LB Kids.

Wiesner, D. (1997). *Tuesday*. Mooloolaba, QLD: Sandpiper.

Wertham, F. (1954). *Seduction of the innocent*. New York: Rinehart.

Yang, Gene L. (2006). *American born Chinese*. New York, NY: First Second Books.

# SOME HELPFUL GRAPHIC NOVEL WEBSITES

www.diamondbookshelf.com
www.firstsecondbooks.com
www.frankwbaker.com
www.graphicclassics.com
www.graphicnovelreporter.com
www.noflyingnotights.com
www.professorgarfield.org
www.toon-books.com

# INDEX

Abadzis, Nick ........ x, 6, 8, 78, 81, 82, 108, 109, 134, 136, 173, 229

Abel, Jessica ............................................2, 12, 13, 107, 229

*Abuela* ................................................................ 56, 229

*A Contract with God*..........................................xvii, 229

aesthetic reading .........................................................9

Afflerbach, P. ................................................... 17, 229

African American Theory ...........................................xx

*After 9/11* .................................................... 90, 173

*Alan's War* ......... 11, 12, 95, 97, 98, 137, 138, 174, 222, 230

*Alia's Mission* ....................................................124, 215, 231

*Amelia Rules*....................................................124, 152, 215

*American Born Chinese*10, 11, 39, 40, 43-45, 47, 48, 51, 56, 58-60, 66, 137, 222, 223, 231

"And the Meaning Is . . ." .....................114, 115, 122, 188

Appollo .....................................x, 27-29, 37, 222, 226, 229

Baker, Frank ............................................................ 103

*Beauty and the Beast*...............................................56, 230

Benson, A. .......................................................... xx, 230

Bercaw, Edna Coe ......................................... 56, 229

body paragraph .......................64, 65, 75, 100, 161, 170

*Bone*........................................124, 174, 215, 221, 223, 231

*Bourbon Island 1730*...... 27-30, 32, 34, 37, 222, 226, 229

"Build It!" ...............................114-116, 122, 189-191, 212

Butzer, C.M. ......................................x, 73, 74, 171, 229

Cammuso, Frank .......................................................229

*Casper the Friendly Ghost* ...................................... 90

*Chiggers*............. 2, 3, 10, 18-20, 37, 110, 137, 221, 223, 230

Clark, R........................................................... xx, 229

Colón, Ernie ........................................... 89, 90, 173, 230

conclusion ...................64, 65, 75, 93, 100, 161, 167, 170

conflict........5, 42, 43, 47-50, 52, 54, 59-62, 134, 149, 150, 154, 156, 218

creative nonfiction graphic novel ........76, 78, 84, 93, 95, 98

critical-reading lens ............................46, 51, 56, 57, 65

critical-reading partnerships...12, 13, 20, 30, 138, 139, 143, 202

    compare and/or contrast partnership ....12, 112, 184, 203

    reference partnership .................13, 112, 185, 204

    story-extension partnership ......13, 112, 138, 186, 206

    potential partnerships ..................... 112, 187, 206

critical theory.................................................................56

Curtis, Jamie Lee ............................................ 56, 229

Cybil Award .....................................................................82

discoveries................70, 72, 85, 87, 88, 91, 166, 167, 174

Dorros, Arthur ................................................................229

*Drawing Words & Writing Pictures* ......................2, 12

Dr. Seuss ......................................................... 56, 229

Dunbar, Polly ................................................. 56, 229

early language learners.....................................125, 126

early production...............................................124, 215

*Ed's Terrestrials*................................124, 215, 231

Eliot, Charles W. .......................................................... xix

Eisner Award .............................................................19, 29

Eisner, Will ........................................................ xvii, 229

elements of story ..... 5, 13, 40, 41, 43, 44, 46, 51, 53, 56, 57, 63-66, 112, 124, 129, 130, 132, 134, 138, 155, 186, 206, 215, 217, 219

emergent readers................................. 125, 127-130

English language learners .............................123-132

Epstein, Daniel Robert........................................ 90

expository writing..............................92, 93, 101, 167

*Everything Bad Is Good for You*..................... 105, 230 falling action ..................42, 43, 47-50, 59-62, 149, 154

Fehlman, R.H. .................................................... xx, 229

Feminist Theory ........................xx, 55, 56, 66, 158, 159

fiction............ 39-66, 114, 118, 149, 152, 154, 158, 221, 222

Fierstein, Harvey .................................................. 56, 229

First Second Books ................................................ 29, 98

Fitzgerald, F. Scott.................................................. 1, 152

fluency..............................17, 44, 123, 124, 131, 215, 221

foreshadowing.... 5, 8, 42, 43, 47-50, 52, 54, 59-62, 134, 136, 149, 151, 154, 157

format.............43, 44, 57, 70, 72, 85, 87, 88, 91, 166, 167

*Frames of Mind*........................................................xx, 229

Garbage Pail Kids ..................................................... 121

Gardner, Howard ................................................... xx, 229

Gownley, Jimmy ................................................. 152, 230

*Grandfather's Journey*............................................56, 231

graphic journalism.................................................... 90

graphic novel balloons.......10-12, 14, 110, 137, 138, 182, 183, 194, 195, 199, 200, 208, 210

    balloon-less balloons............................. 12, 14, 138

    dialogue balloons ................. 11, 110, 137, 182, 200

    sound effect balloons ...........11, 110, 138, 182, 200

    story balloons................... 10, 14, 110, 137, 182, 200

    thought balloons.............. 11, 14, 110, 137, 182, 200

    word balloons .....................................10, 137, 195

graphic novel fiction........ 39-66, 114, 118, 158, 221, 222

"Graphic Novel Media & Me"..... 114-116, 118, 119, 122, 175, 189, 192, 207, 209, 211, 212

graphic novel nonfiction ....67-101, 160, 162, 163, 166, 168, 171

graphic novel vocabulary...... xvi, 1-14, 37, 95, 133-138

Guibert, Emmanuel .. 97-99, 174, 221, 222, 224, 227, 230

gutters ............................. 2-9, 13, 14, 20, 30, 68, 73, 85, 88, 104, 107-110, 116, 133-136, 139, 143, 175-177, 180, 181, 189, 190, 192-195, 198, 199, 208, 210, 211

    action-to-action............. 5, 6, 14, 110, 135, 180, 198

    aspect-to-aspect ........5, 8, 9, 14, 110, 136, 180, 198

    moment-to-moment . 5, 6, 9, 13, 14, 108-110, 135, 136, 180, 198

    non-sequitur.................5, 8, 14, 110, 136, 180, 198

    scene-to-scene ...................... 5, 7, 110, 136

*Halmoni's Day* ........................................................56, 229

Hart, A. ............................................................. xx, 230

Harvey Award ............................................................ 82

Harvey Comics.......................................................... 90

*Heather Has Two Mommies*56, 231

high school ELA.....24-37, 51-68, 71, 85-103, 108, 118-122, 131, 143, 145-148, 154, 155, 158, 162, 165, 166, 168, 170, 171, 173, 174, 192, 207, 222, 226, 227, 230

Hinton, S.E. ................................................... 46, 66, 230

Hobbs, Renee ................xx, 103, 105, 108, 111, 112, 230

Hoffman, D.D. .................................................... xx, 230

*Horton Hears a Who*..............................................56, 229

*I Love My Hair* .......................................................56, 231

"I Write It" ...............................................118, 122, 212

"If I Could Please Respond to This Graphic Novel".. 118, 120, 122, 207, 209

images window 15, 16, 18, 22, 25, 28, 30, 32, 33, 37, 139, 141, 143, 145, 146

informational nonfiction graphic novel .........67-69, 70-75, 84, 85, 87-93, 161, 162, 166, 167

informational/informative writing .... 74, 75, 84, 101

intertextuality .........................................................44

introduction................. 64, 65, 75, 93, 100, 167, 170, 211

Jacobson, Sid.....................................................88-90, 173

*Jellaby*............................................ 124, 215, 222, 223, 231

*Jellaby: Monster in the City* .......................124, 215, 231

Johnson, Stephen .............................................105, 230

Jourdan, Diego ..........................................................231

*Kaput & Zosky*.............................. 124, 215, 222, 223

*Kirkus Review*...........................................................82

Kist, William............................................................108

*Knights of the Lunch Table* .......................124, 215, 229

know-wonder-learn (KWL) chart ..... 78, 79, 95, 127-129, 216

Kress, Gunther ...................................................xv, xx, 230

*Laika*.............. 6, 8, 78, 81, 82, 108, 109, 134, 136, 173, 229

Larson, Hope ..........................3, 10, 19, 137, 221, 223, 230

Lee, Stan ................................................................ 90

lesson ideas...18, 27, 44, 56, 72, 78, 88, 95, 114, 118, 126, 128, 130, 132

Lincoln, Abraham..........................................1, 67, 70, 74

language learning .............................123-132, 215-217

Leavis, F.R. ...........................................................103, 230

Lyga, Barry ................................................ 230

Madden, Matt................... 2, 12-14, 138, 229

main idea....5, 25, 43, 54, 70, 72, 85, 88, 91, 134, 151, 157, 161, 167, 211

*Making Comics* ............................ 107, 174, 230

Marxist Theory .....................xx, 55, 56, 60, 66, 158, 159

Masterman, Len.............................................xx

*Maus I*....................... xvii, 1, 67, 118, 121, 174, 231

*Maus II*.......................... xvii, 67, 121, 174, 231

Mayer, Marianna .............................. 56, 230

McCloud, Scott .....................2, 5-7, 14, 134, 135, 174, 230

media literacy ............................ xx, 2, 103-122, 175-214

media literacy analysis.......105, 112, 184-187, 189-191, 202-206, 213

media literacy construction.107, 175, 176, 189-191, 193

media literacy intention ....108, 110, 177-183, 189-191, 196-201

Meiners, C.J................................. 56, 230

middle school ELA............. 17-25, 40-50, 63, 64, 69-84, 113-118, 139-142, 149-151, 160-165, 175, 188-191, 212-214, 221-225

Mouly, Françoise .................................. xi-xiii, 106, 121

*My Grandparents Are Secret Agents*.........124, 215, 231

Nafisi, Azir.............................................. 15, 231

National Book Award ............................... 45

National Cartoonists Society Division Award...... 82

National Council of Teachers of English (NCTE)..xi, xv, xix, 1, 2, 19, 104, 221, 229, 231

*New Literacies in Action* ............................ 108

new media age ...................................... 39, 230

Newsrama.com................................................ 90

Newman, Leslea ................................. 56, 231

Niles, Steve................................124, 215, 221, 225, 231

nonfiction................. 67-101, 160, 162, 163, 166, 168, 171

Nonfiction Collaboration ......68-70, 72-74, 76-78, 80, 81, 83-89, 91, 93-99, 101, 16-163, 165, 166, 168, 170

Nonfiction Collaboration Journey ....68, 76-78, 80, 81, 83-85, 93-97, 99, 101, 163, 166, 168, 170

Nonfiction Collaboration Stair-Step ..... 68-70, 72-74, 76, 78, 85-89, 91, 101, 160-162, 166

NYPL Book .................................................. 82

Ogle, Donna .................................... 78, 127, 231

panels ...................... 2, 4-9, 13, 14, 20-23, 30-35, 68, 73, 85, 88, 104, 107-110, 116, 133-136, 139-148, 175-180, 189, 190, 192-198, 207, 209, 211, 214

   content panels .......... 4, 5, 14, 110, 133, 178, 196

      image panels ................................4, 133

      word panels ................................4, 133

      word and image panels ...........4, 133

   story panels ..............4, 5, 14, 110, 134, 178, 196

      character panels.........................5, 134

      climax panels...............................5, 134

      combination panels...................5, 134

      conflict panels...........................5, 134

      foreshadowing panels .............5, 134

      plot panels ...................................5, 134

      resolution panels .....................5, 134

      rising action panels ..................5, 134

      setting panels ...........................5, 134

      symbols panels .........................5, 134

      theme panels .............................5, 134

Pantheon Books................................................ 121

Paris, Scott G. ............................. 17, 229

Pearson, P. David............................. 17, 229

*Penguin*................................................56, 229

persuasive writing ................. 63-66, 98, 100, 101, 170

picture book........................27, 28, 56, 124-126, 128, 215

plot ....5, 13, 42, 43, 47-50, 52-54, 59-62, 112, 134, 138, 149, 150, 154-156, 186, 205, 217, 219, 223-227

point of view.....52, 54, 59-62, 64, 100, 154, 156, 223-227

Potok, Chaim............................40, 51, 56, 58, 231

pre-production................................124, 215

pre-writing................................98, 100, 170

*Publisher's Weekly* ............................82

Pulitzer Prize............................. xi, xvii, 67, 121

Queer Theory................................................xx

Reader Response Theory .....................xix, xx

reader's theatre................124, 131, 132, 215, 220

reading comprehension ............xvi, 15-37, 41, 139, 143

reading comprehension windows16, 20-35, 139-149

*Reading Lolita in Tehran* .....................15, 231

Renier, Aaron............................................ 117

*Reinventing Comics*................................... 107, 174, 230 resolution ........5, 42, 43, 47-50, 52, 54, 59-62, 134, 149, 151, 154, 157, 218, 219

retell ................24, 25, 27, 28, 31-37, 84, 144-148, 164

Richards, I.A. ................................................xix, 231

*Richie Rich* ................................................90

rising action.... 5, 42, 43, 47-50, 52, 59-62, 134, 149-151, 154, 156, 157, 218, 219

Roman, Benjamin ......................124, 215, 221, 231

Rosenblatt, Louise......................................xix, 231

Saavedra Mourgues, Juan ..............................231

Sava, Scott Christian ......................124, 215, 231

Say, Allen ................................................56, 231

scaffold................................................56, 63

schema..... 13, 18, 72, 78, 88, 95, 112, 115, 119, 127, 138, 185, 204

*Seduction of the Innocent* ................................xi, 231

Selznick, Brian......................................231

setting................................................5, 21-23, 31, 32, 34, 42, 43, 47-50, 52, 54, 59-62, 110, 134, 140-142, 144, 145, 147, 149, 150, 154, 156, 178, 196, 218, 219

Sfar, Joann ................................98, 221, 222, 224, 227

*Share and Take Turns* ................................56, 230

Simon & Schuster ................................19, 58

Sims, Lesley ................................................56, 231

Smith, Jeff ................................................221, 223, 231

Smith, Dora V................................................xix, 231

speech emergence ................................124, 215

Spiegelman, Art......................xi, xii, 121, 174, 231

*Spiral-Bound*......................114, 116, 117, 189, 231

Stamaty, Mark Alan ................................231

standards....1, 17, 25, 41, 63-65, 68, 75, 84, 92, 100, 103, 118, 120

Steranko, Jim ................................................xvii

*Stories for Little Girls*......................56, 231

story map......................17, 18, 20-37, 139-148, 217, 219

style ................4, 55, 80, 83, 85, 88, 91, 96, 133, 158, 159, 164, 167, 169

sustained silent reading......................xv

symbols......5, 42, 43, 47-50, 52, 54, 59-61, 134, 149, 151, 154, 157

Tarpley, Natasha Anastasia......................56, 231

text potential......................24-37, 143-148

*The 9/11 Report*......................88-90, 92, 173, 230

*The Cat in the Hat*......................56, 229

*The Chosen*......................40, 51, 56, 58, 61, 62, 231

The Committee of Ten................................xix

*The Cryptics*......................124, 215, 221, 225, 231

*The Curious Case of Benjamin Button*......................51, 152

*The English Language Arts*......................xix

*The Human Race*......................56

*The Invention of Hugo Cabaret*......................124, 215, 231

The Literate Eye......................41-66, 149-151, 154-159

*The New London Group*......................xv, xx, 103

*The New York Times* Best-Seller List......................90

*The Newsom Report*......................xix, 231

*The Outsiders*......................40, 43, 44, 46, 49, 50, 230

*The Sissy Duckling*......................56, 229

theme......................5, 42, 43, 47-50, 52, 54, 59-61, 134, 149, 151, 154, 157, 223-227

Thompson, D.......................103, 230

tone......................8, 80, 85, 86, 88, 91, 96, 110, 136, 164, 167, 169

Toon Books ......................xi, xiii, 106, 121, 124, 125, 126, 128, 215, 232

Top Shelf ................................................117

Trondheim, Lewis......................29, 124, 215, 222, 229

*Tuesday* ................................................56, 231

U.S. Census Bureau......................123

*Understanding Comics*......................2, 107, 174, 230

United States Archives Building......................39

validity ................................................85, 86, 89, 167

verbal-linguistic................................................xx

visual-spatial ................................................xx

Wertham, Frederic......................xi, 231

Wiesner, David......................56, 231

*Wolverine: Worst Day Ever*......................124, 215, 230

words window......................15-18, 20, 21, 24, 25, 28, 30, 31, 139, 140, 143, 144

words and images window ...15, 18, 20, 23, 25, 28, 30, 34, 35, 139, 142, 143, 147, 148

writing activities......................63, 64, 74, 84, 98, 100, 118, 120, 132, 164, 207, 212

YALSA ................................................82

Yang, Gene L................................40, 45, 222, 223, 231